THE MAKING OF A NATION: ESSAYS IN INDIAN HISTORY AND POLITICS

Perspectives in History

General Editors

B.N. GOSWAMY
RAVINDER KUMAR
DIETMAR ROTHERMUND

Vol. I Dietmar Rothermund: *Asian Trade and European Expansion in the Age of Mercantilism.*

Vol. II. Dietmar Rothermund: *The Indian Economy Under British Rule and Other Essays.*

Vol. III. Kapil Kumar: *Peasants in Revolt: Tenants, Landlords, Congress and the Raj in the Oudh, 1886-1922.*

Vol. IV. Ravinder Kumar: *The Making of a Nation: Essays in Indian History and Politics.*

Vol. V. Rothermund, Dietmar: *India in the Great Depression, 1929-1939.* (Forthcoming).

Vol. VI. H. Kulke: *Kings and Cults: State Formation and Legislation in India and Southeast Asia.* (Forthcoming).

The Making of a Nation:
Essays in Indian History and Politics

RAVINDER KUMAR

MANOHAR
2026

First published 1989
Reprinted 2021, 2022, 2023, 2026

ISBN 978-81-85054-62-9

Published by
Ajay Kumar Jain *for*
Manohar Publishers & Distributors
4753/23 Ansari Road, Daryaganj
New Delhi 110 002

Printed at
Replika Press Pvt. Ltd.

For
Meenakshi
and
Madhuri

Contents

Preface

The essays on nationalist politics and contemporary history incorporated in the present volume were presented on various occasions over the past five years. Most of them touch upon different facets of contemporary India. What holds these essays together is a vision of Indian society, past and present, which seeks to relate the parts to the whole; focuses upon continuity in the midst of change; and looks upon the endeavour to transform an agricultural society of considerable antiquity into a modern industrial State as one of the most significant developments in the history of mankind during the second half of the 20th century.

It gives me pleasure to present these essays as a perception of India by a student of history.

New Delhi
1988

Ravinder Kumar

Acknowledgements

1. "From *Swaraj* to *Purna Swaraj:* A Review of the Nationalist Struggle in the 1920s and the 1930s" appeared as "Introduction" in a *A Centenary History of the Indian National Congress,* Vol. II, 1919-1935. General Editor, B.N. Pande, Editor of Vol. II, Ravinder Kumar (Bombay, 1985).

2. "A Review of the Historical Literature on the Struggle for Freedom in India, Pakistan and Great Britain" appeared as "Introduction" in *Myth and Reality: The Struggle for Freedom in India,* (1945-47) ed, A.K. Gupta (New Delhi, 1987).

3. "Motilal Nehru: Portrait of a Nationalist" appeared as "Introduction" in *Selected Works of Motilal Nehru, Volume One (1899-1918)* ed. Ravinder Kumar & D.N. Panigrahi (New Delhi, 1982).

4. "Gandhi, Ambedkar and the Poona Pact, 1932" appeared in *South Asia*, Vol. VIII. No. 1 & 2, June-December 1985.

5. "The Role of Urban Society in Nationalist Politics" was presented at a symposium on "Urban History", organized by the Urban History Association of India with the Indian History Congress at its Annual Session at Burdwan 1983.

6. "The Secular Culture of India" was presented at a symposium entitled "The Composite Culture of India and National Integration" held under the auspices of the Indian Institute of Advanced Study, Shimla, in 1984.

7. "The Past as a Mirror of the Future" was delivered as the M.A. Ansari Memorial Lecture at Jamia Millia Islamia in 1984.

8. "Jawaharlal Nehru, the Indian National Congress and the Anti-Fascist Struggle (1939-1945)" was presented at an International Seminar on the Potsdam Conference held under the auspices of the Institute of G.D.R. Historians in 1985. It has appeared in the *Indian Historical Review*, Vol. XI. July 1984-January 1985.

9. "The Historical Roots of Democracy in India" appeared in *Harvard International Review*, May 1985 issue.

10. "The Place of Oral Sources in Historical Research" was presented as "Presidential Address" at a seminar entitled "The Concept and Value of Oral History in Modern Historiography" held by Punjabi University, Patiala in December 1983.

1

From *Swaraj* to *Purna Swaraj*: A Review of the Nationalist Struggle in the 1920s and the 1930s

As peace dawned upon a world weary of war in November 1918, the people of India, who had contributed so substantially to the defeat of Kaiser William's Germany, braced themselves for a new effort to liberate their country from the stranglehold of British imperialism. Even during the course of war, the leaders of the Indian National Congress, who represented the mainstream of nationalism, had drafted a constitution which had been endorsed by the principal classes and communities in the country; and which sought for India a status of autonomy within the British Empire. However, while the British Government was willing to consider a limited measure of political autonomy for India after the conclusion of war, far short of the constitution drawn up by the Congress in 1916, its real intentions were reflected in the enactment of a repressive law, the so-called Rowlatt Act, which sought to deny to the people those basic liberties of speech and person which constitute the bedrock of civilised government in any country.

Yet the desire for political freedom among the people of India was too powerful, at this juncture, to be thwarted by the resources of coercion available to the British Government. As the war drew to a close, the demand for constitutional autonomy, voiced by the Congress in 1916, was reinforced by a number of political movements reflecting the widespread realisation among industrialists, financiers and men of business; among the professional as well as the lower middle classes; and among peasants, industrial workers and tribal communities, that the regime of exploitation set up by the British Government had to be dismantled before their moral and material creativity came into its own. The Home Rule Leagues created by Annie Besant and Bal Gangadhar Tilak reflected this sentiment among the middle and lower middle classes; though membership of the Leagues was by no means confined to men of property and education. The Muslims of India, rich and poor, landlords, merchants, artisans and peasants, were greatly distressed over the threats posed to their religious identity by British policies; and their deep sense of disquiet disposed them to make common cause with other communities in an assault on British imperialism. Most important of all were the rumblings of discontent among workers in industrial cities like Bombay, Calcutta and Ahmedabad; and among the peasants, who suffered through the heavy tax demands of the State, or through the oppressive rentals extracted by the great zamindars and taluqdars, tied through bonds of interest to the British Government.

The Indian National Congress, as it was constituted at this period, was by no means a party capable of drawing different classes and communities in India, particularly the poor in the cities and villages, into a nationwide movement against British imperialism. The leadership of the Congress was, at the commencement of the second decade of the 20th century, drawn from the educated middle classes, especially members of the legal profession, though journalists, educationalists and men of business were not absent from its ranks. As distinct from its leadership, the support base of the Congress was largely confined to the middle and lower middle classes in the cities and towns. True, there had been several occasions, prior to the First World War, when nationalist agitations had penetrated into rural society. The movement against the partition of Bengal, for instance, had spread substantially into the rural districts of the province; and drew the landed gentry and the petty zamindari classes into an agitation marked by widespread hostility towards the alien rulers of the land. Similarly, on various occasions the industrial workers, the peasants, and tribal communities had expressed their hatred of British imperialism in movements characterised by very substantial popular participation. Yet none of these movements, with the exception of the Swadeshi

Movement of Bengal, were initiated or controlled by the leaders of the Congress: The latter did not, at this juncture, possess the vision or the skills to draw such movements into a broad-based programme of political action against the British Government.

The political objectives of the Indian National Congress, in the decades prior to the First World War, were of a piece with its middle-class character. The Congress did not challenge the overall legitimacy of British rule over India. Instead, it argued for the increasing participation, at the all-India and provincial levels, of representative Indians in the legislative councils created by the British Government. The Congress also argued for a broadening of the franchise base and an extension of the powers and prerogatives of these councils. Over and above this, a number of other national issues were taken up by the Congress, prominent among which were the progressive Indianisation of the civil services and the army; the dissemination of mass literacy; and the growth of swadeshi industry. All these objectives, the Congress leadership believed, could be secured through the method of constitutional agitation; which included petitions, appeals and even political campaigns; but precluded any steps that would promote the violation of the laws of the land. Perhaps the character of the Congress in the opening decades of the 20th century is best summed up in a description by Jawaharlal Nehru of one of its annual sessions. "I visited, as a delegate, the Bankipore Congress during Christmas 1912," he states in his *Autobiography*. "It was very much an English-knowing upper class affair where morning coats and well-pressed trousers were greatly in evidence. Essentially it was a social gathering with no political excitement or tension."[1]

I

Whatever be the limitations of the Congress in the second decade of the 20th century, it was nevertheless a national organisation which had already established firm roots in the soil of India. It was also clear that, despite its restricted support base, and its limited political and constitutional objectives, the Congress was capable of being transformed into a mass organisation which could provide political militancy and a firm sense of purpose to the people of India in their struggle for freedom.

It was left to a political actor of truly epic stature, namely, Mohandas Karamchand Gandhi, to effect a dramatic transformation in the dialogue between nationalism and imperialism in India. The life story of Gandhi, who was destined to acquire the mantle of a Mahatma, is too well known to be spelt out at any length in the present context. Suffice it to mention here that the young Mohandas grew up in a devout Gujarati household, where the teachings of the Vaishnava saints, and later, those of Jain philosophers, exercised a powerful influence upon him, and stimulated in his consciousness a sympathetic relationship with popular religious sentiment in India. When Gandhi went to South Africa in 1893, in his professional capacity as a lawyer, he discovered that the Indian community there was subject to a number of discriminatory laws. The humiliation of his countrymen, rich and poor alike, affected him deeply. While he was still in South Africa, Gandhi developed a novel technique of political agitation which he called satyagraha, or moral suasion, through which he sought to persuade the White rulers of the country, by militant yet non-violent means, to extend to their Indian subjects a status of dignity in society. The success with which Gandhi was able to utilise the weapon of satyagraha in South Africa is evident from the relief with which his principal adversary, General Smuts, greeted the news of his departure for India in 1915. "The saint has left our shores, I sincerely hope for ever," he observed.

Perhaps a few observations about the ideological basis and the moral texture of satyagraha as a humanistic vision and as a guide to political action would be appropriate at this juncture. Gandhi subscribed to the view that the religious impulse in man was the noblest impulse in his being. He further equated this impulse with the eternal quest for truth, on the one hand, and the adoption of *ahimsa,* or non-violence, as the basis of individual and collective social relations, on the other. The location of a religious impulse in men, whatever be their vocation, meant that satyagraha could be effectively utilised in all social situations. Turning to the sphere of politics in the extended sense of the term, Gandhi believed that the "weapon" of satyagraha could persuade exploiters and evil-doers to undergo a change of heart, and redress the wrongs, moral and material, which they were inflicting upon others. Since satyagraha rested upon non-violence, and since it aimed at conjuring into existence the 'good society' through a change of heart rather than through the application of brute force, Gandhi was of the view that his technique of political action was not only radically different from that of others, but it also created a bond of sympathy and understanding between the exploiters and the exploited, the rulers and the ruled, at the same time as it resolved social and political problems. Finally, as he put it in *Hind Swaraj*, the most integrated expression of his social vision, satyagraha as a mode of social and political action was particularly relevant to the problems which confronted India in the opening decades of the 20th century. The path to self-determination in India, so Gandhi believed, lay in a bold assertion of autonomy in the face of British imperialism. The alien rulers of the land would have to be bluntly told:

> You have great military resources. Your naval power is matchless. If we wanted to fight with you on your own ground, we should be unable to do so, but if the above submissions be not acceptable to you, we cease to play the part of the ruled. You may, if you like, cut us to pieces. You may shatter us at the cannon's mouth. If you act contrary to our will, we shall not help you, and without our help, we know that you cannot move one step forward.
>
> It is likely that you will laugh at all this in the intoxication of your power. We may not be able to disillusion you at once; but if there be any manliness in us, you will see shortly that your laugh at our expense is an aberration of intellect. We believe that at heart you belong to a religious nation. We are living in a land which is the source of religions. How we came together need not be considered, but we can make mutual good use of our relations. . . . So doing we shall benefit each other and the world. But that will happen only when the root of our relationship is sunk in a religious soil.[3]

Gandhi's assertion that India's salvation lay in the adoption of satyagraha as the basis of political action was put to a critical test soon after his return to India. On the advice of the distinguished nationalist, G.K. Gokhale, whom he regarded as his mentor, Gandhi spent a full year travelling in different parts of the country after his return from South Africa, engaging himself in a dialogue with the urban classes (particularly the intelligentsia) which was, so he discovered, greatly attracted by the goal of national self-determination without having any idea of how they could move towards it. The path suggested by Gandhi; the path of consummating a marriage between religion and politics; of adopting non-violence as the basis of political action, seemed to offer interesting possibilities. It combined militancy of action with a measure of self-constraint singularly appropriate to the resources of power available to the people of India in their struggle against British imperialism. Yet Gandhi, at this juncture, had not achieved a breakthrough in reaching out to social classes which had hitherto remained aloof from national politics. Nor had he come around to the view that confrontation with the British Government was the only means by which the people of India could achieve their political objectives.

All this was to change dramatically during the next few years. As already suggested, the peasantry, the working classes and the tribal communities of India were becoming increasingly conscious of the social and economic exploitation to which they were being subjected, and the relationship between their wretched condition and the regime of imperial rule which obtained in the land. Indeed, throughout the second half of the 19th century, even after the uprising of 1857 had been suppressed with a ferocity unrivalled in the annals of Indian history, the rural classes—peasants as well as tribal communities—had risen again and again against their exploiters, the British rulers of the land as well as their native collaborators, in a bid to create for themselves a life of social dignity and material well-being. Similar struggles for an equitable share of the wealth which was produced in the factories characterised the activities of the working classes in the emerging centres of modern industry like Bombay, Calcutta and Ahmedabad, over a corresponding period. However, the popular struggle of peasants, workers and tribals constituted a domain of activity quite distinct hitherto from the political activity of the Congress, which had reached out primarily to the middle classes, commercial and professional, as well as to the lower middle classes, in the cities and towns of India.

It would be true to say that Gandhi, initially, was no more conscious of the political ferment at work among the popular classes in the cities and villages than the existing leadership of the Congress. The initiative in bridging this gulf and transforming the social character of the struggle for freedom came from the peasantry of a remote district in Bihar, which reached out to Gandhi, in 1916, to seek his assistance in lightening their burden of misery.

Champaran, the district in question, had for long been dominated by European planters of indigo, who forced the peasants of the region to cultivate the land on terms which were oppressive in the extreme. When Gandhi saw for himself the exploitative system set up by the planters, he organised a non-violent movement of great militancy against them. The British Government of Bihar, in the first instance, tried to suppress the satyagraha. But when it failed to do so, largely because of the skill with which Gandhi organised the peasantry, a commission of enquiry was appointed whose findings largely vindicated Gandhi's position concerning the grievances of the peasants of Champaran.

The unrest in Champaran was also reflected in the temper of the industrial and the rural classes in western India. At the very doorsteps of his ashram on the banks of the Sabarmati, Gandhi ran full tilt into the restlessness of the textile workers of Ahmedabad, who were convinced that the factory owners of the city were denying them a fair share of the profits of industry in the form of an equitable wage. Here again, Gandhi was able to persuade the textile workers to mount a struggle resting on the principles of satyagraha, and (as in Champaran) this struggle resulted in a settlement, which seemed to suggest that the path of *ahimsa* offered an effective means of resolving social and political conflict in India. Finally, the peasant proprietors of Kheda in Gujarat, the so-called patidars, were greatly distressed at an increase in their tax obligations arising out of a new revenue assessment of the district by the Government of Bombay. The leaders of the patidars, too, turned to Gandhi for guidance in their predicament. Once again Gandhi was able to present satyagraha as the weapon best suited to waging a militant struggle against the British Government. He was as successful in Kheda as he had been earlier in Champaran and in Ahmedabad.

Although the non-violent agitations conducted under Gandhi's leadership at this juncture were localised in scale, they carried a significance far beyond the localities and the social classes which they affected directly. As suggested earlier, the leadership of the Congress had, hitherto, been concerned primarily with the educated urban classes, professional and commercial. The aspirations or the grievances of the peasantry, the industrial workers and the tribal communities, had made no impact at all upon the organised national movement. Gandhi was the first outstanding leader to recognise the powerful sentiment of nationalism among the popular classes, who saw their poverty and deprivation as something for which the British Government, as well as its collaborators within Indian society, were directly responsible. If these classes were drawn into the arena of nationalist politics, the British Government in India would face a popular movement of invincible strength.

The ideological lessons which Gandhi drew from the local movements which he organised in Champaran, Ahmedabad and Kheda were equally significant. While the time-honoured methods of agitation adopted by the leaders of the Congress before the First World War—representations, petitions and even constitutional agitation—had borne little fruit over the years, there was no reason to believe that a strategy of revolutionary violence would be any more effective. The fact of the matter was that the British Government possessed resources of brute power which were infinitely superior to the resources which the nationalists could possibly muster. The truth of this assertion had been demonstrated by the manner in which the British authorities were able to suppress the outbreaks of revolutionary violence in Bengal, Maharashtra and the Punjab during the first decade of the 20th century. The break-up of the political formations created by the revolutionary nationalists, who believed that through heroic acts of violence they could trigger off a popular uprising against the British Raj, seemed to suggest that a strategy of liberation resting upon political violence had little chance of success in the context of India. The path of satyagraha offered a way out of the dilemma. It combined political militancy with a technique of mass agitation which made it difficult for the British Government to invoke physical force against the satyagrahis. Perhaps Jawaharlal Nehru spoke for an entire generation of young nationalists when he expressed his conviction that satyagraha was the most appropriate method of political action open to the people of India: "Here at last was a way out of the tangle, a method of action which was straight and open and possibly effective. I was afire with enthusiasm. . . . "[4]

II

The possibility of mounting a nationwide agitation based on

non-violence came sooner than Gandhi or his rapidly growing number of followers had anticipated. Even while the war was in progress in Europe, and in West Asia, the British Government had fashioned a dual strategy to meet the challenge of nationalism in India. The liberal face of imperialism was reflected in the Declaration of 1917, which stated that "the policy of His Majesty's Government. . . is that of. . . gradual development of self-governing institutions with a view to the progressive realisation of responsible government in India as an integral part of the British Empire."[5] To substantiate this declaration, a parliamentary committee was set up with the purpose of drafting a new constitution which would give a measure of autonomy to India; and E.S. Montagu, the Secretary of State for India, proceeded to the subcontinent to hold discussions with leaders of different persuasions, and through such discussions, to shape a new system of governance for the country.

While proposals for constitutional reform were being hammered out by Montagu, conservative civilians within the Government of India were engaged in preparing the ground for the enactment of legislation which would greatly enhance the arbitrary authority vested in the hands of the imperial administration. The initiative for such legislation was taken by Sir Reginald Craddock, the Home Member of the Viceroy's Executive Council, who was one of the most reactionary members of the Indian Civil Service. Craddock believed that the values as well as the institutions of liberal democracy were totally irrelevant to India, and he argued that the Government of India should, in no circumstances, loosen its grip over the levers of political power. Referring to the constitutional measures which Montagu and other liberals of his persuasion sought to implement, Craddock observed:

> In India today how can we apply the test of self-determination? How are we to pronounce in which direction it is?. . . There is not a single section in India who believes in or is anxious for democracy. The nearest approach to it is the mob rule, liked by the howling proletariat of the towns which the communist in his malice, and the seditionary in his blindness, are combining to produce in all the large cities. The only people who consistently throughout India acclaim a pure democratic constitution are the Brahmins for they think that even if the Brahmin's hereditary astuteness should not by itself suffice to secure him a monopoly of power the Brahmin's religious curse will supply the deficiency.[6]

Conservatives like Craddock could not stem the tide of constitutional progress in India despite the wide support which they commanded in the ranks of the British community. However, they impressed upon the Government of India the necessity of setting up a commission to assess the strength of revolutionary groups committed to a policy of violence; and to draft legislation which would enable it to deal effectively with what was described as "political crime". The Rowlatt Committee, which came into existence as a result of such pressures, explored the genesis and the strength of the revolutionary movement in India and recommended the adoption of legislation which would enable the Government of India to set aside the due processes of law in dealing with acts of political violence.

The passage of the Rowlatt Bills in the Imperial Legislative Council was opposed by nationalists of all hues. Members with radically different views—loyalists, moderates or extremists—were shocked at the insensitivity of a government which sought to arm itself with such extraordinary powers of coercion at the same time as it was seeking to win over nationalist opinion through constitutional reforms. Gandhi, in particular, was dismayed at the immorality of the whole proceedings; and the episode undermined his faith in the good intentions and in the moral integrity of the British rulers of the land. As he explained to V.S. Srinivasa Sastri, the Liberal leader:

> To me the Bills are the regulated symptoms of the deep-seated disease. They are a striking demonstration of the determination of the Civil Service to retain its grip of our necks. There is not the slightest desire to give up an iota of its unlimited powers, and if the civil service is to retain its unlimited rule over us, the British commerce is to enjoy its privileged position, I feel that the reforms will not be worth having. I consider the Bills to be an open challenge to us. If we succumb we are done for. If we may prove our word that the government will see an agitation such that they have never witnessed before, we shall have proved our capacity for resistance to arbitrary or tyrannical rule. . . . For myself if the Bills were to be proceeded with, I feel that I can no longer render peaceful obedience to the laws of a power that is capable of such a devilish legislation as these two Bills, and I would not hesitate to incite those who think with me to join me in the struggle.[7]

Since the Government of India refused to listen to the words of warning uttered by nationalist leaders within and without the Imperial Legislative Council, Gandhi took a solemn decision to organise a satyagraha, throughout the length and breadth of India, for the repeal of the Rowlatt Act. He further signed a pledge, along with a handful of his close associates, voicing his determination to "refuse civilly to oppose the laws [the Rowlatt Bills] and such other laws, as a Committee hitherto appointed may think fit and we further affirm that in this struggle we will faithfully follow truth and refrain from violence to life, person or property."[8] At the same time, Gandhi wrote an open letter to the people of India, seeking their moral support and urging them to participate in the satyagraha which he was initiating against the British Government.[9]

Gandhi had even prior to 1919 led with conspicuous success non-violent agitations in South Africa and in India. Yet the scale of the Rowlatt Satyagraha was qualitatively different from the scale of the earlier agitations. In the spring of 1919, Gandhi appealed to an entire nation of 400 million to launch an assault upon the British Government of India through a novel technique of political warfare. Furthermore, although Gandhi had set up Satyagraha Sabhas in a few cities to guide the agitation against the Rowlatt Act, he could not at this juncture claim the support of any national organisation like the Indian National Congress. All he had to back his call for a countrywide satyagraha was his reputation for piety, truthfulness and courage among the common people; as well as the widespread hostility of his countrymen to the Rowlatt Act, which symbolised their subject state.

Nevertheless, Gandhi was agreeably surprised at the enthusiasm with which the people of India responded to his call for a satyagraha against the Rowlatt Act. All over the country, Hindus and Muslims, the rich and the poor, businessmen and professionals, industrialists and workers, and artisans and lumpen elements, rose in a mighty movement of protest against the British Government. Broadly speaking, the agitation was stronger in the cities and in the larger towns than in the rural areas; though it reached out to the smaller towns, market centres and even villages in Gujarat and in the Punjab; and to a lesser extent, in the United Provinces and in western Maharashtra. But in the cities and larger towns, too, the satyagraha was supported by different classes and communities to varying extents. In Bombay, the satyagraha was observed in the main by the middle and lower middle classes drawn from the Gujarati and the Muslim communities. In Ahmedabad, Gandhi's adopted hometown, and the site of the Sabarmati Ashram, the mercantile and the professional classes, as well as the workers, Hindus and Muslims, rallied to his support in great numbers. Calcutta was relatively quiet despite its great reputation for being one of the liveliest centres of nationalist politics in India. However, the cities of the south, particularly Madras, witnessed numerous demonstrations of support for the satyagraha. But it was the cities of northern India, Delhi, Lahore and Amritsar, and the numerous district towns of the region, which witnessed the most crowded, the most vociferous and the most enthusiastic demonstrations for the repeal of the Rowlatt Act.

The agitation launched by Gandhi in April 1919 was unprecedented in nationalist history in two respects. First, it was truly subcontinental in character; and secondly, it attracted classes and communities in the cities and towns which had hitherto refrained from participating in nationalist agitations. Moreover, all available evidence suggests that the people who participated in the satyagraha—Hindus or Muslims, the rich or the poor, the middle classes or the lower orders—demonstrated their hostility to the British Government in a manner remarkable for its orderliness and discipline. That the agitation took a violent turn, partly in the cities of western India, but more particularly in the cities of the north, Delhi, Lahore and Amritsar, besides a number of small district towns and rural market centres, was largely due to the attempt of the local British administrators to suppress popular demonstrations, initially through the use of police, but subsequently through calling in the army. The most horrifying incident in the course of the Rowlatt Satyagraha took place in Amritsar where, on 13 April 1919, the army fired upon a peaceful crowd of 20,000 citizens, which had assembled in response to the call of local Congress leaders, killing 397 and wounding 1,143 of them. In the face of such ferocious repression, the agitation against the Rowlatt Act soon ground to a halt. Yet the tumultuous events of April 1919 demonstrated beyond the shadow of doubt that a consciousness of national unity and a sense of national purpose had crystallised among the people of India. They also demonstrated the effectiveness with which Gandhi could reach out to different classes and communities in the country. Moreover, the extent to which people all over India participated in the Rowlatt Satyagraha clearly symbolised the transfer of "moral authority" over the country from the hands of the British Government into the hands of the nationalist leadership. Indeed, this "moral authority" was now vested in the person of Gandhi, who was very soon to assume formal leadership over the Indian National Congress.

III

While the social and economic discontents which affected different classes and communities in India during the opening decades of the 20th century provided the backdrop to nationalist ferment against the British Raj, it would be a gross mistake to assume that such discontents, in themselves, provide a full explanation of demonstrations of popular will like the Rowlatt Satyagraha. Nationalism is as much a moral as it is a materialist phenomenon; and national movements are as much concerned with political and cultural objectives as they are with social and economic objectives. To this axiom the growth of nationalism in India was no exception. The people of India, the elites as well as the popular classes, were increasingly drawn to the belief that their liberation from British rule would enable them to initiate a moral revolution at the same time as it enabled them to create for themselves a new era of material prosperity.

Nothing illustrates the ideological as opposed to the material underpinning of nationalism in India better than the sentiment of Khilafat in the Muslim community; and the manner in which a spiritual crisis drew the followers of Islam, merchants and artisans, the landed gentry and the peasantry, and even the lumpen classes, into agitations against the British Raj. Already by the end of the 19th century, the *ulema* or the clerical classes, and a few other sections of the Muslim community, particularly the minor gentry and the artisans, were attracted by the heady vision of Pan-Islamism. Under the influence of this ideology, such Muslims began looking beyond the frontiers of India, to the Ottoman Empire (whose Sultan claimed to be the Khalifa, or the spiritual head, of Muslims throughout the world) for redefining their religious identity as well as for reassurance at a time when Muslim fortunes in India seemed to be at a low ebb. The hostility to imperialism of such Muslims was reinforced by a growing middle class in the community, which was drawn to the idea of political autonomy for India, for reasons similar to those which stimulated nationalism in the Hindu middle classes.

The leadership of the Muslim community in India, at this juncture, lay in the hands of clerical figures like Maulana Abul Kalam Azad and Maulana Abdul Bari; and secular figures like Mohamed Ali and Shaukat Ali. The outbreak of war in 1914 reinforced Pan-Islamic sentiment in India, since Britain and Turkey found themselves in the position of belligerents. However, it was the defeat of Turkey (along with Germany) in 1918 that conjured into existence a qualitative change in the temper of Muslim politics in India. There was now a growing fear among the Muslims that the Ottoman Empire would be dismembered, as part of the post-war settlement, with grave consequences for the status of Islam in the world community. Faced with this threat to their moral identity, the clerical classes organised themselves into a *Majlis-a-Ulema-a-Hind,* and the secular leaders set up a Central Khilafat Committee. Both organisations had branches throughout the country. The establishment of an alliance between the secular leaders and the *ulema,* who had close links with the community as a whole, was a momentous happening. From the pulpits of hundreds of mosques in cities and towns, the *ulema* spoke to the Muslim community of the grave danger to their religion. Small wonder, then, that Muslims of all classes became very hostile to the British Government, which sentiment was reflected, among other things, in the support which they extended to the satyagraha against the Rowlatt Act in April 1919.

Gandhi was acutely conscious of the sentiments abroad in the Muslim community. He was also aware of the opportunity which these sentiments afforded for a great Hindu-Muslim entente against the British Raj. True, the two communities had already established a united front at the annual session of the Congress in 1916. But this alliance had barely affected classes other than the educated and the professional classes. The Khilafat issue, however, had made a very profound impression upon the poor Muslim classes, like the artisans, the industrial workers and the peasantry. Gandhi was very sensitive to the religious sensibilities of the people, and his vision of the good society, in which the religious impulse represented all that was true and noble in man, encouraged him to look favourably upon the induction of religious grievances for political purposes. As he pointed out before a gathering of Khilafatists in Bombay:

> There are two things to which I am devoting my life—permanent unity between Hindus and Muslims, and satyagraha. . . . The question that I have to answer this evening is: How can I help in having a Mahomedan question emerging out of the late war properly solved? After my arrival in India, I began to find out good Mahomedan leaders. My desire was satisfied when I reached Delhi, and found the Brothers Ali, whom I had the privilege of knowing before. It was a question of love at first sight. When I met Dr Ansari, the circle of Mahomedan friends widened and at last it even included Maulana Abdul Bari of Lucknow. I have discussed the Mahomedan question with all these friends . . . and I feel that this question is the greatest of all . . . for it affects the religious susceptibilities of millions of Mahomedans. . . .
>
> It may be asked why I, a Hindu, bother my head about the Mahomedan question. The answer is that as you are my neighbours and my countrymen, it is my duty to share your sorrow. I cannot talk about Hindu-Muslim Unity and fail to give effect to the idea when the test has arrived.[10]

Notwithstanding the massacre at Jallianwala Bagh and Muslim anger over Khilafat, when the Congress met in annual session in Amritsar late in 1919, Gandhi was unwilling to mount a frontal assault on the British Raj in India. Perhaps Gandhi's moderation was shaped by a number of considerations. In the first instance, the British had announced a new package of constitutional reforms in 1919, which reforms, while they fell short of nationalist expectations, nevertheless substantially increased the powers of popularly elected Indian representatives in the legislative councils. Next, while the statements expressing British intentions about the fate of Turkey in the post-war settlement were the reverse of reassuring, a peace treaty had still to be formulated with those in control of affairs at Constantinople. Last but not least, the British Government had appointed a commission of enquiry into the happenings in the Punjab, and elsewhere, in the course of the Rowlatt Satyagraha; and the report of this committee was anxiously awaited by all sections of opinion in India. For all these reasons, Gandhi was reluctant to declare war on the British Government before it had spelt out its attitude on the great issues of Khilafat and self-determination which were agitating the minds of the people.

The crucial question before the leadership of the Congress at the annual session of 1919 was the attitude to be adopted to the constitutional reforms which had been announced shortly before the session commenced. Along with the reforms came a conciliatory Royal Proclamation which stated: "It is my earnest desire at this time that so far as possible all traces of bitterness between my people and those who are responsible for my government should be obliterated. . . . A new era is opening. Let us begin with a common determination among my people and my officers to work together for a common purpose."[11] C.R. Das, the great Bengali leader, moved a resolution which defined the Reforms Act as "inadequate, unsatisfactory and disappointing." It was also stated therein that "This Congress further urges that Parliament should take early steps to establish full responsible government in India in accordance with the principles of self-determination."[12] While broadly supporting the resolution of C.R. Das, Gandhi moved an amendment in which he suggested the deletion of the word 'disappointing' in describing the Reforms Act, and the addition of a clause welcoming the substance as well as the spirit of the Royal Proclamation. As he in effect observed while moving his amendment: The traditions of India made it obligatory that the integrity of one's opponent be honoured in the first instance. Yet if the British Government overlooked the popular desire for freedom, then it would have to be opposed through the weapon of satyagraha.[13]

Despite the moderation of the Congress leaders at Amritsar in December 1919, the events of the next few months made it clear that the British Government was set upon a collision course with nationalist sentiment in India. The Muslim community was particularly incensed over the Khilafat issue; and Gandhi, who was in close touch with the Muslim leaders, put before them the idea of an agitation resting on the principles of non-violence to redress the wrongs suffered by their followers. The programme of non-cooperation, as put forward by Gandhi, in the first instance to the Muslim leadership, was brilliant in its simplicity of design and pregnant with the most momentous possibilities. It was based upon the assumption that the British Government in India could function only because the people associated themselves with it in a number of ways. If the people refused to co-operate with the British Government; if they rejected the institutions of education, law and administration set up under British aegis; and if they further refused to pay their taxes; then the British Raj would collapse like a house of cards, and the people of India would earn for themselves swaraj. Needless to say, such a programme of action would have to be mounted on a strictly non-violent basis. Otherwise, so Gandhi believed, not only would the people of India reveal a fatal weakness in their moral fibre, but the British Government would exploit its resources of brute strength to suppress the struggle.

Two events of the spring of 1920 were destined to draw the major religious communities, Hindu and Muslim, fully behind the programme of action drawn up by Gandhi. On 15 May 1920, the British Government published the text of the peace treaty with Turkey, along with a lengthy message from the viceroy to the "Muslim People of India" asking them to accept "terms which I fear will be painful to all Muslims".[14] Less than a fortnight later, the Hunter Committee, which had been appointed to look into the unfortunate incidents associated with the Rowlatt Satyagraha, placed its findings before the public. The report, not surprisingly, was a clumsy attempt at justifying the humiliation and worse which the Punjab Government had imposed upon the Punjabis as a whole and upon the citizens of Amritsar in particular. Indeed, so partial were the findings of the Hunter Committee, that its Indian members, who were in a minority, refused to endorse the views of the European members, and came out with a Minority Report which was a scathing indictment of British civil and military authorities.

The publication of the peace treaty with Turkey, and the findings of the Hunter Commission, represented, so Gandhi believed, the utter moral bankruptcy of the British Government in India. He now felt justified in appealing to the people to adopt the path of satyagraha to rid themselves of a government which was 'satanic' in its total disregard of the conventions of civilized governance. A meeting of the AICC at Banaras, on 30 May, decided to call a special session of the Congress, at Calcutta, in September 1920, to debate the proposal for the adoption of non-cooperation. The Muslim leadership of India, which reflected the anger of their constituents at the manner in which they had been betrayed by the British Government, decided to adopt the Gandhian programme, in its entirety, without waiting for the special session of the Congress. At a meeting of the Central Khilafat Committee at Allahabad, on 2 June, at which Gandhi and some other prominent Hindu leaders were present in the capacity of special invitees, a formal decision was taken, whereby the task of organising a non-violent assault on the British Government was entrusted to a small committee consisting of Gandhi, Mohamed Ali and Shaukat Ali.

Despite the support which Gandhi enjoyed from the Muslim community, the Congress session at Calcutta, where the proposal to adopt non-cooperation was to be debated, proved to be a very turbulent affair. Lajpat Rai, a veteran leader of the Punjab and the president of the Calcutta session was opposed to the Gandhian programme, though he refrained from voicing his views in his presidential address. However, when Gandhi formally moved a resolution committing the Congress to non-cooperation, a number of leaders from Bengal, Maharashtra, the Central Provinces, the United Provinces, and the provinces of the south, prominent among them being B.C. Pal, C.R. Das, M.M. Malaviya, Joseph Baptista, M.A. Jinnah and Satyamurti, opposed it. Indeed, Motilal Nehru was alone among the established leaders of the Congress in supporting Gandhi at this juncture. Nevertheless, in contrast to the stance of the leadership, the rank and file delegates who had assembled at Calcutta were largely behind the Mahatma in his call for a non-violent assault on the British Raj; and his resolution advocating the adoption of non-cooperation was upheld by a large majority (1,826 votes against 984).[15]

The popular support for Gandhi, for the attainment of swaraj, and for satyagraha as the weapon most likely to attain this objective, is eloquently reflected in the proceedings of the annual session of the Congress held at Nagpur in December 1920. When the Congress leaders returned to their respective provinces, after the deliberations of September 1920 at Calcutta, they discovered the full extent to which Gandhi's moral authority reached out, over their heads, to different classes and communities in India; and this persuaded them to support a satyagraha movement against the British Government. Even the educated classes of Bengal, which were as passionately nationalistic as they were proud of their commitment to the institutions of representative politics, responded to the Mahatma's charisma in a manner which obliged their leader, C.R. Das, to reconsider his attitude towards non-cooperation, which included, among other things, a ban on contesting election to legislative councils. In Maharashtra, in the Punjab, in the Central Provinces, in the provinces of the south, indeed, throughout the length and breadth of India, nationalist leaders of different persuasions discerned that the message of swaraj had made a great impression upon the popular psyche; and had transformed Gandhi into a truly national figure, eclipsing everyone else on the political stage. The annual session of the Congress at Nagpur, therefore, witnessed an overwhelming demonstration of support for the Mahatma. The resolution committing the Congress to non-cooperation was moved by C.R. Das, who appealed to "every lawyer, every student, every trader, every agriculturist, every merchant, and everybody in the country"[16] to respond to the call for swaraj. The resolution was adopted without a dissenting voice. Gandhi's triumph was complete. He had behind him a great political organisation and the support of the overwhelming majority of the people of India in the epic struggle to be waged on non-violent lines against the greatest imperial power known to human history.

The manner in which the people of India, Hindus, Muslims and Sikhs, rich and poor, zamindars and kisans, capitalists and workers, the educated and the unlettered, fought British imperialism under the leadership of Mahatma Gandhi and the Indian National Congress, is recapitulated in various studies on Indian Nationalism. Suffice it to mention here that the challenge which the non-cooperation movement posed to the British Raj was more serious than any challenge which it had encountered since 1857. Unlike the uprising of 1857, however, non-cooperation rested upon a modern notion of nationalism; and the movement was characterised by a spatial distribution and a social depth absent in the events which convulsed India in the middle of the 19th century. For these reasons, and also because of the extent to which Gandhi's moral influence and the prospect of swaraj reached out to the common people of India, the non-cooperation movement posed to the British Government the most intractable problems of political control and management. Perhaps what the agitation meant to 'faces in the crowd' is reflected with great sensitivity in the following quotations, which describe what the millworkers in Bombay, the peasants of Avadh, and the tribal folk of Gujarat, respectively, *felt* and *believed* during these stormy years.

> Item: While our struggle. . . was going on in this manner [stated A.A. Alwe, a worker in the Bombay Textile industry] the drum of political agitation was being beaten in the country. The Congress started a great agitation demanding rights for India to conduct her own administration. At that time we workers understood the meaning of this demand for swaraj to be only this; that our indebtedness would disappear, the oppression of the moneylender would stop, our wages would increase, and the oppression of the owner on the worker, the kicks and blows with which they belabour us, would stop by legislation, and that as a result of it, the persecution of us workers would come to an end. These and other thoughts came into the minds of us workers, and a good many workers from among us, and I myself, enlisted ourselves as volunteers in the non-cooperation movement.[17]
>
> Item: The currency which Mr. Gandhi's name has acquired in the remotest villages is astonishing. No one seems to know quite who or what he is, but it is an accepted fact that what he says is so, and what he orders must be done. He is a *Mahatma or Sadhu, a Pandit, a Brahaman* [learned one] who lives at Allahabad, even a *Deota* [angel]. One man said he was a merchant who sells cloth at three annas a yard . . . the most intelligent say he is a man who is working for the good of the country, but the *real power of his name is perhaps to be traced back to the idea that it was he who got bedakhili stopped in Pratapgarh*, it is the curious instance of the power of a name.[18]
>
> Item: Some men are possessed by Gandhi [reported the Mamlatdar of Bardoli Taluka in 1922] who asks the people to discard foreign cloth, use khaddar and give up drink, the people say they see Gandhi sitting on village wells and spinning on charkha.[19]

The grand conflict between nationalism and imperialism, at this juncture, was best reflected in the reception accorded to the Prince of Wales when he visited India towards the end of 1921. The royal visit was organised by the British Government with the objective of undermining the nationalist struggle that was in progress; and it reflected the belief in official circles that nationalism was a superficial phenomenon; and that the common people were still loyal to the British Crown. Gandhi handled the royal visit with masterly skill "[We]. . . have nothing against the prince as a man,' he stated. "[but]. . . India will refuse to welcome a representative of a system of which she is sick to death."[20] Symbolically, and with a touch of high drama, precisely when the Prince of Wales landed at Bombay harbour on 17 November 1921, the Mahatma was addressing a large crowd of 60,000 at a meeting in the heart of the industrial suburbs in the city, on which occasion he also applied the torch to a huge pile of foreign cloth which had been collected specifically for this purpose. The progress of the prince through the principal cities of India was, from the British viewpoint, an unmitigated disaster, although the viceroy, Lord Reading, and the members of the British Civil Service, attempted to mask the true magnitude of popular hostility to the royal visitor. Nevertheless, the Prince of Wales wrote to the viceroy about a visit to a university, in particular, in terms which suggested that he suffered from no illusions: "They tried to kid me by filling up the empty student seats with high school boys, boy-scouts and Europeans. I imagine they hoped I would never get to hear of what had been done, or realise what a b.f. they had made of me !!!"[21]

As the movement to wrest swaraj from the British Government gained momentum, Gandhi and the Congress leaders faced difficult questions of control and management of their followers. The mobilisation of the people of a subcontinent as vast as India was a truly stupendous undertaking. This was so partly because non-cooperation rested upon the principles of *ahimsa,* an article of strict faith for Gandhi; but partly also because the Mahatma was apprehensive that outbreaks of violence would provide the British Government with the opportunity, and the justification, to intervene with brutal force, and crush not only the perpetrators of violence, but also the movement as a whole. Moreover, the cleavages of class, community and religion within Indian society could assume a menacing form and erupt into sectarian or communal conflict once violence was accepted as a legitimate instrument of the anti-imperialist struggle. Indeed, even in the city of Bombay, where the Congress possessed a formidable organisation, the demonstrations against the Prince of Wales soon led to violence between Hindus and Muslims, on the one hand, and Parsis and Christians, on the other. Much more serious was the Moplah uprising of Kerala, where a Muslim peasantry, incensed over the issue of Khilafat, attacked the British Government at the same time as it went on a rampage against the superior Hindu rural classes in the region.

The possibility of violence against the British Government, or between different classes and communities within Indian society, haunted Gandhi all the more because he was contemplating, at that time, the use of the most militant weapon available to a satyagrahi, namely, refusal to pay taxes to a government which had lost the moral right to rule. To initiate this phase of the movement, Gandhi had selected the taluka of Bardoli in Surat district. The patidars, the peasant proprietors of this region, had been organised for a non-violent struggle under the leadership of Vallabhbhai Patel, one of Gandhi's principal lieutenants, and the no-tax campaign at Bardoli was expected to shake the edifice of the British Raj to its very foundations.

However, when the patidars of Bardoli were all set to defy the British Government, an act of violence in the United Provinces persuaded the Mahatma to suspend the movement for non-co-operation altogether. The occasion was provided by the peasants of a village called Chauri Chaura in Gorakhpur district, who, when fired upon by the policemen of a local thana, retaliated by burning down the thana and killing their oppressors. Gandhi saw in this ugly episode the symptoms of a deep-rooted malaise. The incident also revealed the extent to which violence had struck roots at the very core of Indian society; and the less than profound impact which the propagation of *ahimsa* had made on the people. From all over the country, whether it was the United Provinces, or Bombay, or Gujarat, or Kerala, or Rajasthan; or the provinces of the Northwest and the Northeast, where substantial Muslim communities, deeply agitated over the Khilafat issue, were located; the perceptions reaching out to the Mahatma suggested that an intensification of the struggle would lead to violent uprisings against the British Raj. Such uprisings would provide the authorities with the pretext to unleash a reign of terror, in which non-violent and legitimate forms of political protest would be put down with the same ruthlessness as violent and "illegitimate" forms of political protest. Moreover, as the example of Kerala demonstrated, the prospect of social conflict between different religious communities was also a prospect which loomed ominously in the horizon. For these reasons, the Congress Working Committee, at a meeting held in February 1922, at the personal initiative of Gandhi, called off the non-cooperation movement, and advised the people to embark upon a programme of constructive activity, having as its objective the regeneration of Indian society.

IV

When the nationalist leaders surveyed the political scene after the suspension of non-cooperation in the spring of 1922, they discovered that the countrywide agitation of epic proportions, initiated by Mahatma Gandhi in the autumn of 1920, had suddenly been transformed into a fragmented and disorganised force. That matters had come to such a pass was hardly surprising. For the leaders, no less than for the rank and file, the suspension of non-cooperation ostensibly appeared to be an ill-advised move; more particularly because it came at a moment when nationalist fervour was at its peak; and the people of India, so it appeared, were ready for a final struggle. Lajpat Rai, the distinguished leader of the Punjab, spoke for many when he wrote to the Congress Working Committee:

> Our defeat is in proportion to the greatness of our leader. . . Mahatmaji pitched his standard too high. . . . To change the hearts of mobs in such a way as to make it impossible for them to indulge in such brutalities without changing the hearts of governments that rule over them, is an impossibility . . . leaders of political campaigns for freedom cannot afford to wear their hearts on their sleeves. . . . [22]

Yet Gandhi, as suggested earlier, had his own reasons for calling off the nationwide movement. In a communication to Jawaharlal Nehru, who had been no less upset at the decision to suspend non-cooperation than Lajpat Rai, or C.R. Das, or Motilal Nehru, he observed: "I assure you that if the thing [i.e., the non-cooperation movement] had not been suspended we would have been leading not a non-violent struggle but certainly a violent struggle."[23]

To suggest a way out of the dilemma, the Congress created a committee, called the Civil Disobedience Enquiry Committee, to review the events of the past two years and to chalk out an appropriate course of action. This committee, on completing its task, found it difficult to recommend a clear plan of action. Its members were unanimously of the view that it was inadvisable to launch a fresh civil disobedience movement in the prevailing circumstances. However, on the crucial question whether members of the Congress ought to contest elections for the reformed legislatures, there was a serious difference of opinion. Some of the members of the committee, the so-called "no-changers", were against entry into the legislatures. Others, who were called "pro-changers", believed that it was advisable, indeed, necessary to contest elections for entry into the legislatures, if only with the objective of wrecking them.

Prominent among the pro-changers were men like C.R. Das, Motilal Nehru, Hakim Ajmal Khan and Vithalbhai Patel. The logic of their position, late in 1922, after the virtual collapse of the non-cooperation movement, needs to be briefly recapitulated at this point. The people of India, Hindus and Muslims, rich and poor, rural and urban folk, had demonstrated an extraordinary solidarity, and a remarkable capacity for self-sacrifice, in response to the Mahatma's call for a non-violent struggle against the British Government. Nevertheless, when the people were all set for a decisive trial of strength, Gandhi, for reasons which were perfectly valid in themselves, had called off the movement. The powerful sentiment for the attainment of swaraj, which had been so skilfully conjured into existence by the Mahatma, in such diverse classes and communities in India, urgently called for a creative outlet; an outlet, moreover, that would help the people attain the objectives which the prophet of non-violence had enumerated in 1920. What could be more appropriate than transferring the nationalist struggle on to the arena of the new legislatures created by the Act of 1919? The essence of the 'pro-changers' strategy lay in capturing the reformed legislatures and utilising them to put an end to British control over India's destiny. The battle for swaraj had been fought earlier through a non-violent confrontation between the satyagrahis and the British Government of India; this struggle was now to be fought in the central legislature at Delhi; and in the provincial legislatures scattered throughout the land. The British Government had created these representative institutions, with their special constituencies and their limited franchise, in order to curb the forces of nationalism. But the pro-changers sought to transform the legislatures into instruments of the national will, which the skilful leadership of the Mahatma had aroused to an unprecedented level of political awareness in the post-war years.

C.R. Das, who, along with Motilal Nehru, spearheaded the move for a new nationalist strategy, put the case for council entry, as he termed it, forcefully in his presidential address before the Gaya session of the Indian National Congress in December 1922.

Defining nationalism as a process "through which a nation expresses itself and finds itself", Das described the freedom movement as the "great purposeful unfolding" of the political destiny of India. That this "purposeful unfolding" of the national destiny was to be achieved through non-violent non-cooperation, the novel weapon of struggle fashioned by the Mahatma, Das argued, was a matter on which no one entertained any doubts. The Constitutional Reforms of 1919 were actually designed to frustrate the movement for swaraj. However, consistently with the principles of non-cooperation, it was incumbent upon all true nationalists to first establish control over the legislatures through the electoral process, and then to destroy them. In the words of C.R. Das:

> I am . . . of opinion that the system of the reformed councils . . . is absolutely unsuitable to the nature and genius of the Indian nation. It is an attempt of the British Parliament to force a foreign system upon the Indian people. . . . Boycott of the reformed councils, to my mind, means that such steps must be taken that these councils may not be there to impede the progress of Swaraj. The only successful boycott of the councils is either to bend them in a manner suitable to Swaraj or to end them completely. That is the way in which I endorse the motion to boycott the councils.[24]

Notwithstanding the oratorical skill with which C.R. Das and other Swarajists presented the case for a change in nationalist strategy at the Gaya Congress, they were unable to win over a majority of the leaders who had responded to the Mahatma's call for non-cooperation in 1920. In view of this, they created a new organisation called the "Congress Khilafat Swaraj Party", with, C.R. Das as president and Motilal Nehru as general secretary. The Swaraj Party, as it was popularly known, proclaimed its overall loyalty to the creed of the Mahatma. But instead of seeking freedom through the weapon of boycott, it sought to undermine the British Raj through obstructing the conduct of business in the new legislatures, which had come into existence as a result of the Reforms of 1919.

Although C.R. Das was the president of the Swaraj Party, he was so deeply involved in the politics of Bengal that the affairs of the party at the national level were largely left in the hands of Motilal Nehru. The election manifesto of the new party, which was issued in October 1923, described the Swarajists as "a party within the Congress, and as such an integral part of the Congress".[25] The Swarajists were committed, through their manifesto, to the cause of India's freedom. But they sought to secure this objective through means slightly different from those suggested by Gandhi. Instead of relying wholly on the boycott of the institutions created by the British Raj, the Swarajists were prepared to carry the struggle into the enemy's camp by entering the councils. The vigorous campaign conducted by the Swarajist leaders in 1923, and the popularity of their stance with the electorate, were admirably reflected in the impressive support which they won in the elections. In the Central Legislative Assembly, the Swaraj Party won 41 out of 101 elective seats. It fared equally well in the provincial legislatures of the United Provinces, Assam and Bengal. Indeed, in the case of the Central Provinces it won an outright majority.

The Central Legislative Assembly which met in New Delhi in January 1924 was the first representation body in which organised nationalist opinion, in the form of the Swaraj Party, could express views on questions relating to the welfare and the destiny of the people. Motilal Nehru, as the leader of the Swaraj Party, was the dominating figure in the legislature. He secured a victory of very considerable proportions when, at the very outset, he was able to draw the Muslims and the Moderate members of the assembly into a loose alliance with the Swaraj Party. The resulting coalition, the so-called Nationalist Party, possessed the strength in numbers to out-vote the official members and government stooges in the Central Legislature. Such a consummation placed in the hands of the Swarajists a most formidable weapon in their campaign to wreck the new constitution from within the councils.

The strength of the Nationalist Party in the Central Legislature, the core of which party was made up of the Swarajists, made itself felt at the very commencement of the new session. The constellation of political groups, which had been brought together by the adroit leadership of Motilal Nehru, embarked upon a well-organised campaign to wrest political concessions from the British Government. The opening shot was fired by a private member who moved a resolution recommending the appointment of a Royal Commission to review the Constitution of 1919 in such a manner as to secure for India the status of a self-governing dominion within the British Empire. Immediately thereafter, Motilal

Nehru presented an amendment to this resolution proposing that a new constitution be framed through a Round Table Conference, drawing upon leaders who represented different schools of political thought in India. As was to be expected, this demand was summarily rejected by Sir Malcolm Hailey, the spokesman of the British Government in the Central Legislature, who argued that the Constitution of 1919 had provided for a machinery of review after a decade, that is, in 1929. But Motilal Nehru would have nothing to do with assurances which amounted to acts of grace on the part of the British Government. Moreover, he was of the opinion that the Constitution of 1919, upon which Hailey had taken his stand, was a piece of legislation designed for the sole purpose of thwarting the aspirations of the people for political liberty. If the British Government could see its way to satisfying these aspirations, then the Swarajists and their allies would extend a hand of co-operation to the alien rulers. But if it took a contrary position, then, Motilal declared, "we shall, like men, stand upon our rights and continue to be non-cooperators."[26]

That the British Government should reject the demand for a Round Table Conference, on the understanding that it would lead to political autonomy for India, surprised no one, least of all Motilal Nehru and the members of the Nationalist Party in the Central Legislature. Yet the Swarajists and their allies were able to score a very substantial victory over the official bloc in the Assembly, when 76 members voted in favour of Motilal Nehru's amendment, and only 48 voted against it. From this victory, the Nationalist Party proceeded to defeat the government and its supporters on a number of issues: for instance, the first four budgetary demands were rejected in their entirety; and a finance bill, too, was thrown out altogether. However, the Constitution of 1919 conferred on the viceroy the power to veto decisions of the legislature. As a result, the Swarajist victories were not productive of any political effect, since the viceroy, on each occasion when the government was defeated, took recourse to the special powers with which he had been invested by the constitution. Nevertheless, the effect of the Swarajist victories, which were broadcast throughout the land by a jubilant nationalist press, was tremendous, and made the British Government look extremely ridiculous in the eyes of the educated classes of India.

With the victories which the Swaraj Party and its allies won over the British Government in the Central Legislative Assembly, the Swarajist stock stood extremely high in nationalist circles. Consequently, C.R. Das and Motilal Nehru made a renewed bid to win over the Mahatma to their viewpoint towards the middle of the year. However, for Gandhi, non-violence was a philosophical truth to which he was deeply committed; and the strategy and tactics of non-cooperation were inextricably linked to his overall view of the human condition. Small wonder, then, that the Swarajist argument that the happenings of 1922—the incident at Chauri Chaura and the consequent suspension of non-co-operation—called for a new look at the political situation; indeed, for a change of tactics in the struggle against imperialism; wholly failed to move the Mahatma. Yet Gandhi was not blind to the fact that differences between nationalist leaders worked entirely to the advantage of the British Government. Later in the year, therefore, he reached an agreement with C.R. Das and Motilal Nehru, whereby their party became an integral constituent of the Indian National Congress. This understanding, which signified a closing of the nationalist ranks, was eventually ratified at the Belgaum session of the Indian National Congress, in December 1924, which was held under the presidentship of Mahatma Gandhi. As he said on this occasion:

> Not much need be said about the status of equality given to the Swaraj Party. I wish I could have avoided it, not because the party is not worthy, but because I do not share its views about council entry. But if I must remain in the Congress, even lead it, I must recognize the facts as they are. It is easy for me to go out of the Congress . . . but it was not, so I thought and still think, in the interests of the country for me to take that step. The Swaraj Party represents, if not a majority, at least a strong and growing minority in the Congress. If I were not to divide the Congress on the issue of its status, I was bound to agree to its conditions, so long as they were not in conflict with my conscience. They are not, in my opinion, unreasonable. The Swarajists want to use the name of the Congress for their policy. A formula has to be found for their doing so without their pledging or binding the no-changers to their policy. . . .[27]

Notwithstanding the spirited opposition which the Swaraj Party and its allies offered to the British Government in the Central

Legislative Assembly during 1924-5, the Nationalist Party conjured into existence by Motilal Nehru was actually a very fragile alliance of disparate political formations. The Party included, besides the Swarajists, Moderates and Muslim members, who were by no means fully committed to the policy of wrecking the constitution from within the councils. Indeed, the provincial leaders who had gathered under the umbrella of the Swaraj Party, particularly those hailing from the Central Provinces and the Presidency of Bombay, also resented the constraints which the strategy of breaking up the constitution from within imposed upon them. These provincial leaders—M.R. Jayakar, N.C. Kelkar and B.S. Moonje, among others—were men who had taken to politics under the aegis of Tilak; and although they had, as a matter of expediency, accepted the Swarajist label in 1922, they were actually "responsivists", who believed in working the constitutional system which had been created in 1919, although their strategic objectives were no different from those of C.R. Das and Motilal Nehru, on the one hand, and Mahatma Gandhi and the no-changers, on the other.

These differences in ideology between different constituents of the Nationalist Party were greatly heightened by the constitutional prerogatives enjoyed by the viceroy and the provincial governors under the constitution of 1919. As mentioned earlier, even though the Swarajists and their allies succeeded in rejecting crucial bills in the central and provincial legislatures, the use of the veto by the viceroy, and the provincial governors, robbed such victories of any political effect. Such a stalemate, not surprisingly, encouraged dissidence to rear its head in the nationalist ranks, particularly on the part of the erstwhile Tilakites. The dissidence of the former Tilakites assumed the form of an open revolt when S.B. Tambe, the Swarajist leader in the assembly of the Central Provinces, accepted nomination to the Executive Council of the Governor. In this act of revolt, Tambe had the tacit if not the open support of M.R. Jayakar, the Swarajist leader of the Presidency of Bombay.

What Mahatma Gandhi and the no-changers who supported his stance had feared in 1922, thus actually came to pass. Nationalists who had fought elections and entered the assemblies, presumably in order to wreck them, found the lure of executive office irresistible, and abandoned the wider objectives which had inspired them to enter into constitutional "dialogue" with the British

Government of India, at the central as well as the provincial levels. The Swarajists who remained true to their mandate thus found themselves on a very slippery path, indeed. However, with C.R. Das no more, Motilal Nehru was quick to see the writing on the wall. He soon came to the decision that an orderly retreat was necessary. On 8 March 1926, therefore, he led the Swaraj Party out of the Central Legislative Assembly, in order to demonstrate that he and his followers would have nothing to do with an imperial government which was so unsympathetic to the popular desire for Swaraj.

The Swarajist walk-out from the Central Legislative Assembly in 1926 bears eloquent witness to the sensitivity of leaders like Motilal Nehru to the winds of change that were blowing through the subcontinent. In 1922, after the Chauri Chaura incident and the suspension of non-cooperation, the social anger of the people, and their desire for a show-down with the British Government called for a programme of action wherein popular sentiment could express itself through militant action. Precisely for this reason, the Swarajists had attempted to transform the central and provincial legislatures into theatres of confrontation between nationalism and imperialism. Yet, by 1926, the legislative arena chosen by the Swarajists for this purpose appeared to be a disadvantageous location for giving battle to the British Government. Indeed, it is difficult to resist the conclusion that the period 1922-6 was, in a manner of speaking, a most trying period for nationalists of different persuasions in India. Not only had the agitation launched by the Mahatma come to an abrupt end in 1922, but cleavages between different religious communities, as well as between different generations of nationalist leaders, had become manifest in the body politic. The most alarming development of the period under review was the breakdown of the Hindu-Muslim entente, which the Mahatma had so skilfully conjured into existence during the heroic days of non-cooperation. This development, in striking contrast to the vindication of the nationalist position in the legislatures by the Swarajists, ensured that Hindus and Muslims spoke with discordant voices on the crucial political issues of the day, thereby seriously weakening the challenge which they could jointly mount to the British rulers of the land. Nor was the communal problem the only problem which confronted Gandhi, Motilal and the leaders of their generation. They further sensed that a younger generation of nationalist leaders—represented best of all by radicals like Jawaharlal Nehru and Subhas Chandra Bose—were becoming increasingly critical of their strategy and tactics. This generation of nationalists wanted to launch a frontal attack on the British Government and secure for the country *purna swaraj*, or complete independence, instead of Dominion Status. Over and above this, as we shall later see, the younger generation of political activists also wanted to transform nationalism from a purely political into a social and economic phenomenon. They believed that the resolution of India's political bondage, as well as of her poverty, could only be achieved by reorganising the polity on socialist principles, whereby the wealth of the country would be collectively owned, and the rewards of labour equitably distributed between different social classes.

In this context of a widening rift between Hindus and Muslims, and between older and younger nationalist leaders, the British Government appointed the so-called Simon Commission, with a membership drawn exclusively from the British Parliament, to review the political progress made by India since the Reforms of 1919. That the British Government did not think it fit to associate any Indian with the Simon Commission, at a point in time when nationalism had become so powerful a force in the country, gives us a rare insight into the lofty arrogance of the imperial psyche. Yet this arrogance was a blessing in disguise for nationalism in India. Practically all classes and communities in the country came together in their hostility to the Simon Commission, Consequently, when in 1928 the members of this exclusively European commission toured the length and breadth of the land, in order to exchange views with political leaders of different persuasions in different regions, they were greeted everywhere by hostile demonstrations, which in their numerical strength no less than in their social composition, recalled the popular enthusiasm against the British Raj in the tumultuous days of non-cooperation.

At the same time as he appointed the Simon Commission, Lord Birkenhead, the Secretary of State for India, challenged the nationalist leadership to devise a constitution for India that would be acceptable to all classes and communities in the country. Behind this challenge lay the assumption that the nationalist leadership in India was drawn from an irresponsible body of men; that the people of the country had still to acquire the consciousness of nationhood; that the great religious minorities, the Muslims in particular, would not make common cause with the Hindus in presenting joint constitutional demands before the British Government; and last but not the least, that Princely India remained largely untouched by the forces that were at work in the provinces of British India.

The challenge thrown by Birkenhead could not be overlooked by the nationalist leaders. A decision was taken at the Madras session of the Congress, in 1927, to draft a constitution for an independent India in consultation with other political groups. In pursuit of this decision, an all-India Conference met shortly afterwards under the presidentship of M.A. Ansari, the distinguished Muslim leader. At this Conference, a Sub-Committee with Motilal Nehru as its chairman and the eminent jurist and liberal politician, Sir Tej Bahadur Sapru, as one of its members, was created to draft such a constitution.

The Nehru Report, as the constitution drafted by Motilal Nehru, with the assistance of Sapru, came to be known, was a document which was destined to play an important role in the political destiny of India. In outlining a political system for India at this juncture, two basic problems had to be resolved. First, any proposed constitution needed the endorsement of the major religious communities, namely, the Hindus and the Muslims. Secondly, the proposed constitution also needed the endorsement of the younger nationalists, like Jawaharlal Nehru and Subhas Chandra Bose, who were pressing for a radicalisation of the national movement, and who had adopted as an immediate objective the attainment of *purna swaraj* by India.

In tackling the communal problem the authors of the Nehru Report adopted an attitude which combined strategic firmness with tactical flexibility in finely balanced proportions. They believed that, in the long run, the communal problem would cease to loom so large and menacingly on the political scene. "We are certain that, as soon as India is free and can face her problems. unhampered by alien authority and intervention, the minds of our people will turn to the vital question of the day . . . . Parties will be formed in the country and in the legislatures on entirely other grounds, chiefly economic, we presume,"[28] observed the Report. Yet, whatever be the strategic prospect, it was clear that, in the immediate future, some tangible assurances would have to be held out to the Muslims if they were to join hands with the Hindus, and the other communities, in presenting common political demands to the British Government. To this end, the Nehru Report made a number of recommendations: first, it suggested that a declaration of rights, assuring religious and political liberty to all citizens of India, be enshrined in the constitution; secondly, it resolved that two new provinces be created, namely, Sind and the Northwest Frontier Provinces, wherein the Muslims would be in a majority; finally, the Nehru Report decreed that the practice of separate communal electorates be abolished, though seats for Muslims were henceforth to be reserved in the central as well as in the provincial legislatures.

V

While Motilal Nehru, and the senior Congress leaders who had rallied around Mahatma Gandhi, laboured to devise a constitution for India which would resolve the communal problem, they were equally concerned about the climate of opinion which was crystallizing around the younger generation of nationalists. This generation of nationalists was not only reaching out to a new ideology as the basis of the struggle for freedom, but it was also impatient of the relatively moderate strategy and tactics of their seniors, and sought to launch forthwith a frontal attack upon the British Government in India.

No one symbolised the idealism and the outlook of the younger generation ot nationalists better than Jawaharlal Nehru. Along with tens upon thousands of young men, very few of whom could claim his upper-class background, Jawaharlal Nehru had been irresistibly drawn to the charismatic personality of the Mahatma during the heady days of the non-cooperation movement; just as he had also been drawn to the revolutionary weapon of satyagraha as the best means of liberating India from British bondage. The suspension of non-cooperation, in 1922, left him baffled and perplexed at the maddening logic which had persuaded Gandhi to call off an agitation of subcontinental proportions. As Jawaharlal Nehru observed in his prison cell: "We were angry when we learnt of this suspension of our struggle at a time when we seemed to be consolidating our position and advancing on all fronts."[29] The unlovely communal strife which characterised the political scene after the suspension of non-cooperation was equally a matter of concern for the nationalist leaders, since it appeared to question the very basis of nationhood for India.

Perhaps the uncertainties which haunted Jawaharlal Nehru, and other young nationalists, at this juncture encouraged them to explore new worldviews in order to arrive at a fresh understanding of the freedom struggle in India. While he was still in Britain, Jawaharlal Nehru had acquired a certain familiarity with Fabian socialism, and with the social and economic vision which the advocates of this movement posed before the intelligentsia. Yet he knew very little about Marxist theory until the middle 1920s, although, as he observed later, he looked upon the "Bolshevik revolution . . . [as] a very exciting episode indeed . . . ."[30] Perhaps the crucial stimulus to Jawaharlal Nehru's intellectual development was provided by the Congress of Oppressed Nationalities at Brussels, which he attended as a representative of the Indian National Congress in 1927. Here was a gathering of the leaders of the nationalist movements of Asia and Africa, under the auspices of the international socialist movement, to discuss question of common interest, and to frame a common attitude towards imperialism. In defining the objectives of the Indian National Congress on the eve of the Brussels meet, Jawaharlal Nehru talked for the first time of the "liberation of the poor and oppressed from all exploitation", over and above the necessity of "freedom from foreign rule".[31] He also gained a new appreciation of the relationship between imperialism and capitalism; of the need for oppressed societies to come together; and, most important of all, of the desirability of building nationalist movements around the aspirations of peasants and workers.

From the Brussels Conference, Jawaharlal Nehru proceeded to Russia, on the strength of an invitation to visit the Soviet Union. This journey was undertaken at a crucial juncture in the reconstruction of Russia on the basis of an entirely novel vision of Man and Society. The boldness of the Soviet experiment, and the manner in which it sought to reshape the moral and material parameters of a polity of very substantial proportions, fired the imagination of Jawaharlal Nehru, more particularly because he was conscious of the strength of conservatism in India. Yet he was not blind to facets of Soviet reality, or to aspects of Bolshevik theory, which were the reverse of commendable. India, with her teeming millions, her age-long problems of poverty and exploitation, heightened by imperial rule, could not but look upon the Soviet experiment with sympathy and interest; and even profit from Russian experience. Yet the epic scale of Indian society, and its historical character as a civilisation of antiquity, called (so Jawaharlal Nehru believed) for solutions which were in keeping with the traditions of India, at the same time as they reached out to a new conception of the "good society", resting upon the twin principles of socialism and popular democracy.

Jawaharlal Nehru's attempt to formulate along novel lines the ideological premises of the freedom struggle in India came at an extremely timely moment. As suggested earlier, the movement led by Gandhi during the years 1920-2 had attracted in great numbers the intelligentsia, as well as the popular urban and rural classes, to the cause of Indian freedom. The notion of militant non-violence, as advocated by Gandhi, had appealed enormously to the people of India. Yet the manner in which Gandhi suspended the non-cooperation movement in 1922, and the communal cleavages which showed up immediately afterwards, caused a good deal of disquiet among the leaders as well as the intelligentsia. What were the bases upon which the different classes and communities of India could come together in a state of nationhood? To what extent was the question of freedom from British rule purely a political question? To what extent, equally, was it also a social and economic question? If, besides the rich and the middle classes, the toiling poor in the cities and in the villages were also to be drawn into the struggle for freedom, then how could their interests be protected in an independent India? How could the traditional loyalties to community and religion—loyalties which were so powerfully manifest in the Indian psyche—be transformed into a new loyalty to a nation-state? Last but not the least, what were the moral and material values which would sustain nationhood in India? These were some of the issues which agitated a new generation of nationalist leaders committed to the liberation of India from British rule.

There were, needless to say, no easy answers to such questions. However, as a result of his explorations in socialist ideology, Jawaharlal Nehru was able to formulate a number of propositions of crucial significance to the freedom struggle in India. He now perceived the liberation movement in India as part of a wider struggle between the capitalist polities of Europe, on the one hand, and the subject societies of Asia and Africa, on the other. He also perceived an organic relationship between the capitalist mode of generating wealth, which characterised the countries of Western Europe, and the phenomenon of imperialism, which obliged such countries to establish relations of political and economic domination over the countries of what is now termed the Third World. Within India, British imperialism had conjured into existence a strong bond of interest with the feudal classes and with sections of the industrial and commercial bourgeoisie. This unholy alliance expropriated for the benefit of imperialism what the peasants and workers produced through the sweat of their labour. The relationship of superordination and subordination between Britain and India provided the basis, so Jawaharlal Nehru believed, of the strategy and the tactics which the Congress could profitably adopt in the anti-imperialist struggle. In the first instance, it was necessary for nationalists in India to establish links with other nationalists in Asia and Africa, in order to devise a common stance in the worldwide struggle against imperialism. Next, the national movement in India would have to overthrow the hegemony of the exploiting classes at the same time as it overthrew the dominance of British imperialism over the subcontinent. Only such a movement, which concerned itself with the interests of the toiling classes in rural and in urban society, would be able to transcend the cleavages of class, community and religion, and lay the basis of a cohesive national polity in India.

While Jawaharlal Nehru was framing his design for the socialist transformation of India, a number of organisations like youth leagues and kisan sabhas were being founded in different parts of the country, under the umbrella of the national movement. The crystallisation of such organisations spoke of the desire of hitherto inarticulate classes for an appropriate share in the distribution of social and economic power. Jawaharlal Nehru sensed the opportunity afforded by this ferment to put forward his new programme of political action as widely as possible. As he observes in his *Autobiography*:

> Everywhere I spoke on political independence and social freedom and made the former a step towards the attainment of the latter. I wanted to spread the ideology of socialism especially among Congress workers and the intelligentsia, for these people, who were the backbone of the

> national movement, thought largely in terms of the narrowest nationalism. . . .[32]

Perhaps the substance of Jawaharlal Nehru's argument is best expressed through extracts from the observations which he made on two such occasions:

> You have probably often condemned British imperialism because you suffered it. But have you thought it is but a manifestation of a world phenomenon? And this world phenomenon is the direct outcome of a system of society which prevails in the greater part of the world today and is called capitalism . . . . We must aim, therefore, at the destruction of all imperialism and reconstruction of society on another basis. That basis must be one of cooperation; and that is another name for socialism.[33]
>
> We are often accused of preaching class war and of widening the distance between the classes. The distance is wide enough, thanks to capitalism. And nothing can beat the record of capitalism in that respect . . . because class war is none of our creation. It is the creation of capitalism . . . by trying ostrich-like to ignore it, we do not get rid of it. Only by removing the classes are we likely to bring peace.[34]

The mood of radical militancy in the younger generation of nationalists was reflected equally powerfully in the person of another rising star in the political firmament of India. Subhas Chandra Bose came from a distinguished family of Bengal; and after a brilliant career at Calcutta University, he proceeded to Britain for higher studies, and competed successfully for the Indian Civil Service in 1920. However, due to the influence of Vivekananda, he was drawn towards the freedom struggle and, in 1921, after quitting the Civil Service, he entered politics under the aegis of C.R. Das.

Bose's distinction as an intellectual, his charismatic presence and his superb organisational skills assured for him in a short span of time a very prominent position in the political scene in Bengal. Indeed, when C.R. Das died in 1925, Bose became a commanding figure in the Provincial Congress Committee, devoting special care to the organisation of the youth as well as of the working class of Bengal. Towards the end of the 1920s, he was one of the few leaders of the younger generation with a reputation that had spread to the far corners of the subcontinent.

Although Bose did not share, in a formal sense, the radicalism of Jawaharlal Nehru, he fully endorsed the hostility of the latter towards the British Government. Indeed, as already emphasised, Jawaharlal Nehru and Subhas Chandra Bose articulated the sentiments of an entire generation of the intelligentsia in their militancy towards imperialism; and in their desire to seek battle with the British Government with the objective of liberating India. At the Madras session of the Indian National Congress, held in 1927, Jawaharlal Nehru sponsored a resolution stating that "The Congress declares the goal of the Indian people to be complete independence."[35] Although such sentiments had been voiced earlier from the platform of the Congress, at the Madras session the resolution reflected the consciousness of the intelligentsia which was ready to translate thought into purposive social action.

VI

While Motilal Nehru was drafting the constitutional proposals which are known to posterity as the Nehru Report, the radical temper of the younger generation of nationalists was an issue of the most serious concern to him. After all, this impulse for an ideological transformation of the nationalist struggle, which refused to have any truck with British imperialism, and which also sought to base the struggle for freedom upon the aspirations of the "wretched of the earth", was spearheaded by none other than his son, Jawaharlal Nehru. To Motilal Nehru, it was clear that in the altered climate of 1928, the erstwhile formula of Swaraj, which Gandhi had defined in so nebulous a fashion, and which he had utilised to draw different classes and communities to the country-wide agitation of the years 1920-2, would no longer meet the approval of the younger generation. Yet Motilal also believed that the slogan of complete independence would be premature, in view of the overall strength of conservative sentiment in the freedom movement. The constitution drafted by him, therefore, stipulated that the status of India within the British Empire should be identical with the status of self-governing colonies like Australia or Canada, which were moving towards the formal attainment of Dominion Status.

Although the Nehru Report was a document which dealt with the crucial issues of contemporary politics with catholicity and vision, its specific proposals failed to win the approval of some significant sections of society in India. Soon after the Report was issued, the leaders of the Congress met in Calcutta in December 1928, to discuss its provisions. The Muslim leaders present at the Calcutta meeting felt that, in view of the plural character of society in India, some of the provisions of the Nehru Report—particularly those recommending a unitary constitution, and the abrogation of communal electorates—would not be acceptable to their constituents. Indeed, in a conference held slightly later, in March 1929, the Muslim leaders presented a radically different prescription for the constitutional future of India. Such leaders envisaged a liberated India as a federal polity, wherein the minorities, particularly the Muslim community, would protect their interests through the mechanism of separate electorates.

In view of the leading role which he had played in preparing a constitutional blueprint for India, Motilal Nehru was the obvious choice for the presidency of the Congress in 1928. As the time approached for the annual session at Calcutta, Motilal sensed the opposition which had crystallised to the constitutional future which he envisaged for the country. Two important sections of society, the Muslim community and the younger generation of nationalists, seemed to have serious reservations about the political future held out in the Nehru Report. To Motilal, as indeed to Gandhi, the latter constituency, that is, the youthful leadership in the nationalist ranks, appeared to be the more important constituency. For, without the support of the youth of the country, there was little prospect of a successful struggle against the British Government of India. Confronted with this crisis, Motilal turned to the Mahatma for guidance as well as for support. How crucial was the role which Gandhi played at this juncture, is vividly reflected in the proceedings of the annual session at Calcutta. In the Subjects Committee, where various issues were debated before they were taken up for discussion in the open session, the question whether the Nehru Report was to be adopted in its entirety, and Dominion Status accepted as the national objective, became a subject of heated discussion. The younger members of the Subjects Committee, prominent among them Jawaharlal Nehru and Subhas Chandra Bose, were insistent in their demand for *Purna Swaraj*. Indeed, but for the Mahatma's presence, and his healing touch, it is doubtful whether the revolt of the younger leaders could have been controlled by the older leaders. As it was, what emerged in the Subjects Committee was in the nature of a compromise. The Nehru Report was accepted in its entirety; but on the crucial issue of Dominion Status, the Congress leadership decided that if the British Government did not concede this demand within the span of a year, they would initiate a movement of civil disobedience to win *Purna Swaraj* for the country. The compromise adopted in the Subjects Committee was then approved in the open session of the Congress.

The decisions taken by the Indian National Congress at Calcutta were as much a triumph for Gandhi, Motilal Nehru and the senior generation of nationalist leaders, as they were a triumph for Jawaharlal Nehru, Subhas Chandra Bose and the younger radicals within the nationalist ranks. An important by-product of the Calcutta Congress was the return of the Mahatma to active politics after an interval of three or four years, during which period he had engaged himself in constructive work in his ashram. As we have indicated earlier, the support which the Mahatma extended to Motilal and the moderate nationalists at Calcutta was crucial for the acceptance, albeit in a modified form, of the clause on Dominion Status by the Congress, at least for the space of a year. Furthermore, it was clear that the Mahatma, with his moral authority enormously enhanced through the programme of social regeneration which he had initiated during the years of political inactivity, would once again lead his countrymen in a non-violent assault upon the British Raj.

The developments within the national movement were followed with close interest by the Viceroy, Lord Irwin. A Tory with sensitive political antenna, Irwin was fully conscious of the winds of the change that were blowing across India. A little earlier, Irwin had committed a monumental blunder in approving the exclusively British membership of the Simon Commission, which had been constituted to review the political development of the subcontinent. However, as Irwin's perception of politics in India sharpened, he realised the extent to which the desire for freedom had taken firm root in the country. "There is quite clearly a strong movement to the Left among educated Hindu political opinion. . ."[36] he wrote to the Secretary of State for India in January 1929. The viceroy was convinced that the situation called for a statesmanlike gesture on the part of the British Government which would clear the climate of distrust that had come to plague relations between the British leaders and the nationalist leadership of India. Irwin commenced toying with the idea of initiating a dialogue, over and above the Simon Commission, between a group of representative Indian leaders and a delegation of British parliamentarians. He also came to the conclusion that it was necessary for the British Government to publicly declare that India would, over the years, acquire a status comparable in all respects to the status of the self-governing dominions of British Empire. Irwin took the opportunity offered by a vacation in Britain, in the middle of 1929, to place his views before the British Government. As a result of these deliberations, Irwin, on his return to India, declared that the British Government would soon call a Round Table Conference to discuss the political future of India; and further that "the entire issue of India's constitutional progress was the attainment of Dominion Status".[37]

Irwin's declaration of 1929 was superbly timed. It obliged Mahatma Gandhi, Motilal Nehru and other leaders of the Congress to re-examine the decision of the Calcutta Congress, that if Dominion Status was not bestowed upon India by 1929, then an agitation for *Purna Swaraj* would be mounted against the British Government. As a result of the conciliatory gesture by the viceroy, a group of nationalist leaders assembled at Delhi to hammer out a common response to the viceregal declaration. At this meeting, predictably, Mahatma Gandhi, Motilal Nehru and their peers differed from Jawaharlal Nehru and Subhas Chandra Bose, who were for an outright rejection of the Irwin declaration. However, the Delhi Manifesto, which was drafted by the more moderate nationalists, welcomed the proposal for a Round Table Conference on the understanding that such a "conference is to meet not to discuss when Dominion Status is to be established, but to frame a scheme of Dominion Status."[38] A meeting between Irwin and Gandhi, along with Motilal Nehru and others, held shortly afterwards, nevertheless revealed a wide gulf between the nationalist position and the position of the British Government towards the question of political autonomy for India.

The annual session of the Indian National Congress, held in Lahore in the last week of December 1929, under the presidentship of Jawaharlal Nehru, was largely a vindication of the stance adopted by the radical nationalists *vis-á-vis* the liberation movement.

In his presidential address, Jawaharlal Nehru, for the first time in the history of the Congress, held out a socialist critique of the world situation, as well as of the Indian problem, before the assembled delegates. Emphasising the international context in which the capitalist democracies of Western Europe had come to dominate the rest of the world, through the extensive empires which they had carved out in Asia and Africa, Jawaharlal Nehru pointed out that the struggle for the freedom in India, although it had to be fought by the people of the subcontinent, was an organic constituent of a wider struggle between imperialism and nationalism in the contemporary world. Nor did he make a secret of his ideological commitments: "I must frankly confess that I am a socialist and a republican, and am no believer in kings and princes, or in the order which produces the modern kings of Industry, who have greater power over the lives and fortunes of men than have the kings of old and whose methods are as predatory as those of the old feudal aristocracy."[39] Given his commitment to a socialist vision, Jawaharlal Nehru's perception of the internal problems of India, which called for urgent attention, was forthright and unambiguous:

> India means the peasantry and labour, and to the extent that we raise them and satisfy their wants will we succeed in our tasks and the measure of the strength of our national movement will be the measure of their adherence to it. . . . [The] Congress, it is said, must hold the balance fairly between capital and labour and zamindar and peasant. But the balance has been and is terribly weighted on one side and to maintain the status quo is to maintain injustice and exploitation. The only way to right it is to do away with the domination of any one class over another.[40]

Such radical statements from the presidential chair clearly reflected a qualitative transformation in the temper of the nationalist movement. This transformation was equally vividly reflected in the adoption, also at the Lahore Congress, of a resolution which stated that the goal of the Congress was "complete independence"; and which authorised the national leadership to launch a movement of civil disobedience, under the leadership of Mahatma Gandhi, having as its objective the liberation of India from British rule.[41]

The deliberations of the Lahore Congress thus placed a heavy responsibility upon the Mahatma. The decision to entrust the destiny of India at so crucial a juncture to Gandhi, the veteran of numerous non-violent struggles, also reflected the locus of sentiment within the premier national organisation. If the moderate leaders of the Congress were willing to accept the initiative of Jawaharlal Nehru in defining the ideological content of the anti-imperialist struggle, they were equally convinced that such a struggle had to be waged by a judicious combination of firmness and flexibility through the weapon of non-violent protest fashioned by the Mahatma.

As the sole leader of a satyagraha reflecting the aspirations of a nation of 400 million, Gandhi selected his battleground and his tactics with great care. He first placed before the viceroy, Lord Irwin, a list of demands designed to mobilise behind the call for *purna swaraj* broad sections of society, particularly men of business and industry, the professional classes, and peasants and workers. But the principal item, a fantastically simple item, in this list of demands, upon which Gandhi focused his attention, was the repeal of the tax upon salt, which product was a state monopoly. The decision to focus upon salt, a prosaic product of daily consumption, may at first blush appear quixotic in the extreme. But as subsequent events were to demonstrate, the Mahatma revealed himself as a tactician of genius in selecting the issue upon which the civil disobedience movement was to hinge in the first instance. Prosaic salt may well have been. Yet it was a product closely linked to the daily life of millions of peasants and workers, for whom the trifling quantum of the salt tax was a sum of considerable magnitude. Moreover, the refusal to pay the salt tax was singularly well-designed to heap ridicule upon the authority of the British Government in India.

Gandhi was equally skilful in selecting the locality in which he violated the salt laws, as a signal to the entire nation to unleash a non-violent assault upon the British Raj. He initiated a *padayatra* from Sabarmati Ashram in Ahmedabad, in the company of 78 trusted associates representing different religious communities and regions in India. This *padayatra* took Gandhi and his band to the remote coastal village of Dandi on the Gulf of Cambay, where the satyagrahis 'manufactured' salt in defiance of the laws of the land. The rural districts through which Gandhi marched were the setting for two of his earlier campaigns; and the peasantry of the region was utterly devoted to the Mahatma. The march was a monumental success. At one level, it taught the local peasants the meaning of satyagraha and swaraj. "Who can help liking this poor man's battle? The cruel tax is no respecter of persons. It is, therefore, as much the interest of the Mussalman as that of the Hindu to secure its abolition. This is the first fight undertaken in the name of God and for the sake of the millions of the paupers of this country,"[42] Gandhi stated repeatedly in the course of the march. So much for the local peasantry. But at the national level, the daily accounts of Gandhi's march, and his words of advice to the rural folk of Gujarat, reached out to the people of India through the speeches of Congress activists and through nationalist newspapers, thus preparing the entire nation for the struggle.

The civil disobedience movement which Gandhi initiated at Dandi on 6 April 1930, through the symbolic manufacture of salt from sea-water, was in some respects comparable to the movement which he had organised a decade earlier. As in 1920, the Mahatma reached out to a diversity of classes and communities in a society of epic scale. Again as in 1920, the movement was articulated by the Indian National Congress, through organised networks in cities, townships and *casbahs,* in a substantial proportion of the half a million villages of the subcontinent. Over and above this, Gandhi's moral authority, plus the grievances which affected the peasantry and tribal communities in different parts of the country, where the Congress lacked a formal presence, simultaneously triggered off populist agitations of primordial fury, which had very little to do with non-violence as a mode of political action. Yet, there were two significant differences between the agitation of 1920-2 and that of 1930-1. The industrial and business elites of India, formally organised in the Federation of Indian Chambers of Commerce and Industry (FICCI), rallied to Gandhi's call in 1930 in a manner they had refused to do earlier, partly due to the economic distress caused by the great depression of 1929, and partly also due to a clearer perception on their part of their economic interests. If industrial and commercial participation presented an accretion of strength to the nationalist movement, then the alienation of the Muslim leadership and the Muslim community, with the distinguished exception of Khan Abdul Ghaffar Khan and the Pathans, was a source of serious disquiet to Gandhi and his associates. Since the Muslim leaders had refused to endorse the Nehru Report, they also refrained from persuading their followers to seek involvement in the civil disobedience movement, thus posing before Gandhi and the Congress a problem to which there appeared no easy solution.

The widespread support which the civil disobedience movement received from different classes and communities—from industrialists and businessmen; from the professional classes and the *petite bourgeoisie;* and from peasants, workers and tribal communities—greatly undermined the authority of the British Government over India. The reaction of a civil servant, who visited Bombay during the spring of 1930, was by no means atypical of the profound pessimism which seized hold of the British in India when the agitation was at its height:

> There is no doubt about the great strength of the Civil Disobedience Movement in Bombay City [stated Sir Harry Haig]. The Gujaratis have thrown themselves into it with all their hearts, and by their activities and demonstrations have created the belief among themselves, which is not without its effect upon others (Maharashtrians, Parsis and even Europeans), that a national movement has been started which will prove irresistible. The success of the movement, the wide and intense support it is receiving, has surprised everyone. The Congress House openly directs the movement of revolt against Government, Gandhi caps fill the streets, volunteers in uniform are posted for picketing with the same regularity and orderliness as police constables. . . . It is not surprising that all this intense feeling, with its open and apparently successful defiance of Government, has produced a profound impression in Bombay as a whole. Nothing, perhaps, has done more to deepen that impression than, the series of processions that have been organized by the Congress. Their numbers, the discipline, the organization and the brushing aside of the ordinary functions of police control of traffic have combined to produce a vivid impression of the power and the success of the Congress movement.[43]

Small wonder, then, that the viceroy, Lord Irwin, came to believe that the First Round Table Conference of British and Indian leaders, which met in Great Britain to decide the constitutional future of India, lacked the moral authority to take any major decisions without the participation of representatives of the Indian National Congress. The way out of the impasse, as Irwin saw it, was to draw Gandhi and the Congress leaders into a constitutional dialogue; and to fashion out of such a dialogue a system of politics which could protect British commercial and strategic interests in India, at the same time as it met the basic demands of the Congress led national movement. Whether such a reconciliation between nationalism and imperialism was at all possible was an altogether different question.

One aspect of Gandhi's greatness lay in his willingness to explore every possible solution to a problem. Hence, he had a series of meetings with the viceroy in the autumn of 1930, to explore the possibility of an understanding, whereby the Congress could participate in the Round Table Conferences and call off the non-violent agitation which had succeeded in demonstrating, beyond the shadow of a doubt, how much popular support it enjoyed in the country. Of course, Gandhi's earlier demand, that the consultations in Britain between British and Indian leaders should relate to the 'substance of Indian independence', had, in a manner of speaking, already been conceded, since the First Round Table Conference had unanimously endorsed the idea of a federal polity, in which the provinces of British India and the princely states would participate as constituent and largely autonomous units. However, in opening up a dialogue with Irwin, as the first step towards a political truce, Gandhi's real concern lay with the radicals within the Congress, represented best of all by Jawaharlal Nehru, who fervently believed that the civil disobedience movement needed to be carried through to the bitter end.

Outside the Congress, at this juncture, yet within the wider framework of the freedom struggle, stood revolutionary nationalists like Chandrasekhar Azad, or Bhagat Singh or Surya Sen. Such men were totally committed to the notion of a violent instead of a non-violent assault on British imperialism. The revolutionary nationalists were drawn close to a socialist position in the late 1920s, though their new ideological orientation did not rule out dramatic acts of terrorist violence, which were designed to undermine the authority of the British Government, and to persuade the common people of India—particularly peasants, workers and the intelligentsia—to rally to the nationalist cause. The vision which inspired such men was admirably expressed in a pamphlet entitled *The Philosophy of Violence,*[44] written by the revolutionary activist Bhagwati Charan Vohra, and this vision was not without influence upon the wider community, particularly the intelligentsia. At the same time as the followers of Gandhi violated British laws through satyagrahi action, the revolutionary nationalists in different parts of India assaulted officers of the British Government; or made spectacular demonstrations in assemblies; or captured, if only for a brief while, British treasuries in the mofussil; in a bid to undermine the fabric of the British Raj. The activities of such revolutionaries complemented the non-violent campaign of civil disobedience; and their effect upon popular consciousness was no less decisive than the effect of the satyagraha movement.

Notwithstanding the complexity of the nationalist struggle over which he presided, the Mahatma was able to reach a settlement with the viceroy, which is popularly known as the Gandhi-Irwin Pact. According to this settlement, the Congress was to suspend the civil disobedience movement. The British Government, on its part, would release activists from prison and annul the ordinances which declared the Congress and its sister organisations unlawful bodies. Moreover, the Congress was to participate, along with the representatives of other Indian parties, in the scheme of constitutional reforms to be discussed at the Second Round Table Conference: "Of the scheme thus outlined federation is an essential point; so also are Indian responsibility and reservations or safeguards, in the interests of India, for such matters as, for instance, the defence; external affairs; the position of minorities; the financial credit of India; and the discharge of obligations."[45] The settlement can in no manner be construed as an unalloyed victory for Gandhi. The Mahatma had to concede several significant points to the viceroy. Moreover, radical and youthful nationalists, within the Congress or without it, looked upon the conduct of negotiations with the British Government as politically inexpedient. Yet the spectacle of Lord Irwin parleying with Mahatma Gandhi was not without its gains for the cause of nationalism. For the representative of the King Emperor, and the spokesman of the greatest imperial power known to history, to embark upon a dialogue, on terms of equality, with the undisputed leader of the liberation movement in India was in itself a great triumph for the latter.

Gandhi attended the Second Round Table Conference as the sole representative of the Indian National Congress and the most outstanding leader from India. In this capacity, the Mahatma was pitted against British politicians of distinction, as well as against fellow-Indians, handpicked by the imperial authorities, to represent the counterpoised constituencies of class, community and religion, which the British Government had all along exploited to retard the constitutional progress of India. In a memorable speech before the Federal Structure Committee of the Round Table Conference, Gandhi spelt out the substantive issues facing the assembled delegates, British and Indian, in terms which admitted of little ambiguity. Proceeding, in the first instance, to spell out the sources of the populist strength of the Congress, he stated:

> The Congress is, if I am not mistaken, the oldest political organisation we have in India. It has had nearly fifty years of life . . . it is what it means—national. It represents no particular community, no particular class, no particular interests. It claims to represent all Indian interests and classes . . . .
>
> [Above] all, the Congress represents, in its essence, the dumb, semistarved millions scattered over the length and breadth of the land, in its 70,000 villages, no matter whether they come from what is called British India or what is called Indian India. Every interest which, in the opinion of the Congress, is worthy of protection, has to subserve the interests of those dumb millions; and so you do find now and again apparently a clash of interests. But, if there is a genuine real clash, I have no hesitation in saying on behalf of the Congress, that the Congress will sacrifice every interest for the sake of the interests of these dumb millions. It is, therefore, essentially a peasant organisation, and it is becoming so progressively.[46]

Given the constituency of tens upon millions of peasants for whom he spoke as the sole representative of the Indian National Congress, the Mahatma was of the view that the attainment of the objective of *Purna Swaraj,* which his party had set itself, was the only possible means of resolving the "Indian problem". The recognition of India as an independent polity, by His Majesty's Government, was by no means incompatible with a mutually beneficial partnership between Britain and India as members of an Empire transformed into a Commonwealth of Nations. As against this, the continuation of a master-slave relationship was so distasteful to the people of India, that Britain could perpetuate it only through brute force. Such a prospect was morally repugnant and politically disastrous. "Take that nation [India] and this nation [British] together," the Mahatma observed, "and I again ask myself and ask you whether. that an India free, completely independent as Great Britain is, whether an honourable partnership between the two cannot be mutually beneficial, even in terms of the domestic affairs of this great nation. And so, in that dreamy hope, I have approached the British Isles, and I shall still cherish that dream."[47]

Not surprisingly, Gandhi's attempt to raise the constitutional dialogue between British and Indian leaders to an altogether new level foundered on the rocks of imperialist manoeuvre and sectarian intransigence. As indicated earlier, the delegates to the Round Table Conferences were so chosen by the British Government as to ensure that every religious and communitarian cleavage in the social fabric of India would manifest itself to thwart any national consensus which might threaten imperial hegemony over the subcontinent. As against the nationalist viewpoint of the Mahatma, three cores of discontent, each one of them resting upon a distinctive political formation, crystallised in the course of the deliberations over India's constitutional future. The representatives of Princely India, although they had welcomed the notion of a federation at the First Round Table Conference, were now extremely coy about the precise terms upon which the princely states could participate in such an arrangement. The leaders of the Muslim community voiced the fears of their constituents at the prospect of an autonomous federation, and sought assurances that Muslim interests would not be overwhelmed in such a polity by the dominant Hindu community. Perhaps the third locus of opposition to the nationalist worldview was the most disturbing of all, if only for the reason that it had not surfaced earlier in constitutional dialogues. The representatives of the Depressed Classes, whose cause Gandhi had espoused over the years, repudiated their link with Hindu society, and called upon the British Government to accord them the right to vote in separate electorates in the political system which was to be devised for India.

That the Mahatma should find the deliberations of the Second Round Table Conference frustrating was hardly surprising. The very composition of the Indian delegation guaranteed that the genuine voice of nationalism, reflecting the aspirations of the common people, would be lost in the cacophony of divisive voices raised by the representatives of Princely India, on the one hand, and those of communitarian and religious constituencies, on the other. Precisely for this reason, it was vital that a leader with a commanding presence, capable of transcending the limitations of class, community and religion—and who could this be other than Mahatma Gandhi—should put before the political elite of Britain the passionate desire of the people of India to shape their own political destiny. Such an exercise was worthwhile, even though the British Government, weighed down as it was by the problems of the Great Depression, failed to react to Gandhi's stirring call for a statesmanlike gesture in response to the growing strength of nationalism in India.

Small wonder, then, that after Gandhi's return to India, the civil disobedience movement was taken up once again by the Congress. That the second phase of this agitation, which sought to paralyse the British Government through non-violent action, should manifest itself in a slightly muted note was only to be expected; for the coercive power available to the imperial authority was sufficient to break the resistance of satyagrahis through sheer attrition. At the same time, the British Government did not permit the non-cooperation of the Congress to assume the proportions of a veto. Quite the contrary. Yet another Round Table Conference, the third in the series, was held in 1933; and the various sub-committees of the conference, which were assigned specific responsibilities, proceeded with their allotted tasks, in order to provide the basis for a major piece of legislation, concerning the system of government in India, to be presented to the British Parliament for its approval.

Perhaps the Franchise Sub-Committee of the Round Table Conference was saddled with the most difficult task of all. The reasons for this are easy to discern. In a democratic polity, the electoral system substantially influences the manner in which power is exercised by different classes and communities. To heighten the divisions of society in India, and to stem the rising tide of nationalism, the British had created a system of separate communal electorates, the first beneficiaries(?) of which were the Muslims of the subcontinent. What the Muslims attained in 1909, B.R. Ambedkar, the refractory leader of the Depressed Classes, claimed on behalf of his community before the Franchise Sub-Committee. Needless to say, this demand was forcefully opposed by Gandhi and other Indian leaders present at the Second Round Table Conference.

Since the Franchise Sub-Committee could not come to an agreement about the structure of the electoral system, the matter was resolved by the so-called Communal Award of Ramsay MacDonald, the British Prime Minister. This award, which reflected the extent to which the British Government married the rhetoric of a vacuous liberalism with the reality of a ruthless imperialism, contained a new element, over and above those elements which had hitherto characterised the structure of constitutional reform in India. Besides conferring separate electorates upon the Muslims and other religious communities, the Prime Minister's Award also conferred separate electorates upon the Depressed Classes. Gandhi discerned in the Communal Award a sinister design to foster yet another cleavage in Indian society. He was not against the reservation of seats for the Depressed Classes, so long as the caste Hindus, too, were entitled to vote in such reserved constituencies. But to create separate electorates for the Depressed Classes, the Mahatma believed, was to break up Hindu society into antagonistic and warring social fragments and ensure the perpetual subordination of the Depressed Classes by the caste Hindus:

> To appreciate the harm that separate electorates would do them one has to know how they [the Depressed Classes] are distributed amongst so-called caste Hindus and how dependent they are on the latter. So far as Hinduism is concerned, separate electorates would simply vivisect and perpetuate it. . . .
>
> You will have to appreciate my feelings in the matter by remembering that I have been interested in the condition of these classes from my boyhood and have more than once staked my all for their sake. . . .
>
> But I know that separate electorates is neither a panacea nor any remedy for the crushing degradation they have been ground under. I, therefore, respectfully inform His Majesty's Government that in the event of their decision creating separate electorates for the Depressed Classes [becoming operative] I must fast unto death.[48]

The "fast unto death" which Gandhi undertook on 20 September 1932, to effect a cancellation of the Communal Award, as it concerned the Depressed Classes, shook Hindu society to its very foundations. The leaders of the community were appalled at the prospect of the Mahatma sacrificing his life in order to atone for the indignity and worse which the Hindus had heaped upon the Depressed Classes over the centuries. Prominent men like Tej

Bahadur Sapru, Madan Mohan Malaviya, M.R. Jayakar and a host of others, representing orthodox or liberal opinion within Hinduism, hastily arranged a conference to seek a solution to the problem. Over and above this, outstanding Depressed Class leaders like B.R. Ambedkar, M.C. Rajah and P.N. Rajbhoj, also addressed themselves to the business of mapping out an appropriate place for their community within Hindu society.

The meetings between the caste Hindu and the Depressed Class leaders resulted in an agreement which rendered the creation of separate electorates for the lowly Hindu castes, as set out in the Communal Award, wholly unnecessary. From the very outset, it was clear to the Hindu leaders who mediated in the situation that the Mahatma's stance was a most reasonable one. As he had suggested to Sir Samuel Hoare, the Secretary of State for India, he was prepared to concede to the Depressed Classes the reserved seats which they could legitimately claim as their own. What horrified him was the introduction of separate electorates for such classes. Such a provision would not only introduce a fatal cleavage within Hindu society, but it would also prove detrimental to the interests of the Depressed Classes, dependent as they were for their moral and material welfare upon the upper caste Hindus. The only way to improve the lot of the lowly castes, Gandhi believed, was to bring about a "change of heart" within Hindu society, so that the upper castes would accord a status of dignity to the lowly castes. Any attempt at creating a distinctive Depressed Class constituency through the mechanism of separate electorates would bring down upon them the wrath of the superior Hindu classes on whom they were so utterly dependent.

The Mahatma's fast unto death aroused the conscience of wide sections of Hindu society. "To find a parallel for [sic] the anguish of September 1932 we have to go back to Athens twenty three hundred years ago when the friends of Socrates surrounded him in prison and urged him to escape,"[49] observed Chakravarti Rajagopalachari, a distinguished leader of the Congress very close to Gandhi. All over the country, in the citadels of orthodoxy in the plains of the Ganga or the Kaveri, organised Hinduism, its conscience touched to the quick, came out in support of the Mahatma, and threw open temples and other sacred premises to members of the Depressed Classes. The six days during which Gandhi fasted within Yeravada Central Prison brought about a more fundamental change in Hindu society than was true for as many decades prior to 1932. It was as though a moral power of overwhelming proportions had transformed the Hindu social order and persuaded the superior castes to accord a new status of dignity to the lowly castes whom they had exploited for centuries.

B.R. Ambedkar was the most militant of the Depressed Class leaders at this juncture. He had belittled from various platforms Gandhi's attempt at bringing about a social and moral revolution within Hinduism. But even Ambedkar found himself unable to resist the Mahatma when he undertook a fast unto death to secure a cancellation of the Communal Award. After a series of meetings between the caste Hindu and the Depressed Class leaders, an agreement was reached whereby the Communal Award was rendered superfluous. According to this agreement, which is known as the Poona Pact, Ambedkar and the Depressed Class leaders gave up the provision of separate electorates in exchange for the right to select a panel of candidates from their community, one of whom could then be formally elected by high and low caste voters jointly. Gandhi thus succeeded in neutralising a grave threat to the unity of Hindu society; over and above which, he generated among his co-religionists a moral fervour which provided the basis for a transformation of social relations within Hinduism.

VII

While the Poona Pact between the caste Hindu and the Depressed Class leaders represented a substantial victory for nationalism, it would be a mistake to imagine that British imperialism was vanquished once and for all through this agreement. Indeed, despite the assurances which Lord Irwin, the viceroy, had given to the nationalist leaders on the eve of the First Round Table Conference, the Conservative Party in Britain, which featured so prominently on the political scene, was opposed to the devolution of power into Indian hands. During the early 1930s, therefore, a great debate convulsed the Conservative Party as to whether it was necessary to concede more power to the leaders of the national movement in India. Ranged on one side were men like Winston Churchill, who vociferously opposed any constitutional progress in the subcontinent. Churchill believed that the Congress-led nationalist movement was a very weak force that enjoyed no support other than that of the professional, commercial and industrial classes. A slightly different stance was adopted by liberal conservatives like Sir Samuel Hoare, who held the view that the rising tide of nationalism in India was a phenomenon which could no longer be overlooked. While it is true that the "liberal" conservatives triumphed over the "die-hards" in the Conservative Party, the victory of the former by no means ensured the emergence of India as an independent polity in the not too distant future.

This was so for a number of reasons. While the liberal conservatives would have nothing to do with the policies of die-hards like Churchill, there is little reason to believe that they wanted to preside over the liquidation of the British Empire in India. Perhaps their intentions *vis-á-vis* India, and the role which they envisaged for Britain in the subcontinent, are best reflected in the terms of a constitutional bill which was soon introduced in the British Parliament. Hoare and conservatives of his persuasion were no longer interested in exercising direct administrative control over the sprawling provinces of India, as the British had done for the past century and more. Hence, they were willing to concede considerable autonomy to the legislatures, resting upon limited franchise rights, in the provinces of British India. However, such autonomously ruled provinces were to be drawn into a federal polity over which Britain would exercise overarching economic and strategic dominance. To ensure such dominance, the constitutional system envisaged by the British Government drew upon the minorities, and upon Princely India, in such a manner as to ensure that the representatives of nationalism within the federal polity would be held in check by the representatives of the minorities and Princely India.

The motives which underpinned the constitutional system embodied in the Government of India Act of 1935 were by no means hidden from the leaders of the Indian National Congress. Throughout the years under review, therefore, Gandhi maintained unrelenting political pressure upon the imperial authorities through a civil disobedience movement of national proportions, though it was not possible for him, after his return from the Second Round Table Conference in December 1931, to sustain an agitation of the same momentum as the one which he had initiated in the spring of 1930. Gandhi was fully supported by radical nationalists like Jawaharlal Nehru in his assessment of British imperial purpose and British constitutional design. Yet some of the Congress leaders believed that it would be pointless to wage an endless struggle against British imperialism; and they wanted to cash upon the possibilities thrown open by the constitutional system created in 1935. The prospect of autonomy within the provinces, these leaders argued, offered the Congress an opportunity to promote national interests at the same time as it prepared itself for a final assault on the British Government.

The national movement led by the Congress, as it had gathered strength under the aegis of Mahatma Gandhi and Jawaharlal Nehru, in the years surveyed in this essay, was an admirable instrument for such an assault upon British imperialism, leading to the liberation of India from a century and a half of political bondage. Even before 1920, the year in which Gandhi rose to national prominence, the Congress had grown into an organisation reaching out to the far corners of the subcontinent, and drawing classes and communities belonging to different religions and cultures into the mainstream of nationalist activity. Yet, if the Congress support base prior to 1920 was countrywide, it nevertheless rested largely upon the professional and the commercial classes. The tens of millions of the poor in the cities and the villages of India, the overwhelming majority of the population of the country, had very little to do with it. Under the leadership of the Mahatma, however, the Congress was not only revitalized organisationally, but it also succeeded in drawing the workers, peasants and tribals into the struggle against the British Government. Over and above this, the Mahatma put before the people a novel method for waging political struggles, which drew upon traditional moral resources, at the same time as it moulded these resources into an ideological weapon appropriate to the transformation of a civilisation of antiquity into a modern nation. Gandhi's was a magnificent achievement, which not only strengthened the national movement, but also made it clear to the British that their empire in India was doomed to destruction. Nor did his achievements end here. Alone among his contemporaries, he attempted to disseminate the sentiment of nationhood among the Depressed Classes and tribal communities, and draw them into a closer relationship with the mainstream of Indian society. Indeed, the extent to which Gandhi's call for an anti-imperialist struggle reached out to the lowly Hindu castes, and to the tribal folk, was a clear indication of his success in creating a popular movement of invincible power for the liberation of India.

The contribution of Jawaharlal Nehru to the growth of the national movement was no less significant than that of Mahatma Gandhi. To appreciate this contribution, it is necessary to dwell briefly upon the 1920s, the period when Jawaharlal was drawn into nationalist politics. Even a superficial look at the non-cooperation movement reveals that Gandhi succeeded in mobilising the people in a nationalist struggle in a manner they had never been mobilised before. Yet the Mahatma's resounding success posed several crucial questions, some of which called for urgent answers during the years following the suspension of non-cooperation. Could the question of liberation from British rule be resolved simultaneously with the problems of class exploitation and class domination within Indian Society? Or was it necessary to postpone the resolution of internal problems till such time as the struggle against imperialism had resulted in a victory for the nationalist cause? Gandhi never came to grips with such issues in 1920-2, despite his success in shaking the edifice of British rule to its very foundations.

The socialist vision which Jawaharlal Nehru propagated among the people of India sought to provide a novel ideological poise to the national movement. Jawaharlal believed that it would be a fatal mistake to defer the resolution of economic conflict within Indian society till such time as freedom had been attained. He further believed that the exploitation of the lowly by the rich classes within India was inextricably linked to the exploitation of the subcontinent as a whole by Britain. As Jawaharlal observed on more than one occasion, the Indian problem was merely one manifestation of a worldwide conflict between nationalism and imperialism; and any strategy for the liberation of enslaved societies like India would be simultaneously called upon to resolve the problem of social inequity within such societies. Such a perception of the struggle for freedom was a pre-condition to a liberation in which the creative powers of the people would become the basis of their moral and material welfare. The speed with which the radical ideas of Jawaharlal Nehru spread among the intelligentsia and the underprivileged classes suggests that the people of India were anxiously searching for a revolutionary ideology as the basis of the freedom struggle. The Indian National Congress, which under Jawaharlal Nehru's inspiration was drawn to such an ideology, and which enjoyed the support of millions of the citizens of the subcontinent, was therefore admirably equipped to lead India to political independence and to a non-violent social revolution.

NOTES

1. Jawaharlal Nehru, *An Autobiography* (London, 1953, Reprint), p. 27. (Henceforth cited as *Autobiography.)*
2. W.K. Hancock, *Smuts: The Sabgyube Years* (Cambridge, 1962), p. 345.
3. M.K. Gandhi, *Hind Swaraj* (Ahmedabad, 1938), pp. 161-3.
4. *Autobiography*, p. 41.
5. Declaration by Secretary of State for India, 20 August 1917: A.C. Bannerjee (ed.), *Indian Constitutional Documents 1757-1947*, Vol. III (Calcutta, 1961), pp. 1-3.
6. Sir Reginald Craddock, *The Dilemma in India* (London, 1926), p. 259.
7. M.K. Gandhi to V.S. Srinivasa Sastri, 9 February 1919: *The Collected Works of Mahatma Gandhi* (henceforth cited as *Collected Works*), Vol. XV, pp. 101-2.
8. For the text of the Satyagraha Pledge, see *Collected Works*, Vol. XV, pp. 101-2.
9. Letter by M.K. Gandhi, 26 February 1919: *Collected Works*, Vol. XV, pp. 102-3.
10. Speech by M.K. Gandhi, 9 May 1919: *Collected Works*, Vol. XV, pp. 296-7.
11. Royal Proclamation: *The Indian Year Book 1920* (ed.), Stanley Reed (Bombay, n.d.), pp. 669-70.
12. Quoted in M.R. Jayakar, *The Story of My Life*, Vol. One 1873-1892 (Bombay, 1958), p. 306.
13. Ibid., pp. 307-9.
14. *Indian Annual Register:* Letter from Viceroy to the Muslim People in India, 15 May 1920, p. 185. For terms of the Turkish Peace Treaty, see ibid., pp. 185-6.
15. Ibid., Part III, p. 112(j).
16. Ibid., Speech by C.R. Das in support of NCO Resolution, 30 December 1920, Part III, p. 180.
17. *Proceedings of the Meerut Trial:* Statement by A.A. Alwe.
18. *National Archives of India* (henceforth cited as NAI): Home Department, Deposit, File No. 13/21.
19. Quoted in J.C. Coe, Tribe, Caste and Nationalist Politics in Surat District, 1920-25 (Ph.D. Thesis, University of Sydney, 1984), p. 135.
20. Letter by M.K. Gandhi: *Young India*, 6 July 1921.
21. Quoted in S.D. Waley, *Edwin Montagu (*Bombay 1964), p. 264.
22. Quoted in B.R. Nanda, *The Nehrus* (London, 1962), p. 201.
23. M.K. Gandhi to Jawaharlal Nehru, 19 February 1922: *Collected Works*, Vol. XXII, p. 436.
24. Presidential Address by C.R. Das, Gaya Congress, 1922.
25. B.R. Nanda, *The Nehrus* (London, 1962), p. 207.
26. *The Legislative Assembly Debates,* (Official Report), Vol. IV, Part I (Delhi, 1924), p. 370.

27. Presidential Address by M.K. Gandhi, Belgaum Congress, 1924.
28. Quoted in R. Coupland, *The Indian Problem 1833-1935* (Oxford, 1943), p. 89.
29. *Autobiography*, p. 81.
30. Quoted in R.C. Dutt, *Socialism of Jawaharlal Nehru* (Delhi, 1981), p.22.
31. Statement to the Press at Brussels, 9 February 1927: *Selected Works of Jawaharlal Nehru* (henceforth referred to as *SWJN)*, Vol. II, pp. 270-2.
32. *Autobiography*, p. 182.
33. Presidential Address by Jawaharlal Nehru before Bombay Presidency Youth Conference, 12 December 1928: *SWJN*, Vol. III, pp. 203-10.
34. Presidential Address by Jawaharlal Nehru before All India Trade Union Congress, 30 November 1929: *SWJN*, Vol. IV, pp. 49-55.
35. Quoted in B. Pattabhi Sitaramayya, *The History of the Indian National Congress*, Vol. I (1885-1935).
36. Quoted in Lord Birkenhead, *Halifax: The Life of Lord Halifax* (London, 1965), p. 263.
37. Statement by Lord Irwin, 31 October 1929: *Speeches and Documents on the Indian Constitution 1911-47*, Vol. I, Selected by M. Guryer and A. Appadorai (Oxford, 1957), pp. 225-7.
38. *Collected Works:* Vol. XLII, p. 81.
39. Presidential Address by Jawaharlal Nehru, Lahore Congress, 1929.
40. Ibid.
41. J.M. Brown, *Gandhi and Civil Disobedience* (Cambridge, 1977), pp. 76-80.
42. Speech by M.K. Gandhi, reported in *Young India*, 3 April 1930.
43. *NAI:* Report by Sir Harry Haig, 25 May 1930: Home Political Volume V/257/30.
44. See Nandkishore Nigam, *Balidan (Sacrifice)* (Delhi), pp. 56-8.
45. Pattabhi Sitaramayya, op. cit., p. 436.
46. Speech by M.K. Gandhi before Federal Structure Committee, 15 September 1931: *Collected Works*, Vol. XLVIII, pp. 13-20.
47. Ibid.
48. M.K. Gandhi to Samuel Hoare, 11 March 1932. Pyarelal, *The Epic Fast* (Ahmedabad, 1932), pp. 99-103.
49. Pyarelal, *The Epic Fast*, p. VII.

2

A Review of the Historical Literature on the Struggle for Freedom in India

The emergence of India as a sovereign state in 1947 was one of the crucial events of the 20th century. It is hardly surprising, therefore, that a substantial body of historical writing has appeared over the past four decades on different facets of this development. Some of these writings focus upon the conflict between British imperialism and Indian nationalism at the national, regional or local level(s). Others, touch upon the quality of social cleavages and political cohesion within Indian society, more particularly as they pertain to the emergence of Pakistan, or the integration of the Princely States in the Indian Union. Others, yet again, explore the changing locus of social and economic power within Indian society, and raise issues concerning the dominance of the rich and the propertied within the alliance of classes and communities that went into the making of a national movement of truly epic proportions. All told, therefore, the literature on the liberation movement is comprehensive in the questions which it poses; wide ranging in the ideological vision which informs it; and conflicting in the insights which it offers. Perhaps the time is now opportune to review this literature and cull out of such a review an overall understanding of the manner whereby the people of India liberated themselves from British rule.

A striking feature of the historical literature on the liberation movement in South Asia is the articulation of three distinctive national viewpoints by the scholars who have contributed to it. This should occasion no surprise; for historical scholarship inevitably reflects national viewpoints and national aspirations. There is little reason to believe that scholars within a national polity necessarily agree with each other on questions of focus and interpretation. Nevertheless, even the differences in perception within a national scholarly community belong to a common universe of discourse. As against this, historical explanations offered by scholars drawn from different countries seldom lead to conclusions which offer a common ground for a dialogue.

Since historical literature on the recent past emanating from Pakistan is known least of all, it may be profitable to commence our review by examining the insights which it offers pertaining to the retreat of British imperialism from South Asia, and the emergence of two (and, later, three) national polities in the region. Perhaps the basic framework of "nationalist" historiography in Pakistan was laid down by the officially sponsored series entitled *A History of the Freedom Movement*[1] (hereinafter referred to as *Freedom Movement in Pakistan)*. The initial contributions to this series deal with the position of Muslim communities in India in the 19th century, when British rule was firmly established over the subcontinent. The historians of Pakistan have argued that different sections of Muslim society were, at this juncture, totally unreconciled to the *Pax Britannica:* the aristocracy and the landed gentry, since they had suffered displacement as the ruling classes; the religious intelligentsia, because of the umbilical cord which tied it to the latter; the artisan and weaving communities, because imperialism brought with it deindustrialisation and a diminution in their social status; and the peasantry in the north-west and the north-east, since alien rule had resulted in its impoverishment. Although Muslim hostility to British rule was not expressed in substantial movements of revolt—with the conspicuous exception of the Uprising of 1857—it nevertheless manifested itself in a variety of fragmented and populist movements, like the Wahabi movement, or the agitation of Titu Mir, or the Faraizi upsurge, which convulsed society in the 19th century.

Since Muslim communities were by and large hostile to the *Pax Britannica,* the contributions to the *Freedom Movement in Pakistan* have further argued that, towards the close of the 19th century, two distinct trends were discernible within Islam in India.

Several prominent Muslims, drawn from liberal elements within the landed gentry, attempted to transform the religious vision of their coreligionists with the objective of modernising the community. In contrast to this, the religious intelligentsia of Islam sought to generate an overarching solidarity between different sections of Muslim India, with the objective of undermining British rule. The Pan-Islamic movement generated by the religious intelligentsia gained substantial strength, not only among the landed, the commercial and the professional classes, but also among the artisans and the peasantry. By the second decade of the 20th century, this trend gave birth to a militant upsurge, whose leaders joined hands with Hindu nationalists in an attempt to dislodge British rule over the subcontinent. However, so Pakistani scholars believe, the non-cooperation movement, in which the Muslims made sacrifices wholly out of proportion to their demographic strength, was a chastening experience for Muslim India. There was a genuine danger of Muslim interests being subordinated to the interests of the dominant Hindu community. Hence the bitterness in relations between Hindus and Muslims which characterised the political scene in the aftermath of the non-cooperation movement. The experience of an alliance with the Hindus during 1919-22, served as a warning to the Muslim leadership and the Muslim masses, that they would have to fashion their political destiny separately from Hindu India, if the vision of the good life, as decreed by Islam, was to be realized. The definition of a distinctive political identity stimulated a sharp debate within the Muslim intelligentsia in the late 1930s, and this debate culminated in the adoption of the demand for a separate homeland, i.e., Pakistan, by the Muslim League in 1940. Thereafter, the vision of Pakistan was communicated to the elite no less than to the popular classes within a remarkably short span of time. Small wonder, then, so it is spelt out in the *Freedom Movement in Pakistan,* that when the British Government declared its decision to pull out of the subcontinent after the Second World War, it faced a distinctive Islamic nationalism which was no less robust than the nationalism of the Indian National Congress. The British were obliged to acknowledge the strength of Muslim sentiment for a separate homeland; and as a result of this, Pakistan came into existence in August 1947.

The overall perspective spelt out in the *Freedom Movement in*

Pakistan (I shall comment upon its historical validity later) provides, even today, the context within which Pakistani scholarship approaches the recent history of the subcontinent. For instance, despite his libera (bordering on the radical) preconceptions, a scholar like Khalid B. Sayeed portrays a causal chain of events in *Pakistan: The Formative Phase* which does not question the framework sketched out above.[2] Nor do any of the scholarly studies which are available question the basic thesis advanced in the *Freedom Movement in Pakistan.*[3] What Pakistani scholars have accomplished, however, is the detailed exposition of the trends spelt out in the official historiography. The manner in which the Muslim League won the support of the elite and popular Muslim classes, in the Punjab and in Bengal, during the 1940s, is the subject of a number of explorations.[4] In the case of the Punjab, fascinating light has been thrown on the networks of influence, controlled by the landed gentry, or by religious leaders, which were the basis of popular support for the Muslim League. Similarly, the tension between a predominantly Hindu rural gentry (linked to the Congress) and the Muslim peasantry of Bengal enabled the League to draw into its embrace the poorer agrarian classes in that region. Equally illuminating are scholarly studies which dwell upon the 19th century, and focus attention upon subterranean movements of protests among artisans and the lowly rural classes. While none of this literature challenges the perspective of the *Freedom Movement in Pakistan,* very recently scholars have explored the character of popular Islam in Bengal prior to 1947; and in doing so, they have highlighted the crystallisation of a distinctive identity, which was Bengali and Islamic in equal proportions.[5] The growth of such a consciousness in the late 19th century, particularly among the rural classes, explains cleavages between Hindu and Muslim Bengal just as much as it also explains the emergence of Bangladesh in 1971.

Perhaps the historical literature on the freedom movement in Pakistan, which is briefly reviewed above, is as illuminating as it is misleading a guide to the recent history of the subcontinent. The assertion that the Muslim communities of India were, by and large, hostile to British rule is an assertion which needs to be explored sympathetically. Behind such a view, however, lie assumptions about the quality of social cohesion within Muslim India which are borne out not at all by the evidence available to us.

Indeed, it would be difficult to conceive of solidarity between classes as far removed from each other in their economic status and in their social sensibility as the landed gentry of Uttar Pradesh and Bihar; or the tribal communities of north-west India; or the artisans and craftsmen who fabricated goods for popular or elite consumption in the cities of Hindustan; or the mercantile groups which resided in the port cities of western and south-western India. Except for a brief span of time in the 1940s, these classes, notwithstanding their allegiance to Islam, pulled in very different directions and harboured very different visions of the good life. The decisive factor here was the overarching presence of the imperial power, whcih promoted dissension *between* Hinduism and Islam (as it promoted dissension *within* the communities of Hinduism and Islam) for the purposes of political control over the subcontinent. The objective of this strategy of "divide and rule" was not to break up the subcontinent into antagonistic polities. Its objective was to render a society of 400 million and more amenable to imperial control. However, this strategy reinforced the strength of political formations, like the Muslim League, which sought to aggregate the Muslim communities of India into a separatist posture. Yet the fragility of such an aggregation is eloquently reflected in the fact that the Muslim League—the political organisation responsible for a coming together of different Islamic communities—was literally wiped out of existence a few years after the genesis of Pakistan. The fragility of the separatist alliance, which makes nonsense of the claim that Muslim India constituted a cohesive social community, is equally reflected in the events of 1971, when the Muslims of north-east India decided to carve out a separate state for themselves. We get no clues to the reasons behind such a development in the very substantial literature created by Pakistani scholarship, on the dissolution of the British Empire and the partition of the subcontinent, which has appeared over the past few decades.

I

Although British interest in South Asia has of late been expressing itself increasingly in popular literature of "nostalgia for the Raj"[6] genre, historical writings on the struggle for freedom in India, emanating from Great Britain, are sufficiently distinctive to merit separate consideration in any scholarly review of the subject. To the extent this literature deals with British imperial strategy in the decade preceding 1947, two viewpoints merit special attention. In an essay which C.H. Philips[7] wrote on the partition of India some fifteen years ago, he put forth the argument that as soon as nationalism achieved maturity in South Asia, British statesmen not only recognised it as a legitimate force, but they also strove to channelise it in a creative direction. The fruits of this labour were reflected in the Government of India Act of 1935. This Act accorded recognition to three distinctive political forces in the subcontinent: Hindu India, the elite and the popular classes, which had come together under the aegis of Gandhi and the Congress; Muslim India, which had rejected the leadership of the Congress after the brief honeymoon of 1920-22, and sought fulfilment through a political strategy different from that of the Congress; and finally, Princely India, which was untouched by the leaven of nationalism and desired to retain for itself a distinctive position within the framework of an autonomous Indian polity. The Constitution of 1935 reflected the desire of British statesmanship to weld together these three disparate political forces into a single polity. Despite British attempts to forge Indian unity—needless to say, on terms that would do no violence to the identities of the three distinctive constituents of political society in India—the prescription held out in the Act of 1935 failed in securing its objective. The responsibility for this failure, so Philips argued, lay with the Congress; insofar as its leadership was unsuccessful in assuring the Muslims that their interests would be protected in a united India. Moreover, this line of reasoning assumes that the Muslims of India, rich and poor, zamindars and peasants, merchants and artisans, constituted a cohesive community which it fell upon the Congress to draw into a creative partnership with other communities. The Congress may have been unequal to the task of uniting Hindus and Muslims; yet behind such a failure, according to Philips, lay two distinctive, indeed, antithetical religious cultures; which resulted in the emergence of two Nations once the unifying fabric of the *Pax Britannica* had been undermined.

A decade after Philips had pronounced upon the factors which led to the liberation and partition of India, another British scholar essayed upon an analysis of the reasons behind this development. Low's exploration of the processes whereby India emerged as an independent polity focused upon the dominant peasant communities, which controlled social and economic power within rural society, over a long span of historical time.[8] The *Pax Britannica,* like earlier polities in the subcontinent, rested upon these rural classes, whose support it cultivated through a package of policies and a network of institutions at the same time as it appropriated a substantial proportion of the wealth produced by them. But by the 1930s, the Congress, under the leadership of Gandhi, was able to detach these classes from British rule, and draw them into a nationalist alliance. The British Government failed to see how its rural base had been undermined until the provincial elections of 1937. These elections, which were shaped by the votes of the recently enfranchised peasants, made it clear that the dominant rural classes had been won over to the cause of nationalism. Thereafter, according to Low, it was a matter of time before the British quit the subcontinent, since it was impossible for any government, particularly an alien government, to hold India against the wishes of this powerful constituency. Nevertheless, the rural support of the Congress, which rested principally in the Hindi speaking provinces, but also reached out to Gujarat, Maharashtra, Andhra, Tamil Nadu, and some other provinces, was conspicuous by its absence in the north-eastern and also in the north-western regions of the subcontinent. In these regions, at least for a brief span of time, the Muslim League succeeded in winning over the rural gentry and the peasantry to a separatist stance. As a result of this, the Congress could not prevent the partition of the subcontinent into the two sovereign states of India and Pakistan in 1947.

Over the past two decades, a steady stream of scholarly monographs has emerged from Great Britain. These studies attempt to spell out and to further refine the two perceptions which have been sketched out above. Some of these historical works also seek to explain the break-up of empire in South Asia through developments within the polity and economy of Great Britain. It has been suggested, for instance, that Britain's economic stake in India declined sharply over the second quarter of the 20th century, so that British statesmen of the period no longer attached the same importance to India as an integral part of an imperial system.[9]

Moreover, this diminishing stake in the Indian economy was accompanied by a sharp decline in the strength of British personnel in the civil service through which the vast territories of South Asia were controlled.[10] Taken altogether, such writings suggest that the reason for the British withdrawal from the subcontinent lay in social, political and economic developments within Great Britain, rather than in the growth of a powerful nationalism within the subcontinent.

Whatever be their perception of the metropolitan factors behind the loss of empire in India, British historians of South Asia have also paid substantial attention to the growth of nationalism within Indian society. A considerable body of scholarship on this theme has appeared under the inspiration of some historians associated with Cambridge.[11] These writings portray a highly cleavated and fragmented society as the dominant reality behind the nationalist upsurge in India. Within this social order characterised by faction and cleavage, according to the Cambridge historians, well entrenched elites who controlled social, economic and political power were able to jockey themselves into positions of leadership in the national movement, and make it an instrument of their sectarian economic interests. The most striking feature of this scholarship is the premium it puts upon "acquisitive" as against "moral" man; the lowly place which it accords to ideology as the motivator of action; and the distorted picture which it presents of faction and cleavage along caste and religious lines, within Indian society. Indeed, scholars subscribing to this school of thought are wholly blind to the moral vision which brought together different classes and communities in a movement of epic strength, and thereby obliged the British Government to dismantle its empire over India.

II

If British scholars tend to exaggerate the divisiveness of society and the fragmentation which characterised the national movement in South Asia, then Indian historians often magnify the political cohesion which was achieved in the course of the anti-imperialist struggle. Indeed, in the liberal and nationalist historiography of the struggle for freedom, there is an emphasis upon certain themes, to the exclusion of others, which results in a distorted understanding of the liberation movement. Perhaps the shortcomings of such a perception can best be appreciated through a terse narration of its content.[12]

By the first quarter of the 19th century, it is argued, the institutions of western education and western values had conjured into existence an intelligentsia which desired to initiate changes within Indian society, with the objective of reconstituting it on liberal and rational principles. The organisational efforts of this intelligentsia were initially local in character; next, they achieved a regional dimension; and finally, in 1885, a "parliament of Indian nationalism" came into existence under the rubric of the Indian National Congress. Apart from the intelligentsia, liberal members of the landed gentry and the commercial classes also participated in this seminal process, which sought to achieve, by the end of the 19th century, autonomy for India within the British Empire.

Although liberal scholars regard the crystallisation of the Congress, in 1885, as an important landmark in the growth of the liberation movement, they simultaneously concede that, initially, the Congress represented only a small proportion of the diverse classes and communities which constituted Indian society. The Swadeshi movement of 1905 was partly launched with the objective of broadening the support base of the Congress. Nevertheless, the mobilisation of the toiling classes—workers, artisans, peasants and tribals—was only brought about by Gandhi, who drew upon an idiom of politics interlaced with popular religious symbols and could, therefore, reach out to classes which did not respond readily to nationalist appeals couched in the secular political idiom of the West. Indeed, liberal historiography goes beyond this to suggest that Gandhi was also successful in creating a multi-religious alliance between Hindus, Muslims and Sikhs against British imperialism. The combined strength of the different classes and communities which participated in the non-cooperation movement, during the years 1920-22, under the aegis of the Mahatma, seriously weakened the fabric of British rule over India. Gandhi's reluctance to countenance violence, however, obliged him to withdraw in February 1922 the movement of protest which he had earlier set in motion. Yet this retreat was followed by renewed assaults upon the British Raj over India, in the 1930s, and in 1942, till in 1947 the British Government decided to withdraw from the subcontinent. The dawn of freedom in 1947 was a great triumph for the people of India. But this triumph was flawed through the simultaneous partition of the subcontinent. The partition was largely a result of the policy of 'divide and rule' pursued with consummate skill by the British Government; though it also resulted partially from religious cleavages in the fabric of Indian society which the national movement had failed to heal.

While the liberal vision of the national movement continues to dominate historical writing in India, recent researches have substantially modified the picture sketched out by its protagonists. Most of this recent scholarship is inspired by a vision which seeks to restructure Indian society upon radical principles at the same time as it is undergoing an industrial transformation.[13] At the very outset, radical scholarship enlarges the horizons of nationalist historiography by going beyond the elite classes, and focusing upon the anti-imperialism of peasants, sharecroppers, agricultural labourers, tribals, industrial workers and artisans, to list only some of the disaffected popular classes. Indeed, these exercises in "history from below" suggest that the lowly classes as a whole—although they lacked an understanding of the means through which the polity could be radically reorganised—were seething with discontent under British rule, and were desirous of establishing control over the political economy of the subcontinent. Indeed, the intelligentsia, the landed gentry and the commercial classes, despite their exposure to western ideas and to the ideology of nationalism, were initially inclined to look upon British rule with a measure of sympathy. Nothing reflects this better than the Uprising of 1857, when throughout the valley of the Ganga, the erstwhile aristocracy, plus the religious intelligentsia and the peasantry, rose in a mighty movement of armed protest against British rule; while the commercial and educated classes clung to the coat tails of the British Government, fearful about their future in the event of an overthrow of British rule over the subcontinent.

While focusing on the initial loyalty of the intellectual and commercial elite to British rule, radical historiography is not blind to changes in elite consciousness towards the close of the 19th century. These changes are best reflected in the founding of the Congress in 1885. Nevertheless, the most significant contribution of radical scholarship rests in its appreciation of the manner in which the national movement was transformed, from an elite to a mass movement, in the first quarter of the 20th century, and the implications of such a development.

The populist transformation of the national movement in the third decade of the 20th century was a process which drew heavily upon the cultural traditions of Indian civilisation. Over the centuries, the influence of moral actors of outstanding stature has repeatedly drawn the popular classes into social movements designed to transform mass consciousness and reorganise the orders of society. In the 1920s, Gandhi utilised this cultural resource with conspicuous success, and he drew into his epic agitations, rural and urban classes with conflicting interests and religious communities subscribing to different visions of the good society. Such unity among the rich and the poor within the national movement (so argue radical scholars) enabled the former to establish their dominance over the movement as a whole. The Gandhian mode of political organisation; the Gandhian concept of trusteeship; and the Gandhian vision of autonomous rural communities as the basis of the political order made a very substantial contribution to this state of affairs. As a result, although the countrywide agitations which characterised the liberation movement successfully mobilised the toiling classes, their participation in the struggle came about under the dominance of the privileged social orders. Equally significant was the fact that the mobilisation of the peasantry; the workers and the tribal communities by Gandhi rested upon an appeal to their religious sensibilities and upon a belief that the spiritualisation of politics would greatly strengthen the cause of liberation. Not only, therefore, was the national movement launched under the hegemony of the privileged classes; but it also reinforced the religious identity of those Hindus, Muslims and Sikhs who participated in the anti-imperial agitations. The radical critique of the liberation movement, therefore, concedes the strength in numbers of the popular front which Gandhi was able to forge in the course of the struggle against British imperialism. Yet this populist strength was achieved through an idiom of politics and through an organisational strategy which subordinated the poor to the rich classes; and widened cleavages between different religious communities by conferring upon their members an heightened consciousness of their distinctive identities.

III

Most of the recent writings on nationalist history rest upon the scholarly perceptions outlined above, and they seek to further illumine the processes underlying the emergence of India as a sovereign state, at the same time as the subcontinent was partitioned into two political entities under British aegis. What was the strategic vision of the British Government during the culminating phase of the Raj in India? How did the leaders of the Congress frame their objectives *vis-à-vis* the British Government no less than *vis-à-vis* the Muslim League? Over and above this, how did the mainstream leadership look upon emerging political groups of a radical complexion? Closely related to this was the issue: what were the forms of consciousness—particularly as they related to nation and community—which shaped the values of different classes and religious groups within India? And finally, to what extent was communalism a social growth which sprang from the womb of Indian society; and to what extent was it "conjured into existence" by the British Raj? These are some of the questions to which such writings address themselves; and they rely not only upon evidence drawn from conventional historical sources but also upon imaginative literature to identify the values of different classes and communities and the manner in which (if at all) they contributed to the partition of India.

Perhaps the first question worthy of reflection relates to the strategic objectives of the British Government. Here it is important to remember that the emergence of two sovereign states in 1947 should not lead the historian to a Whiggish view of the preceding decades. Indeed, it is rewarding to look at the Constitution of 1935, for the evidence it provides about imperial motivations, after British statesmen had recognised the existence of a powerful national movement in India. It is arguable—and we would so argue—that even after the British had recognised the strength of the national movement, their conception of how this movement could be contained was radically different from what even moderate Congress leaders looked upon as minimum nationalist objectives. Contrary to Philips's interpretation of the Constitution of 1935, this Act in fact sought to create a polity which would be tied in bonds of enduring subordination to the British Empire. This is not to question the view that the British Government, in the 1930s, perceived three distinct political constellations within the subcontinent—the Congress, which had drawn the Hindu communities into a stance of nationalism;

Muslim opinion, which was distrustful of the Congress and sought ways to ensure political and cultural autonomy for itself; and Princely India, in which the focus of loyalty was still provided by the traditional ruling families—whatever be the validity of this view. This is merely to suggest that the British Government sought to create two effective arenas of political action for the containment of nationalism. Through the device of provincial autonomy, the British sought to break up the Congress into tame regional formations, which would rest content with the limited initiative vested in provincial governments, leaving to the federal centre the task of shaping the overall destiny of the subcontinent. To ensure such a state of affairs, the centre contemplated by the Constitution of 1935, was so devised that nationalist spokesmen in the federal government would be counterpoised by the spokesmen of Princely India and the great religious minorities, most prominently of all, the Muslim community. The Constitution of 1935, in brief, was not a charter of freedom for India, as Philips would have us believe. Instead, it was a design for the break-up of nationalism as an all-India movement and its relegation to the provincial arena of political action. At the same time, this constitution sought the permanent political, economic and strategic subordination of India to Great Britain.

The struggle between Indian nationalism and British imperialism, during the decade preceding 1947, was essentially a struggle regarding the quality of independence which India would enjoy after liberation. The British Government was prepared to yield the shadow of power to organised nationalism, by creating for the Congress an arena of political activity at the provincial level. By that very logic, British imperialism sought to undermine nationalism as an all-India phenomenon. The leaders of the Congress saw through the British design in all its subtlety—and worse—irrespective of their reaction to this design. Men like Jawaharlal Nehru saw the trap with great clarity and were, therefore, unequivocally opposed to any involvement in the institutions of provincial governance created by the Constitution of 1935. Instead, they proposed the election of a Constituent Assembly which would be vested with the responsibility of hammering out a new system of government. Such an assembly would cut through agonising negotiations with the British Government, and enable the people of India to shape their destiny through a truly representative institution resting upon the popular will. Nehru's stance was irreproachable in its revolutionary logic. But even conservative leaders of the Congress, willing to work the Constitution of 1935, were by no means prepared to lend themselves to the British design. Hence the institution of a "High Command" in the Congress; which ensured that the Congress governments installed in the provinces conducted themselves in accordance with the wishes of the national leadership. It is hardly fortuitous that few outstanding leaders of the Congress accepted office under the Constitution of 1935. It is also amusing to see the premiers of various provincial governments (as they were then called) rushing to Wardha, or elsewhere, at the call of the High Command, very much like errant school children being summoned by a censorious headmaster. Such firm party discipline ensured the integrity of nationalism as an all-India phenomenon. It also demonstrated that, despite differences, leaders of various hues within the Congress were united in their determination to destroy British imperialism and create a cohesive polity in India.

How can our portrayal of imperial policy be squared with the view, often expressed by historians within India, that the British Government supported the pretensions of the minorities and was, therefore, responsible for the partition of the subcontinent? There can be no simple answer to this question. It is true that the constitutional reforms shaped by the British Government were designed to promote dissension within Indian society. Such tactics are frequently employed by imperial governments in order to strengthen their hold over subject societies. Indeed, communal cleavages were by no means the only cleavages which the British attempted to exploit within India. Thus, various attempts were made to detach the landed interest from the professional classes; and from the 1920s, the British handled the emerging capitalist classes with great care, in order to prevent them from rallying around the nationalist cause. Yet such cleavages were invoked, not with the intention of undermining the unity of India, but to abort the growth of nationalism within the subcontinent. Nevertheless, whatever may have been the objective of extending support to the minorities, such support pitchforked political parties resting upon communalism into prominence. The classic instance is that of the Muslim League, the support of whose pretensions greatly assisted the British Government in thwarting the Congress.

Yet this support, in turn, helped the League in establishing its hold over the Muslim communities of India.

When the British Government finally recognised the untenability of its Raj over India, after 1945, organised communalism had also grown into a Frankenstein whose pretensions were difficult to overlook. Yet there is little evidence to suggest that this was even attempted. On the other hand, the fantasy of exercising indirect control over the subcontinent died hard. In an important contribution, a scholar suggests that even after the creation of India and Pakistan, the British attempted to so arrange matters that a measure of imperial control would be a substantive reality for both the new dominions.[14] At the same time, some British strategists were of the view that global imperial interests would best be served through the maintenance of "friendly" relations with Pakistan. Indeed, another contribution on this theme suggests that the fate of the North-West Frontier Province, in 1947, is the most eloquent testimony to the existence of such a design.[15]

IV

At this juncture, it would be profitable to recapitulate the manner in which various classes and communities within Indian society were drawn into the anti-imperialist struggle by the Congress. When the national movement underwent a populist transformation in the third decade of the 20th century, the mobilisational techniques through which peasants, workers, artisans and tribals, among others, were drawn into the struggle possessed some distinctive features which, as already suggested, were not without their influence upon religious cleavages and class dominance within Indian society. As the leaders of the Congress reached out to new regions and localities within the subcontinent, they turned to dominant men and powerful social groups everywhere, and utilised their power, their influence and their commitment to nationalism to recruit new social classes and broaden the bases of the struggle. Such a *modus vivendi* for the aggregation of an anti-imperialist alliance was productive of the most spectacular results, so far as the mobilisation of the popular classes in the cities and in the villages was concerned. The striking success of the nation-wide agitations of the 1920s and the 1930s bears eloquent witness to this assertion. However, such access to mass constituencies through the mediation of dominant interests posed serious problems pertaining to relations between the propertied and the impoverished classes; just as it also created a movement in which, notwithstanding the concern of leaders like Mahatma Gandhi and Jawaharlal Nehru for the poor, the initiative lay with those who possessed substantial wealth and controlled the levers of economic power in society. Indeed, there is reason to believe that by the 1930s, upper and middle class interest had crystallised within the national movement in a manner which ensured that the lowly classes, urban and rural, participated in nationalist agitations only under the hegemony of the propertied classes.[16] There was no dearth of locality and region based popular movements, within the wider framework of the liberation struggle, which offered the prospect of remedying the situation. At least three of the essays in a recent work on nationalist history deal with agitations which were simultaneously radical and national.[17] Yet other essays in this work also suggest that the dominant pan-Indian nationalism, on the eve of independence and partition, was middle class in character; and that this nationalism was fully capable of meeting the challenge of radical movements (which never acquired other than a fragmentary or localised character), at the same time as it acquired the strength to destroy British rule over the subcontinent.

What features in nationalist historiography as the "communal question" is not unrelated to the "class question". Indeed, the fact that the liberation movement was basically middle class in character and tied to the vision of a market economy probably fed into the widening gulf between Islam and Hinduism within the subcontinent. Perhaps—and this is speculative—if the liberation movement had rested upon the moral and material interests of the lowly classes, then notwithstanding differences in cultural traditions and religious vision, the communities of Hinduism and Islam could have been drawn into a cohesive political society when the struggle against imperialism terminated in 1947.

What is the basis of such an assumption? No ready answer can be given to this question. Yet it is significant that radical nationalism, wherever it made its presence felt, was much more successful than middle class nationalism in creating bonds of unity between Hindus and Muslims. Wherever the leaders transformed nationalism from a political to a social and economic proposition; wherever they held out a vision of India wherein equity would determine the distribution of the gross national product between different classes and communities; a large measure of unity was achieved between Hindus, Muslims and other religious communities. The communal question was partially a psychological question. It flowed from the fear of domination by the so-called majority, the Hindus. This fear tied different sections of Muslim society in a tenuous unity that had very little basis in social reality. Yet the position which the propertied classes had acquired—nowhere is this reflected more clearly than in the essay on the growing strength of the Marwari bourgeoisie[18]—seems to suggest that by the 1930s their dominance over politics was difficult to displace. For this very reason, the leaders of the national movement were unable to provide a satisfactory answer to the communal question. Only a radical national movement held the possibility of forging unity between different religious communities; and since the liberation movement in India was middle class in character, it failed to tame the monster of communalism.

Yet the radical scholar may offer too facile an analysis of communalism and the complex issue of unity between different religious communities within India. Recognising the ubiquity and complexity of communalism, some historians have turned to creative literature on the themes of independence and partition to seek illumination. Perhaps a few observations are appropriate before the insights provided by imaginative literature to the historian of the national movement are explored. The explanations offered by the social sciences, whether radical or liberal in their conceptual underpinning, suffer from some shortcomings which spring into bold relief when questions pertaining to social consciousness and political identity are explored. The analytical categories of the social sciences are disaggregative of reality; and social scientists rely substantially upon induction in arriving at generalisations. There is, in the social sciences, the further assumption that the arithmetic sum of perceptions of disaggregated reality can provide a rounded understanding of the whole. Such an assumption is particularly misleading when the subject of enquiry touches upon problems of social consciousness and its reflection in political action. Small wonder, then, that both liberal and radical historiographies appear inadequate when dealing with problems arising out of religious and communal conflict. The creative writer, however, seeks to grasp reality through cognitive processes different from those of the social scientist or the historian. His perception does not depend upon an initial process of disaggregation, for purposes of ready analysis, and the subsequent aggregation of fragmentary insights into a mechanical whole. Instead, the imaginative writer seeks to explore reality as a totality. He, therefore, reveals a sensitivity to problems of consciousness and identity which is seldom equalled by the more formal disciplines of the social sciences.

The communal question, for all these reasons, can be fruitfully explored through works of literary imagination created during the decades under review. What light is thrown by such literature upon the communal psyche; or its articulation in the consciousness of "faces in the crowd"; or its reflection in political action? Those writings which explore imaginative literature in the 1940s, with particular reference to communalism, point to a social milieu of nightmarish starkness and terrifying atavism that provided the backdrop for the religious warfare which traumatised the subcontinent on the eve of independence.[19] Indeed, such writings also point to the existence of diverse and deeply stratified religious identities, drawn into relationships of hostility, distrust and rejection, which were unrelated to any overarching pan-Indian consciousness. Perhaps this picture is overdrawn; since there were arenas of political action where Hindus, Muslims and other religious communities came together in an alliance against British imperialism. Despite such unity, however, the identities of Hindus, Muslims and Sikhs were so articulated, that even when different communities came together for common political objectives—and there are many instances of joint action—the underlying distinctions between men subscribing to different spiritual visions stood boldly etched in the background.

What, in conclusion, are the insights offered by recent nationalist writings? It would be appropriate to state that some recent writings present a novel picture, at the national no less than at the local level, of society in India on the eve of independence and partition. The great strength of the national movement, and this strength needs to be highlighted, lay in the support which it drew from an enormous range of social classes and communities; and the skill with which its leaders defeated the British design of drawing India into an enduring relationship of subordination to the Empire. But if the liberation movement was successful in some areas, there is reason for disquiet in other domains. A major objective of the national movement was to create a unified and cohesive polity in the subcontinent. This was successfully accomplished so far as the Princely States were concerned; but not for Muslim India. Unity between Hindus and Muslims eluded the national leadership. Perhaps the communal problem, as suggested above, was tied up with the class question. The liberation movement in India was successful in drawing the popular classes into an anti-British struggle; yet dominance within the movement, so scholars believe, lay with the propertied classes. This dominance provided fertile ground for sowing the seeds of distrust between Hindus and Muslims. But the question must be asked—and the essays which explore imaginative literature pose this question—whether, over and above the dominance of property, the existence of distinctive social identities also stood in the way of political unity between Hindus and Muslims. The multiplicity of cultures and identities within Indian society is a phenomenon with which the historian is familiar. The play of this plurality upon the liberation movement created problems to which there were no easy solutions. Indeed, the seriousness of these problems is reflected in the fact, that four decades after the attainment of independence, the people of India are still grappling with the seminal issue of national unity. Yet despite such flaws the liberation of India in 1947 was a stupendous achievement which opened the possibility of transforming the human condition within the country.

NOTES

1. *A History of the Freedom Movement (Being the Story of Muslim Struggle for the Freedom of Hind-Pakistan) 1707-1947*; Vol. I, Parts I and II; Vol. II, Parts I and II; Vol. III, Parts I and II. Republished by Renaissance Publishing House, New Delhi, 1984.
2. K.B. Sayeed, *Pakistan: The Formative Phase 1857-1958* (London, 1968).
3. See, for instance: (a) Chaudhri Muhammad Ali, *The Emergence of Pakistan* (Lahore, 1973); (b) S. Qain Hussain Jafri, (ed.), *Qaid-i-Azam: Correspondence with Punjab Muslim Leaders* (Lahore, 1977); (c) Choudhry Khaliquzzaman, *Pathway to Pakistan* (Lahore, 1961); (d) Matlulul Hasan Saiyid, *Mohammad Ali Jinnah: A Political Study* (Lahore, 1962), and (e) Mukhtar Zaman, *Students' Role in the Pakistan Movement* (Karachi, 1978).

4. See Imran Ali, "Relations Between the Muslim League and the Punjab National Unionist Party 1935-47", *South Asia*, No. 6, December 1976; and A. Gilmartin, "Religious Leadership and the Pakistan Movement in the Punjab," *Modern Asian Studies*, Vol. 13, Part 3, July 1979.
5. R. Ahmed, *The Bengal Muslims, 1871-1906* (Delhi, 1981).
6. See W.H. Morris-Jones, "The Jewel in the Crown," *Pacific Affairs*, Vol. 58, No. 2, Summer 1985, pp. 287-92. Even while accepting the populist character of this literature, Morris-Jones attempts to give it a serious moral purpose.
7. See C.H. Philips, "Introduction," in C.H. Philips and M.D. Wainwright (eds.), *The Partition of India: Policies and Perspectives 1935-47* (London, 1970).
8. See D.A. Low, "Introduction: The Climactic Years" in D.A. Low (ed.), *Congress and the Raj: Facets of the Indian Struggle 1917-47* (London, 1977).
9. The classic statement of this thesis is to be found in B.R. Tomlinson, *The Political Economy of the Raj 1914-1947: The Economics of Decolonisation in India* (London, 1979).
10. D.C. Patter, "Manpower Shortage and the End of Colonialism: The Case of the Indian Civil Service," *Modern Asian Studies*, Vol. 7, Part I, January 1973, pp. 47-73.
11. The three principal studies created by this group are: (a) A. Seal, *The Emergence of Indian Nationalism*. (b) J. Gallagher, G. Johnson and A. Seal (eds)., *Locality, Province and Nation: Essays on Indian Politics 1870-1940* (Cambridge, 1973). (c) C. Baker, G. Johnson and A. Seal (eds). *Power, Profit and Politics: Essays on Imperialism, Nationalism and Change in Twentieth Century India* (Cambridge, 1981).
12. Perhaps the classic statement of the liberal-nationalist view is to be found in Tarachand, *History of the Freedom Movement in India*, 4 Vols. (Delhi, 1961-72).
13. The Radical view of the freedom struggle has been voiced with sensitivity and rigour by Sumit Sarkar, *Modern India 1885-1947* (Delhi, 1983).
14. See article by P.S. Gupta entitled "Imperial Strategy and the Transfer of Power" in A.K. Gupta (ed.), *Myth and Reality: The Struggle for Freedom in India, 1945-47*, (New Delhi, 1987). The present essay is an introduction to this volume.
15. See article by Baren Ray entitled "Pakhtun National Movement and Transfer of Power in India" in A.K. Gupta (ed.), op. cit.
16. See R. Kumar, "From Swaraj to Purna Swaraj: Nationalist Politics in the City of Bombay (1920-1932)" in D.A. Low (ed.), *Congress and the Raj: Facets of the Indian Struggle, 1917-47* (London, 1977) and Gyanendra Pandey, *The Ascendency of the Congress in Uttar Pradesh 1926-34* (Delhi, 1978).
17. See articles by Radhakanta Barik, Gautam Chattopadhyay and Ranajit Das Gupta in A.K. Gupta (ed.), op. cit.
18. See article by Omkar Goswami in A.K. Gupta (ed.), op. cit.
19. See articles by Alok Rai, Tapati Chakravarty, S.S. Hans and R.K. Jain in A.K. Gupta (ed.), op. cit.

3

Motilal Nehru: Portrait of a Nationalist*

There are individuals cast in a truly heroic mould whose lives mirror the historical experiences of a generation as a whole. Motilal Nehru was one such outstanding individual. He was born at a time when the British Empire was at the height of its power and glory in India. He grew up in a social, political and intellectual milieu which was very largely the creation of the British Raj. But despite the distinction which he achieved in his chosen vocation of law, he was drawn towards a stance of militant nationalism, which led him to reject British rule over India as something unworthy of a proud and ancient country. What prompted Motilal Nehru to exchange a life of privilege, as a successful lawyer, for a life of sacrifice, as a distinguished participant in the struggle for India's freedom? To what extent was this transformation due to the exploitative character of the British Raj? To what extent, equally, was it a result of Motilal's changing perception of British rule over India? In posing such issues before those who possess a scholarly interest in our struggle for freedom, I seek to answer some crucial questions concerning the life and times of one of the most distinguished figures of the age of nationalism in modern India.

Any enquiry into the origin of the Nehrus can draw upon a very rich body of historical literature. But perhaps our most reliable guide would be Jawaharlal Nehru himself. "We were Kashmiris," he

*I am deeply obliged to my colleague, Dr Hari Dev Sharma, for going through an earlier draft of this essay and suggesting a number of stylistic and substantive changes in the text.

points out in his *Autobiography*. "Over two hundred years ago, early in the eighteenth century, our ancestor came down from that mountain valley to seek fame and fortune in the rich plains below. . . . Raj Kaul was the name of that ancestor of ours, and he had gained eminence as a Sanskrit and Persian scholar in Kashmir. He attracted the notice of Farrukhsiar during the latter's visit to Kashmir, and, probably at the Emperor's instance, the family migrated to Delhi, the imperial capital, about the year 1716. A *jagir* with a house situated on the banks of a canal had been granted to Raj Kaul, and, from the fact of this residence, 'Nehru' (from *Nahar,* a canal) came to be attached to his name. Kaul had been the family name; this changed to Kaul-Nehru; and, in later years, Kaul dropped out and we became simply Nehrus."[1]

The descendants of the scholarly Raj Kaul led relatively uneventful lives in an age which witnessed a political development of outstanding significance, namely, the decline of Mughal imperial authority over north India. Yet the Kaul-Nehrus, too, were not unaffected by the declining fortunes of their imperial patrons, and we have reason to believe that the *jagir* which had sustained the family earlier suffered a diminution in value over the years. The male members of the family, therefore, turned to professional employment to sustain themselves and their dependents. Motitlal Nehru's grandfather, Lakshmi Narayan Nehru, accepted the office of a vakil with the East India Company at Delhi, and his son, Gangadhar Nehru, held the position of kotwal of Delhi, when the Uprising of 1857 erupted with a tragic intensity that was to play havoc with the lives of thousands of men and women in the erstwhile imperial capital.

What the events of 1857, particularly the sack of Delhi by the British in the month of September, meant to the citizens of the former capital of the Mughals, has been graphically described by the distinguished poet, Mirza Asadullah Khan Ghalib, in his memoirs. When the British entered the city, Ghalib states in this account, "they killed the helpless and weak and they burnt the houses. . . . Seeing their anger and fury the townpeople turned pale (with fear and horror). Hordes of men and women, commoners and noblemen, passed out of Delhi from the three gates and took shelter. . . outside the city. There they remained, hoping at a later time, either to return to Delhi, or to move to another town."[2]

Among those who quit the city of Delhi in 1857 was Gangadhar Nehru, then barely thirty years of age. The Nehrus, like hundreds of other respectable families of the erstwhile capital, had lost all their belongings in the course of the sack. Homeless, jobless and bereft of all earthly possessions, Gangadhar trekked with his wife, Indrani, his two sons, Bansidhar and Nandlal, and his two daughters, Patrani and Maharani, to the city of Agra. Here he sought to restore the fortunes of his family. But fate willed otherwise. Gangadhar passed away in February 1861 at the relatively young age of thirty-four. Three months later, on 6 May 1861, his widow gave birth posthumously to a third son, Motilal. The widow Indrani, according to a family tradition, was a woman of great courage and will power. In this hour of adversity, deprived of the loving care of her husband, she probably needed all her resources of courage to ensure that the family under her charge was able to re-establish itself in a style of life appropriate to its status and dignity.

Fortunately for Indrani, her two elder sons, Bansidhar and Nandlal, although in their teens, were able to extend invaluable support to their mother in managing the affairs of the family. Bansidhar, the eldest, sought employment in the judiciary, and rose to a position of considerable eminence in the vocation of his choosing. Nandlal, the younger, first taught in a school for some time, and then went to the Princely State of Khetri in Rajasthan, in the capacity of Dewan. After some time at Khetri, Nandlal returned to Agra, and set himself up as a lawyer in the *Sadr-Diwani-Adalat.* When the *Sadr-Diwani-Adalat* was transferred to Allahabad, where it was soon renamed the High Court of the North-Western Provinces, Nandlal moved to this city. In the absence of a father, it was Nandlal who really brought up Motilal. And between the two, there "grew up a knot of affection, a happy blend of the filial and the fraternal, of which the Hindu joint family, with all its faults, furnishes probably the best example."[3]

I

The city of Allahabad to which Motilal came as a child, under the care of Nandlal, was the newly created capital of the North-Western Provinces (contemporary Uttar Pradesh),[4] and an important centre of political, social and economic life in the region. Motilal was a spirited child, of lively temperament and of incisive intelligence, who also possessed a firm will of his own. All these qualities combined to make a most favourable impression on those who came into contact with him. That the young Motilal grew in Allahabad was a fact of very considerable significance, since this city provided the setting in which he could realise to the full his potential, first in the profession of his choice and next, as a distinguished soldier in the cause of India's freedom. It is to the examination of the distinctive social and political milieu of Allahabad, and indeed, of the North-Western Provinces as a whole, in the last quarter of the nineteenth century, that we shall next turn briefly, before we resume once again our exploration of Motilal's life and achievements.

The great cities and the rural districts of the North-Western Provinces, which provided the setting for Motilal's career, also constituted the stage for a remarkable experiment in colonial politics by the British Government of India. To appreciate the full implications of this experiment in colonial politics, as we have called it, we shall recapitulate briefly the structure of politics and society in the region under consideration prior to the establishment of British rule. Before the British advent, the territories which went into the making of the North-Western Provinces, were controlled by a number of successor States to the Mughal Empire, of which the most prominent State was that of Avadh. The ruling class in this successor State—the land owning aristocracy of Muslim elites as well as of superior Hindu castes like Rajputs and Brahmans (particularly the former)—drew its political legitimacy from the court of Lucknow, and partook of a rich and composite Hindu-Muslim culture, which was reflected in life-styles, in courtly etiquette, in secular and religious architecture, and last but not the least, in literature and in the arts. Further, this ruling class in turn rested upon small principalities of very considerable antiquity, controlled by Rajput chiefs, who were also the heads of powerful clans. The individual members of these clans were distributed over entire rural districts in the capacity of petite zamindars, and partook of a traditional culture which gave to the North-Western Provinces, particularly to the eastern districts, their reputation for being the great heartland of Hindu culture.

When the British first established themselves in the North-Western Provinces, they pursued a policy of stripping the aristocratic classes of their 'proprietal' rights over the land, and bestowed these rights on a petite zamindari class in the villages, in the hope that the latter would become ardent supporters of the *Pax Britannica*. But the Uprising of 1857 shattered British hopes of buying the loyalty of the petite zamindari class in the villages through such a policy. Instead, in the rural districts of Avadh and the neighbourhood, both the dispossessed landed aristocracy, and the recently enfranchised petite zamindars in the villages, who were often linked to the former through bonds of kinship, rose in a mighty movement of armed revolt against the British Raj. We can gain some idea of the depth, and the intensity, of the uprising in these regions from the fact that it took the British Government more than a year after the fall of the centres of urban resistance, like Lucknow and Kanpur, to suppress the resistance of the landed aristocracy and the petite zamindars.

The British drew several important conclusions from their experience of the Uprising of 1857 in Avadh and in the North-Western Provinces. First and foremost, they rejected the policy of dispossessing the landed aristocracy—the Talukdars, to give them their proper name—and reinstated them in their former estates, as the instruments of British rule over the region. The Talukdars were henceforth looked upon as "the natural leaders of the people"; and British administrators regarded them as the great bastions of stability and order in rural society. Indeed, they further regarded the Talukdars as the instruments of economic progress and social prosperity in the region. The Talukdars, as a class, thus became the lynch-pin of British policy in the region, and they acquired a very central position in the imperial scheme of things. "Where else . . . in India [an ecstatic British supporter of the regime asked in 1906] can be found more true happiness and ease under British rule, more solid progress, more unquestioning loyalty? Where such smooth relations between the rulers and the ruled, between the party of order and the party of change? Where a better measure of agrarian peace? Where a more effective combination of old sanctions and young aspiration?"[5]

To accord a central place to the landed aristrocracy in reconstructing the fabric of society in Avadh and in the North-Western Provinces, in the closing decades of the nineteenth century, is not to overlook seminal developments elsewhere in the region. Indeed, the cities of the region, Lucknow, Agra, Kanpur, Varanasi, and most important of all for our purposes, Allahabad, too, were the setting for crucial developments in the period under review. We shall now reflect briefly upon social changes in these urban centres.

Allahabad, as the seat of the provincial government since 1858, and the High Court since 1866, witnessed a remarkable expansion of its social, political and economic horizons in the last quarter of the nineteenth century. For over and above its importance as an administrative and judicial centre, the city was also the base of substantial Khatri and Bania magnates, who were money-lenders, businessmen, and landlords rolled into one, and whose predominant position in the city—a position underpinned by their designation as *raises*, or urban notables—was reflected as much in the world of high finance and business, as it was reflected in their patronage of religious and cultural activities, and in their dominance over local politics and civic affairs. Indeed, it was these *raises* or urban notables, with their roots in the city, rather than the land-owners of the rural districts, who constituted the most influential section of Indian society in Allahabad.

A class of growing significance in Allahabad was the professional class, whose members were attached to the institutions of administration and the judiciary, as well as to the schools and colleges in the city. This class was largely recruited from the service communities—*prabasi* Bengalis, or Muslim elites, or Kayasths, or local or emigre Brahmans—whose members constituted an intelligentsia that had traditionally found employment in the administrative institutions of revenue, police or justice. In a situation where important positions in the bureaucracy were monopolised by British members of Civil Service, the legal profession offered a very good opportunity for advancement to able and ambitious young men of the traditional service communities. Initially, the Allahabad Bar had been dominated by British barristers, who were admitted as advocates of the High Court. But by 1877, a second tier of lawyers, called pleaders or vakils, had organised themselves into a vakils' association, and many young men drawn from the service communities were able to carve out a niche for themselves at this level of the legal profession. The volume of litigation was rising sharply in the period under consideration, owing to the new property relations which the British Government had established after 1857, and there was a great flow of legal briefs from the rural districts to the courts in the city. Here, although competition was fierce, was an avenue for advancement open to young men of ability and enterprise; an avenue, moreover, through which such men could acquire substantial fortunes at the same time as they established themselves in the public life of the city, and indeed, of the province.

II

Motilal commenced his schooling at Khetri, where he resided as a ward of his elder brother, Nandlal. His first teacher was Kazi Sadruddin, an oriental scholar attached to the princely court of Khetri, from whom he acquired a proficiency in Persian that was to stand him in good stead later in life. Thereafter, he moved to Kanpur, to his eldest brother, Bansidhar, and completed his preliminary education at a local high school. On passing the Matriculation Examination, he sought admission to the Muir Central College at Allahabad.

The Muir College of Allahabad, where Motilal sought admission for higher education, was the premier educational instituion in India, in the last quarter of the nineteenth century, outside the presidency cities of Bombay, Calcutta and Madras. The College had been established in 1873, on the initiative of Sir William Muir, the Lieutenant Governor, and some of the leading citizens of Avadh and the North-Western Provinces. The objectives which inspired the establishment of this institution of higher learning were eloquently summed up by Sir Arthur Lyall, a successor of Muir, on a later occasion. "The College commemorates," Sir Arthur observed, "the firm, earnest, and statesman like trust placed by Sir William Muir and other leading personages—the principal chiefs and the most enlightened representatives of different classes in our society—the trust placed by them in the sure and certain progress and spread of higher education in this part of India; their belief in its great public advantage, and in its promise and potency of future development. And if we may pretend to read a meaning in the style and proportion and design of the architecture of this College, we may say that it foreshadows and anticipates the speedy expansion of higher education under the combined impulses of Eastern and Western ideas and traditions and the advancement of learning to a greater dignity and more imposing position among us."[6] The founders of the Muir College also recruited a very distinguished faculty for the institution, prominent amongst whom were scholars like Augustus Harrison, the Principal; W.H. Wright, the Professor of English Literature; Maulvi Zakaullah, the Professor of Vernacular Literature; and Pandit Adityaram Bhattacharya, the Professor of Sanskrit.

Motilal's sojourn at the Muir College, and the opportunity of interaction with scholarly men like Harrison and Wright, exercised a decisive influence over his intellectual development. Already as a child, Motilal had been introduced to the literary and religious heritage of the East, by his teacher at Khetri. His tenure as a student at the Muir College opened up before him, at a very impressionable age, the vast treasure-house of western learning, both speculative and empirical. Motilal was by no stretch of imagination a bookworm. Nor was he given to fanciful flights of imagination. However, his robust intelligence, lively and incisive in equal proportions, imbibed certain English values which were to guide him in his subsequent career, as an outstanding lawyer, as well as a nationalist leader of distinction. He acquired a strong admiration for English culture and institutions; for the principles of liberty and progress which upheld the fabric of society and moulded the minds of men in the late Victorian era; and for the moral rectitude which inspired Englishmen in their private and public life in their own country. Over and above this, Motilal developed a rational attitude towards life, which led him to question, and even to reject some of the outmoded and archaic values and institutions of Hindu society. Yet it needs to be stressed, at this juncture, that despite the admiration which Motilal had acquired for English values, as they were interpreted to him by his mentors at the Muir College, he remained firmly anchored to the rich, composite Hindu-Muslim culture of the North-Western Provinces, which shaped in particular the style of life of the Kashmiri Brahmans who had settled in this region.

Without completing his courses of study at the Muir College, Motilal appeared for the vakil's examination, and topping the list of successful candidates, set himself up as a junior under the watchful eye of Prithinath Chak, a very well-established lawyer at Kanpur, who was also a close friend of the Nehru family. However, a district court like the one at Kanpur offered insufficient incentive to young Motilal, who dreamt from the outset of establishing a first rate reputation for himself in the profession. In 1886, therefore, after serving in the district courts at Kanpur for three years, as an understudy of Prithinath Chak, Motilal moved to Allahabad, and set himself up in the legal profession in the city.

The decision to practice law in Allahabad, the seat of the Government of the North-Western Provinces, and the seat also of the High Court, was profound in its implications for Motilal's future. More than any other vocation (as we have already pointed out), the profession of law offered able young men drawn from Indian society an opportunity to make their mark in life. Of course, this is not to suggest that a fortune and a reputation in the legal profession were easily acquired. Quite the contrary. Precisely because success at the Bar had so much to offer—the stakes were so high—the profession was highly competitive. Already by the 1880s, the primacy of the English barristers at the High Court in Allahabad was being challenged by a number of Indian members of the Bar, drawn from the traditional intelligentsia, or hailing from the landed gentry of the region. Prominent among such men were *prabasi* Bengalis like P.C. and L.M. Banerji; Nagar Brahmans from Gujarat like (later Sir) Sunderlal Dave;[7] Kayasths like Jwala Prasad, Sachchidananda Sinha, and Ram Prasad; and Banias like the scions of the well-known Rai Balmukund family. Also amongst such men was a select group of the Kashmiri Brahmans of whom Tej Bahadur Sapru, Bishambar Nath, and, of course, Motilal Nehru, were the most prominent.

Motilal did not possess the connections that would ensure for him instant success in the legal profession. But in a couple of years, while he was still in his early thirties, he had acquired a practice of Rs. 2,000 a month, a very substantial sum of money in the last quarter of the nineteenth century. He was also one of the four outstanding vakils who were raised to the rank of advocates of the Allahabad High Court in 1896; and slightly more than a decade later, in 1909, he received permission to appear before the Judicial Committee of the Privy Council in Great Britain, the highest judicial body in the British Empire. Motilal was a civil lawyer; and most of the cases which came his way concerned disputes over property, or succession, within the great talukdari families of Avadh. From what we have stated earlier about the pre-eminent position occupied by the Talukdars in society in the region, it follows that a lawyer like Motilal, who drew his professional work mainly from the aristocracy, was destined to rise to the very top of his profession.

What are the attributes which make for success as a lawyer? In law, as indeed, in other professions, it is difficult to provide a wholly satisfactory answer to such a question. Yet the qualities which went into the making of Motilal's success are not entirely unknown to us. First and foremost, Motilal was endowed with a powerful intellect, incisive and penetrating in equal proportions. Secondly, he possessed a great capacity for sheer hard work, burning much midnight oil over legal tomes, and studying in detail the briefs which came his way in increasing numbers with the passage of time. Further, Motilal had a physical presence which captivated all those who came into contact with him in his professional life. His striking good looks, his graciousness of manner and his aristocratic demeanour, taken in conjunction with the intellectual qualities to which we have already drawn attention, made him one of the most outstanding members of the Allahabad Bar. According to one of his younger contemporaries: "Pandit Motilal was handsome. He dressed fastidiously. He was by no means eloquent, but keen in debate and incisive in argument . . . when Pandit Motilal was in court and on his legs, the atmosphere seemed surcharged with sunshine".[8] Dr. Rajendra Prasad, who first met him as a colleague in a legal suit, found in him "a lawyer of a very high order . . . . "[9] A colleague in Allahabad, Sachchidananda Sinha, rated him as "one of the greatest . . . (advocates) that India has ever produced . . . . "[10] And a Chief Justice of the Allahabad High Court, an Englishman with little sympathy for Motilal's politics, observed: "He (Motilal) had a profusion of gifts; knowledge came easily to him and as an advocate he had the art of presenting his case in its most attractive form. Every fact fell into proper place. . . . Many of you will remember his handling of the Etawah case . . . . No man at any bar in the world could have done better than Pandit Motilal."[11]

III

At the same time as he established himself as a lawyer of distinction, Motilal was also engaged in laying the foundations of a rich and rewarding family life. In an age when the innocence of childhood gave way to the responsibilities of adult life, without experiencing the carefree phase of youthful freedom. Motilal married in his late teens. His young bride, Swarup Rani, came of a Kashmiri family of Lahore, and she was, in the words of a biographer of the Nehrus, "petite, with a 'dresden china perfection' of complexion and features. . . ."[12] Motilal and his bride were blessed, in the first instance, with a son, who unfortunately did not survive for long. On the 14th of November, 1889, a second child, also a son, was born to the young couple. He was given the name of Jawaharlal.

The birth of a son in a Hindu household has a very special ritual as well as temporal significance. Since Jawaharlal was also the eldest child in the family, he became the focus of his parents' affection, and the repository of their hopes and aspirations for the future of the Nehru family. Between the father and the son, in particular, there came into being a bond of affection which held them together in an especially close relationship. This bond of affection between Motilal and Jawaharlal was characterised by a blend of admiration, esteem and regard on the part of Jawaharlal; and a deeply tempered love, parental and solicitous, on the part of Motilal. Yet in the texture of his personality, no less than in the cast of his features, the young Jawaharlal drew as much upon his mother as he drew upon his father. Particularly did Jawaharlal inherit his sensitive eyes, the eyes of a Hamlet, introspective and soulful, searching and questioning, from the gentle Swarup Rani, who in a quiet and unobstrusive manner, filled the Nehru household with the warm presence of a devoted wife and a loving mother.

Motilal's affection for his family, and his increasing success at the Bar, were vividly reflected in the style of life which he pursued as a distinguished member of the legal profession at Allahabad. As soon as he had established himself in his vocation, Motilal shifted from his residence at Mirganj, in the heart of Allahabad, to a spacious bungalow located at Elgin Road, in the Civil Lines. From Elgin Road, in turn, he moved in 1900 to a palatial residence at Church Road, near Bhardwaj Ashram, not very far from the confluence of the Ganga and the Yamuna. Anand Bhavan, or the "Abode of Pleasure," as this residence was christened, spoke in unmistakable terms of the success of its master, and the prominent position which he occupied in the city of Allahabad. We have referred earlier to the composite Hindu-Muslim culture which

Motilal had inherited as a Kashmiri Brahman. This heritage was enriched, by the progressive adoption in the Nehru household, at the personal initiative of Motilal, of the style of life of the upper classes in England.

It was a most gracious way of life, elegant and cultivated, and it involved much party-going and entertainment. A contemporary picture of Motilal, at the steering wheel of his car, with some members of his family by his side, a smartly turned out domestic servant standing beside the car, has so distinctly Edwardian a flavour, that it might well have been taken in a countrytown in England in the first decade of the twentieth century. Yet in Motilal, the adoption of a western style of life coexisted with a great love for things Indian, particularly for the poetry and the literature of the country. Moreover, Swarup Rani provided the Nehru household an anchorage with the traditions of Hinduism, that secured for young and old alike, a deep and enduring relationship with a culture of great antiquity and sophistication. This anchorage, needless to say, conferred a rare poise and dignity upon the various members of Motilal's family.

The diverse cultural influences which Motilal drew into his domestic world, as a matter of deliberate choice, are reflected most clearly of all in the education of Jawaharlal, who was the focus of his hopes and his aspirations for the future. In his *Autobiography* Jawaharlal speaks of the "stories from the old Hindu mythology, from the epics . . . that my mother and aunt used to tell us. My aunt . . . was learned in the old Indian books and had an inexhaustible supply of these tales, and my knowledge of Indian mythology and folklore became quite considerable."[13] At a more formal level, Motilal requested the great oriental scholar, Pandit Ganganath Jha, to teach his son Sanskrit. Besides, two English governesses were engaged in succession to instruct Jawaharlal in English and in the rudiments of arithmetic; and they were followed by the appointment, in the capacity of a tutor, of an Irish-French theosophist, F.T. Brooks, who apart from inculcating in the mind of his ward an interest in theosophy, introduced him to English poetry and literature, and also to the sciences. Finally, in 1905, Motilal secured admission for Jawaharlal at Harrow, in the belief that the liberal education given at such a prestigious public school would adequately equip him for a career of distinction in his life.

It is likely that the decision to provide Jawaharlal with an

English education was taken by Motilal during the course of his first visit to Great Britain in 1899. The ostensible reason which took Motilal to Great Britain was a dispute between the Raja of Khetri, whom his late brother Nandlal had served as Dewan, and the ruler of Jaipur. He arrived in London armed with introductions from the Raja of Khetri, and apart from attending to the business which had brought him to this great metropolis, he was also able to "(make) some friends among the nobility and society of England. . . . "[14] Among those Motilal saw in London was Sir Muncherjee Bhownaggree, an Indian M.P.; Sir W. Lee-Warner, a Member of the India Council and Sir G. Seymor-Fitzgerald. With the Boer War in progress, affairs in India interested few apart from old India hands like Lee-Warner. But the orderliness of life in the premier city of the British Empire; a first-hand experience of British society and its institutions; and a personal exchange of views, on men and affairs, with some distinguished individuals in Great Britain, heightened the admiration which Motilal already possessed for things English. All this must also have impressed upon him the desirability of providing his son with an education in a public school, and later in a British university, that would enable him to make his mark in life.

On his return from Great Britain, Motilal confronted a situation which throws a flood of illuminating light upon contemporary society in India. This situation also illumines Motilal's position in the Kashmiri community, and the strength of his liberal commitments. For a citizen of India in the late nineteenth century, a journey to Great Britain was a momentous undertaking. Only men well-placed in society, men of considerable means, could undertake this journey. Such a journey could also be expected to be an enlightening experience, even for an individual not as well equipped as Motilal to appreciate the novel intellectual and political culture to which he was likely to be exposed. Above all, a journey to Great Britain was also a declaration of faith in a liberal way of life, if only for the reason that travel beyond the frontiers of the country was regarded as polluting, and brought down upon the head of an individual who embarked upon such a venture, the serious disapproval of the conservative elements in society.

To the widespread belief in Hindu society that travel overseas was polluting, the Kashmiri community of Allahabad was no exception. Even before Motilal's journey to the West, the visit to Great

Britain of a Kashmiri lawyer, Bishen Narayan Dar, had split the community into two warring factions. Motilal had as a matter of course thrown his support in favour of the liberal camp. On his return from Great Britain, Motilal, too, faced ostracism at the hands of the orthodox section of the Kashmiri community. But he stood firm as a rock, refusing to perform the purificatory ceremonies through which more pliable men, who had violated orthodox sentiment by travelling overseas, bought peace. "My mind is fully made up," Motilal wrote in righteous indignation to Prithinath Chak. "I will not (come what may) indulge in the tomfoolery of *Praschit.* No, not even if I die for it. I have been provoked and have been dragged from my seclusion into public life. But my enemies will find me a hard nut to crack. I know what your *biradari* (caste) is and if necessary, in self-defence, I will ruthlessly and mercilessly lay bare the tattered fabric of its existence and tear it into the minutest possible shreds."[15]

Motilal's first visit to Great Britain in 1899, and his second visit in 1900, were in the nature of exploratory tours. He was now at the very height of his professional career, as highly respected for his legal acumen as he was respected for his wide culture and his warm hospitality. A leading citizen of Allahabad, he could count as his friends all those who mattered in the capital city of the United Provinces. Indeed, even the British *herrenvolk* of the civil service acknowledged his outstanding stature: and men of the distinction of Sir Harcourt Butler, later the Lieutenant Governor of the United Provinces, and Sir John Edge, the Chief Justice of the High Court at Allahabad, maintained cordial social relations with him. By the first decade of the twentieth century, Motilal, in his early forties, had travelled very far, indeed, from a young lawyer who arrived in Allahabad less than two decades ago, full of promise and ambition, yet with little by way of inherited wealth, or the connections, that usually went into the making of a successful legal career.

In 1905 Motilal travelled for the third time to Great Britain. This time he was accompanied, as became a successful man of the world, by his wife and his son, as well as by his four year old daughter, Swarup. The journey was partly a vacation, a much needed break from the stresses and strains of a busy professional life in Allahabad. But it was also undertaken to secure admission for Jawaharlal in a suitable school in Great Britain. A diary

Motilal maintained during his travels reveals how welcome was the vacation after the uninterrupted labour of four years. After making arrangements for Jawaharlal to stay in London, and prepare for the entrance examinations at Harrow, he travelled to the health resorts of Europe, in order to make the most of the brief moments of leisure available to him. In September 1905, Motilal returned to London, and completed the formalities for the admission of his son to Harrow. Yet the moment for parting from Jawaharlal, now sixteen years old, was a sorrowful one. It was with a heavy heart that Motilal wrote a poignant letter to his only son, whom he was leaving behind in an alien land: "You must bear in mind that in you we are leaving the dearest treasure we have in this world, and perhaps in other worlds. We are suffering the pangs of separation for you simply for your own good . . . it is simply a question of making a real man of you. . . . "[16]

IV

Motilal's ascent to a position of preeminence in the Allahabad Bar was achieved in the context of the quickening pulse of politics in the country. Although the quick flow of briefs, and the hectic pace of his professional life, left Motilal little time or leisure for politics, these developments could not but affect his appreciation of British rule over India. Indeed, the rising tempo of political activity in India, in itself a consequence of the sharpening political consciousness of different classes and communities, was to draw Motilal into the very vortex of public life, transforming in the process the distinguished lawyer into a valiant soldier in the cause of India's freedom.

The biographers of Motilal have probably erred in assuming that his involvement in public life can be attributed entriely to developments in politics at the national level. The facts in this regard are a matter of common knowledge. We know, for instance, that when the Indian National Congress met at Allahabad in 1888, among the delegates present at the session was 'Pandit Motilal Nehru, Hindu, Brahman, Vakil, High Court, N.W.P.' Next year, in 1889, Motilal was elected to the Subjects Committee of the Congress. He featured again on the Subjects Committee at Nagpur in 1891. And when the Indian National Congress met at Allahabad for the second time, in 1892, Motilal, by now a prominent member of the local Bar, was the Secretary of the Reception Committee. Yet in the next decade, Motilal did not figure in the list of delegates at the annual sessions of the Indian National Congress. Why? "These were the years when he was forging his way to the top of the Bar, and hardly had the time or the inclination to stray into the bye-ways of politics. Nor was the political atmosphere electric enough to evoke a response in him," states one of his biographers. Yet to explain Motilal's entry into national politics, simply in terms of attendance of the annual sessions of the Congress, is to completely overlook the local political milieu of Allahabad, which played so important a part in shaping his awareness, on the one hand, of the growing aspirations of the people of India, and on the other, of the strategic and tactical objectives of British imperialism. This milieu has been portrayed with rare sensitivity in a recent scholarly study.[17] The crystallisation of communal identities in the region; the establishment of the institutions of local self-government; the creation of centres of higher education, through official or through denominational initiatives; the activities of local agitators, patronised by men of wealth and standing in the community, who sought to create in the minds of the people a new consciousness of their cultural and religious heritage; all these developments contributed to radically altering the political climate of the city of Allahabad, and, indeed, of the region as a whole, during the closing decades of the nineteenth century.

This is not to suggest that the activation of local and regional politics in Allahabad, led the men who mattered in the city—the *raises* or urban notables; the substantial men of business and finance; and the leaders of the professional classes—into a collision course with the British rulers. True, the efforts of local agitators, plus the climate of competitive politics conjured into existence through the establishment of civic institutions, resting partly upon electoral principles, created an altogether new milieu in the capital of the North-Western Provinces. But the policies adopted by the Provincial Government, particularly during the tenure of Sir Antony Macdonnell as Lieutenant Governor, were astutely designed to establish a working alliance between the prominent men of the city and the region, on the one hand, and the British *imperium*, on the other.

The conciliatory face of the British Raj in the politics of the North-Western Provinces, and of the city of Allahabad, during the last quarter of the nineteenth century, went a long way towards reinforcing the favourable view which Motilal entertained of British political institutions and British social values as a young man. As we have already indicated, he was deeply influenced by his English teachers during his tenure as a student at the Muir College. The legal profession which he had adopted with such conspicuous success, was a profession which was conjured into existence by the British *imperium* in India; and it created in its practitioners a deep appreciation of those institutions of law and politics which underpinned British rule over India. The adoption by Motilal of a western style of life, despite his deep attachment to the indigenous culture of which he was so distinguished a product, reflected his growing identification with British values. This identification was reinforced by the visits which Motilal paid to Great Britain, at a time when she was at the zenith of her imperial glory.

We have little reason to believe that there was any tension, till the close of the nineteenth century, between the relatively quiet political milieu of Allahabad and the North-Western Provinces, on the one hand, and the mainstream of nationalist politics, as reflected in the activity of the Indian National Congress, on the other. The Congress, in the first two decades after its inception, was largely (though not exclusively) an organisation reflecting the aspirations of the educated and the professional classes in India. As such, it did not question the bonds which linked India in a relationship of subordination to the British Crown. Instead, in the period under review, the activities of the Indian National Congress were directed towards securing for the classes on which it rested a larger share of political and economic power; furthermore, the Congress was also wedded to the methods of constitutional agitation for securing its objectives.

The constitutional dialogue between the British Government of India, on the one hand, and the leadership of the Indian National Congress, on the other, was seriously disturbed by new developments in nationalist politics in the first decade of the twentieth century. The historical literature on nationalism in India refers to this development as the emergence of "extremist politics" in the country. Recent researches, however, have revealed that this strand of politics reflected the entry of new social classes—particularly in Bengal, Maharashtra and the Punjab—into nationalist politics; classes whose political culture was different from the political culture of the professional classes; and who were willing to adopt more militant methods of agitation in their struggle against British imperialism.

The politics of extremism, whatever be its precipitating cause, was hardly visible in the city of Allahabad. A few members of the local Arya Samaj; a small number of individuals drawn from the lower middle class; a few *prabasi* Bengalis; and a section of the student community; these elements constituted the support base of extremist politics in Allahabad. However, the visits paid to the city in 1907, first by B.G. Tilak, and then by G.K. Gokhale, dragged Allahabad into that tension within nationalist politics—the tension between the moderates and the extremists—which had already created a crisis in the ranks of the Indian National Congress. Yet the men who mattered in Allahabad and in the North-Western Provinces, prominent among them Motilal, refused to bow before the extremist storm. Indeed, these local notables, who spoke for the politically articulate classes in the region, had already decided to hold a provincial conference in Allahabad, in order to demonstrate their solidarity with the moderate leadership within the Indian National Congress. That Motilal was chosen to preside over this conference speaks eloquently of his pre-eminent position in the province, as well as of his ideological stance in nationalist politics.

Motilal's presidential address before the provincial conference held in Allahabad on 29 March 1907, was a remarkable *tour de force,* which needs to be highlighted for two reasons. First, because it presents a sensitive analysis of the seminal issues in contemporary politics in India; and secondly, because it vividly outlines Motilal's perception of the relationship between imperialism and nationalism in the country. Motilal commenced his address with a declaration of faith in the good intentions of the British towards India. "John Bull," he observed, "means well—it is not in his nature to mean ill. . . . It takes him rather long to fully comprehend the situation. But when he does see things plainly, he does his plain duty, and there is no power on earth ... that can successfully resist his mighty will."[18] In view of the unexceptionable motives which inspired British rule over India, what (Motilal asked the question) was the appropriate line of action to be adopted by men of goodwill in India, men who looked forward to the day when India took her rightful place in the community of free nations? The ranks of the Congress, the great party of organised nationalism in India, were divided into two conflicting groups on this issue. There were the moderates, who sought to rely upon time-honoured methods of constitutional agitation to secure increasing control over the levers of political power for those who represented the people of India. And there were the extremists, who represented a new spirit in the country, which was especially attractive to the young and the impetuous; a spirit, moreover, under whose influence men sought to destroy, through militant action, the fabric of British rule over India.

Motilal hesitated not at all in rejecting the stance of the extremists, even though he identified himself wholly with their objective of securing political freedom for India. The two tactical weapons which the extremists were advocating as singularly appropriate to the Indian struggle for freedom, he observed, were those of swadeshi and boycott. The first of these weapons, the weapon of *swadeshi*, was wholly commendable; indeed, it was a weapon which every patriotic Indian ought to adopt to the extent the social and economic development of India enabled him to do so. But boycott, even when confined to the economic sphere, was an instrument that could possibly prove to be counter-productive. When boycott was also applied to the arenas of politics and education, as the more vocal extremists were inclined to do, it could lead the country to total disaster. "I for one tremble to think," Motilal observed, "of the condition of things which would prevail if all our Government schools and colleges were to be closed, all Municipal and District Boards abolished, and the elected element of the legislative council done away with. Where shall be we then. The answer is plain enough; nowhere. We cannot even occupy the position reached at the beginning of British rule, when the institutions I have just mentioned did not exist. . . . We must bind ourselves (in order to struggle against the British Government) to methods which are at all times perfectly constitutional and legitimate."[19]

V

The assumption that British rule over India rested upon liberal principles, that the statesmen who controlled the destiny of the British Empire would respond positively to the growth of national consciousness in the country, went a long way towards shaping the attitudes of men like Motilal, who had adopted a moderate position within the Indian National Congress in the period under review. In the course of his address before the provincial conference, Motilal actually drew upon Macaulay's rhetorical statement, voiced in the House of Commons in 1832, that the day when India acquired the ability to govern herself through representative institutions would be "the proudest day in English history", in justification of his favourable assessment of British motives. More tangibly, Motilal and the moderates were aware of the constitutional reforms which were being hammered out in Great Britain contemporaneously, under the guidance of a liberal Secretary of State, John Morley, who was believed to be sympathetic to Indian aspirations. Here, the moderates believed, lay concrete evidence of the good intentions of Great Britain towards India; here, they further argued, also lay an unrivalled opportunity to build a bridge of understanding between political opinion in India and Great Britain, that would ensure the slow but sure elevation of India to the status of a self-governing community.

Yet the moderate strategy, to which Motilal subscribed without any reservations at this juncture, rested upon far too flattering an appreciation of the strength of liberal sentiment, or the intentions of liberal statesmen, within the British Government. It refused to take note of the special interests in Great Britain and India—the diehard imperialists in both the major British parties; the rentier classes with substantial investments in India; the textile magnates of Lancashire; the expatriate commercial groups in Calcutta, Bombay and Madras, with their metropolitan links; and most important of all, the solid ranks of the civil service— that were opposed to any devolution of power into the hands of Indian leaders.

The retrogressive influence which the special interests in Great Britain and India were able to exercise over the constitutional reforms of 1909 needs to be spelt out at this juncture. Constitutions, it is well known, are powerful instruments of political engineering, and they reflect the ideological commitments no less than the political objectives of their framers. The promise which liberal British statesmen, whose rhetoric often outstripped their power, had held out to India was the promise of constitutional reforms, which emphasised the importance of territorial constituencies, and the *de jure* equality of the individual members of a political society. The only reservation voiced by such statesmen, a reservation which the moderates in India endorsed, lay in the restriction of the franchise to those who had acquired a measure of education, and could, therefore, be expected to exercise their prerogatives in full knowledge of how democracy functioned. But over and above the liberal tradition, British statesmen could also draw upon a Whig tradition of politics, which looked upon political society as consisting, not so much of a loose aggregate of individuals, as of a number of interacting and interlocked corporate social interests. According to Whig principles, the legitimate bases for a constitution were these corporate social interests rather than the individual constituents of the social order. Territorial constituencies, and the *de jure* equality of individuals, held no place in a Whig polity. Instead, a constitution resting upon Whig principles sought to induct a number of corporate interests in the political system; and the weightage accorded to a particular interest in the constitution depended upon its wealth and power rather than upon its strength in numbers.

The moderates in India, whose sentiments Motilal voiced in 1907, looked forward to a package of reforms inspired by liberal principles. What they got instead was a Whig constitution which suffered from two fatal flaws. First, it completely failed to recognise the strength of nationalist sentiment in India. Secondly, it drew upon the most conservative classes in Indian society, which could be relied upon to counterbalance the nationalism of the professional classes, in a bid to reinforce the British Raj over India. The conservative spirit of the constitution of 1909 has been widely recognised so far as the creation of communal electorates is concerned. But the imperialist net was cast much wider than is commonly believed. Apart from the communal interest, which understandably looked to the British for support, other conservative elements in Indian society—the landed interest, or the commercial interest, or denominational and sectional interests—too were drawn into the political system, as a counterpoise to the professional classes, and other social groups, which were becoming restive of British control. Further, even the communal interest was very narrowly conceived in terms of the rich, property owning classes, mainly rural in character, which could be relied upon to support the *status quo* in society. The reforms of 1909, in short, constituted a repudiation of the liberal promises which had been held out to the political classes in India earlier. Furthermore, it was the first step towards the creation of a political system in the country, which would enable the British Government to exercise overall control over India, even when the husk of political authority had been transferred into the hands of Indian leaders.

Whatever hopes Motilal and the moderate leaders may have entertained of liberal British statesmen like Morley, they had very little illusions about the constitution of 1909. "Morley's long promised reforms have at last been published," Motilal stated in August 1909. "They are . . . just the opposite of reforms . . . . The avowed object of the so-called reforms is to destroy the influence of the educated classes, but the law of the survival of the fittest is too strong even for Morley."[20] Yet despite such a realisation, Motilal and the moderates of his persuasion were willing to extend a hand of cooperation to the British Government in India, if only to demonstrate their willingness to meet the Imperial Government more than half way, in ensuring the orderly progress of politics in the country.

Motilal was elected to the Provincial Legislative Council in 1910, and he now spent an increasing proportion of his time in public activity, both inside as well as outside the legislature. His place in the political firmament was still with moderates like Pherozeshah Mehta, G.K. Gokhale, or S.N. Banerjea. But the quickening pulse of politics in the country, partly owing to the unrest generated by the partition of Bengal, and partly also owing to the ferment which affected the Muslim community, was bringing about a qualitative change in his political stance. Indeed, not only was his involvement in politics growing apace, but also his perception of the character of British rule over India was undergoing a fundamental change.

Perhaps the frustrating experience of confrontation with British civilians in the provincial legislature was crucial here. This experience made it unequivocally clear to Motilal, if he had any doubts earlier, that no genuine devolution of power was possible so long as the British Civil Service in India could have things its own way. His very first involvement in a debate over the budget, as a member of the Provincial Legislature, indicated the shape of things to come. Motilal voiced a very mild criticism of the manner in which the executive had deemed it fit to raise revenues from the impoverished people of the United Provinces. But even such a mild criticism earned for Motilal the hostility of the treasury benches; and the limited powers transferred to the elected representatives, in a constitution conjured into existence by one of Great Britain's most liberal statesmen, prevented him from exercising any constraint upon the executive. "We had no right to reply," Motilal observed, "and the important debate was wound up by the Governor who patted (on the back) the *Khushamdis* (Sycophants) and the officials."[21] This experience was repeated on a number of occasions over the next few years. Motilal, with his deep knowledge of law and the principles of administration, and with his equally deep commitment to liberal values, was one of the most forceful members of the provincial legislature. On a variety of important issues, like the representative character of the legislatures; or primary education; or the position of women in society; he argued persuasively for the adoption of more liberal policies on the part of the executive. But all to no effect. Indeed, as we shall later see, the frustrating experience of legislative politics at this juncture left a permanent impression upon Motilal; and when he participated in such activity at the level of the Central Legislature in the 1920s, it was with the avowed purpose of destroying, from within such institutions, the whole edifice of British rule over India.

VI

The outbreak of the First World War in September 1914, gave Motilal an opportunity to reaffirm his loyalty to the British Government. Yet in doing so, he drew attention to the differences between the educated classes, on the one hand, and the British Government of India, on the other, on the question of devolution of power. The fact of the matter was that there was a new spirit abroad in the country; and Motilal was as much affected by this spirit, as were a whole generation of his countrymen, who were very soon to rise in revolt against the political relationship which tied them in bonds of subordination to Great Britain.

The new spirit, to which we have referred above, manifested itself in two distinct spheres of political activity in India. Even before the outbreak of war, the Muslim community in India had been greatly agitated by the hostility of Great Britain towards the

Turkish Empire. As a result of this, a powerful section of the Muslims in India sought to reject their erstwhile stance of loyalty in politics, and to make common cause with the leadership of the Indian National Congress against the British Government. The quest for Hindu-Muslim unity led to the Lucknow Pact of 1916, and this agreement enabled the leadership of the two communities to resolve their political differences, and to agree upon a package of constitutional demands to be jointly placed before the British Government of India. No less significant than the Hindu-Muslim understanding of 1916, was the movement for Home Rule, which erupted upon the national stage with dramatic intensity in the second decade of the twentieth century. The moving spirit behind this development was Annie Besant, the theosophist turned nationalist, whose charismatic personality and oratorical skills enabled her to utilise the organisational network of the Theosophical Society to draw the intelligentsia, particularly men of the younger generation, into a militant posture of defiance towards the British Government of India. Besant raised the cry of Home Rule for the first time in 1916; and in a remarkably short span of time, this slogan was taken up by an entire generation of militant young men, to whom the politics of moderation, as practised by a senior generation of nationalists, spoke of a spirit of mendicancy unworthy of the people of India.

Motilal was deeply involved in both these issues, which transformed the quality of nationalist politics in India during the course of the First World War. He was a very keen advocate of Hindu-Muslim unity, and he fully realised how the British Government exploited the differences between the two communities in order to frustrate nationalist demands. Even though Motilal was not directly involved in the negotiations which led to the Lucknow Pact of 1916, we have reason to believe that the wider agreement between the two communities, "of which the Lucknow Pact was a part, . . . [was] hammered out at a meeting in his house in Allahabad."[22] Besant's movement for Home Rule failed to elicit his support in the first instance. But when the Governor of Madras, Lord Pentland, interned Besant in a bid to stifle the movement, the educated classes of India rose in revolt against his high-handed action, and demanded of the British Government her immediate release. Motilal was one among a number of prominent men who joined the Home Rule League at this juncture, and his stature in public life ensured for him the presidency of the Allahabad Branch of the Home Rule League. "The country is in the midst of a crisis," Motilal pointed out to the supporters of Home Rule in Allahabad. "The Government has . . . declared a crusade against our national aims. . . . Let us raise aloft the banner of Home Rule League and 330 million throats voice forth the motto of Home Rule."[23]

Motilal's espousal of Home Rule was a clear indication of the fact that, slowly but surely, he was moving away from the moderate position which he had taken for a decade and more in nationalist politics. In doing so, Motilal was partly responding to a groundswell which he discerned around himself, and partly also giving a creative expression to this groundswell. The British Government, too, was not unaware of the changing temper of the people of the country. Already in August 1917, a statement had been made in Parliament, to the effect that the British Government was committed to "the increasing association of Indians in every branch of the administration" and "a progressive realisation of responsible government in India." To gain an understanding of the climate of politics in the country, Edwin Montagu, the Secretary of State, paid a personal visit to India towards the end of 1917, in the course of which he held consultations with some of the important leaders, including Motilal Nehru. Montagu, who was a liberal of the same hue as Morley, rejected the joint demand of the Indian National Congress and the Muslim League, that the substance of autonomy be conferred on India forthwith, through the creation of popularly elected legislatures in the provinces, and at the centre, with control over the respective executive wings of government. Instead, in the proposals which he put forth, Montagu advanced the novel idea of "dyarchy" in the provinces, whereby the provincial executives would be partly controlled by the Governor, and partly answerable to legislatures elected on a restricted franchise.

Montagu's timid proposals for constitutional reforms further widened the gulf between Motilal and his erstwhile associates of the moderate party. When the proposals came up for consideration before the Provincial Legislative Council in August 1918, Motilal refused to accept them as they stood. He argued that the time was ripe for all executive functions, with the possible exception of law and order, to be placed in the hands of elected ministers responsible to the legislatures. Anything short of such a measure would mean that the British Government was afraid of entrusting responsibility to the people of India. "We cannot learn to walk unless you give us the opportunity to exercise the function," Motilal observed. "If we keep lying down all the time then good-bye to all benefits of the exercise."[24] Motilal reiterated this position at the special session of the Indian National Congress, held in Bombay shortly afterwards, to consider the proposals for reform of the Secretary of State. None of the more prominent moderate leaders—men like T.B. Sapru or D.E. Wacha or S.N. Banerjea—were present on the occasion, to hear him speak on the need for the British Government to adopt a more imaginative approach to the Indian question than had hitherto been the case. The breach between Motilal and the moderates was now complete. Henceforth he was to associate himself, more and more, as an outstanding figure in his own right, with the new consciousness in politics that was flowing across the country.

The leading spokesman of this new consciousness in politics was Mohandas Karamchand Gandhi, who was very soon to be elevated to the status of a Mahatma by his fellow-countrymen. The event which projected Gandhi to the national scene, as a truly epic figure, was the decision taken by the British Government in 1919, to enact laws that sought to deny to the people of India those basic liberties of person and speech which constitute the bedrock of civilised government. The Rowlatt Bills which the British Government introduced in the Central Legislature in 1919, antagonised all sections of society in the country, rich and poor, Hindu and Muslim, the professional classes and the *petite bourgeoisie.* When the British Government showed itself to be wholly insensitive to popular sentiment, Gandhi decided to initiate a countrywide movement of protest, along non-violent lines, against the repressive laws upon which the alien rulers of India had set their heart. To provide organisational coherence to such a movement, Gandhi organised satyagraha sabhas throughout the length and breadth of the land. One of the centres chosen for such a sabha was Allahabad, the hub of cultural and political life in the province.

The creation of a satyagraha sabha in Allahabad, as a point of focus for the organisation of an agitation against the Rowlatt Bills, confronted Motilal with a serious dilemma. His son, Jawaharlal, to whom he was deeply attached, and who had since his return to India in 1912 been drawn increasingly into nationalist politics, decided to join the satyagraha sabha of Allahabad. The idea of defying the laws of an alien government, which had lost its moral legitimacy, through non-violent yet militant means, appealed enormously to the youthful imagination of Jawaharlal. "When I first read about . . . (Gandhiji's) proposal in the newspapers, my reaction was one of the tremendous relief," states Jawaharlal in his *Autobiography*. "Here at last was a way out of the tangle, a method of action which was straight and open and possibly effective."[25] Yet Motilal did not share, at this juncture, his son's enthusiasm for the militant non-violence of Gandhi. Nor did he entertain any exaggerated hopes of what could be achieved through an agitation resting upon the technique of satyagraha. True, Motilal had already cut himself adrift from the moderates, his erstwhile friends, and he had espoused the cause of radical nationalism at the Bombay session of the Indian National Congress. But he was still not prepared to adopt extra-constitutional methods of agitation, which involved a frontal collision with the British Government of India. Perhaps a lifetime spent in the profession of law had created in Motilal's consciousness a deep respect for legal values and legal institutions, as well as for the orderly procedures of governance, and this regard for legality and propriety was not to be shaken loose all of a sudden by the subtle logic of the Mahatma. Besides, it is important to remember that Gandhi, despite his achievements in South Africa, and despite also the extraordinary position which he had earned for himself in India in a remarkably brief span of time, since his return from South Africa in 1915, was still something of an unknown quantity in Indian politics in 1919. Furthermore, it still remained to be seen how potent a weapon was the weapon of satyagraha, and to what extent would non-violence contribute to the success of the struggle for freedom in India.

Whatever reservations Motilal may have entertained about the Rowlatt Satyagraha of 1919, the brutality with which the authorities in the Punjab suppressed the popular agitation against the Rowlatt Act drew from him strong condemnation of the British Government. The atrocities committed by British officials—the massacre at Jallianwala Bagh in particular—sent shock-waves of horror throughout the country, and all sections of society revolted against the humiliation, and worse, inflicted upon the people of the Punjab. Motilal had very close ties with the Punjab, and some of his friends, prominent among them, Lala Harkishen Lal, the distinguished financier and entrepreneur, became the victims of official fury at the bold expression of their nationalist fervour by the Punjabis. Even before Gandhi, and the leadership of the Indian National Congress could make any move to extend support to the people of the Punjab, Motilal appealed to Montagu, the Secretary of State for India, and Lord Sinha, a Member of the Indian Council, for permission to render legal assistance to the hapless victims of British vindictiveness in the province.

The happenings of April 1919, in Amritsar and elsewhere drew Motilal into the very eye of the storm, as a member of the committee of enquiry created by the Indian National Congress to look into the reign of terror unleashed by the Government of the Punjab. The membership of this committee proved to be a very fateful experience for Motilal. It brought him into close contact with the Mahatma, and it gave him a revealing glimpse of the remarkable combination of the visionary and the realist which went into the making of his personality. Furthermore, membership of the committee of enquiry also obliged Motilal to take a fresh look at the character of British rule over the country. It was clear to Motilal, as he travelled about the Punjab in 1919, talking to leading men as well as to ordinary citizens, that behind the liberal facade of the Raj, lay a frightfulness, a capacity for blind repression, for brutal action, which could surface at the slightest assertion of their will by the people of the country. There is little reason to believe that Motilal, even before 1919, harboured any great illusions about the nature of the British Raj. He had outgrown his moderate views well before the events of 1919. But the traumatic experience of travelling around the Punjab, in the wake of the Rowlatt Satyagraha, opened his eyes still further to the brutality of British rule over India.

How deeply Motilal was affected by what he saw in the Punjab, in 1919, is vividly reflected in his presidential address before the annual session of the Indian National Congress, which was held in Amritsar towards the close of the year. At the very commencement of his address, Motilal referred to the tradition of authoritarianism which had characterised British rule over the Punjab since its very inception. The Punjabis had discovered in the person of Sir Michael O'Dwyer, the Lieutenant Governor of the province in the period under consideration, someone whose insensitivity to nationalist opinion marked him out in a region where British civilians could hardly be accused of suffering from an excess of liberalism. When the pent-up feelings of the people of the Punjab found expression in the satyagraha launched by Gandhi in April 1919, the Government of the province reacted with primitive fury, and initiated a policy of repression, the like of which had not been seen in India since 1857. The tragic events associated with the Rowlatt agitation in the Punjab, Motilal observed, held lessons for the people of India as well as for the British rulers of the land. "To us (Indians) they point to the path of steadfast endeavour, the path of sacrifice and patient ordeal. That is the only way to reach our goal. To Englishmen, they teach the oft-repeated truth that tyranny degrades those who exercise it as much as those who suffer under it .... It is for England to learn the lesson and put an end to conditions which promote occurrences (like the Punjab atrocities) in her own dominion. If our lives and honour are to remain at the mercy of an irresponsible executive and military, if the ordinary rights of human beings are denied to us, then all talk of reform is mockery. Constitutional reform without free citizenship is like rich attire on a dead body. Better to breathe God's free air in rags than be a corpse in the finest raiment."[26]

Motilal's reappraisal of the nature of British rule over India, as he saw it reflected in the frightful happenings at Amritsar and elsewhere in the Punjab, coincided with some seminal developments in politics in India. We have already drawn attention to the grave disquiet which affected the Muslim community in India, over the hostile attitude of the British Government towards Turkey. Since Turkey was one of the vanquished powers in 1918, the Muslims of India became extremely anxious about the fate of the *Khilafat*, and the security of the holy places of Islam, which had hitherto been looked after by the Turkish Government. The Muslim leaders, prominent among them the brothers, Mohamed Ali and Shaukat Ali, Maulana Abul Kalam Azad and Maulana Abul Bari, turned to the Mahatma to lead their community in a movement of non-violent protest against the British Government. Motilal, whose cultural roots tied him in close bonds of sympathy to the Muslim community, shared their apprehensions about British good faith towards the Turkish Empire and the institution of *Khilafat*. These apprehensions were heightened by the callousness of the British Government towards the sufferings of those Punjabis who had participated in the Rowlatt Satyagraha. When the official committee of enquiry, or at any rate its British members, placed their findings before the authorities, they put responsibility for the unfortunate happenings in the Punjab squarely on the shoulders of the Mahatma and his followers. These extraordinary conclusions were accepted without any reservations by the Government of India. So furious was Motilal at the indifference of the British Government to the sufferings of his countrymen, that he wrote to Jawaharlal: "My blood is boiling ever since I read the summaries (of the Hunter Report) you have sent me. We must hold a special Congress now and raise a veritable hell for the rascals."[27]

Yet Motilal's fury at the misdeeds of the British Government did not win him over immediately to the views of Gandhi. The Mahatma was seeking, at this juncture, to rally Hindus and Muslims behind the programme of non-cooperation; a programme which exhorted the people to withdraw forthwith from the institutions of the British Raj—educational, administrative and judicial—and thus ensure its destruction within a year. In view of the prominent position occupied by Motilal in public life, the Mahatma was anxious for his support. He had in Jawaharlal, Motilal's son, an enthusiastic convert to the novel technique of political agitation which he was seeking to apply to the struggle for political freedom in India. Nevertheless, Motilal took some time before he decided to extend support to the idea of non-cooperation, though once he had made up his mind, he plunged into non-violent warfare against the British Government with a sense of commitment which was characteristic of his personality.

Motilal's conversion to Gandhian politics, and his acceptance of the programme of non-cooperation, has been the subject of considerable speculation by scholars who have written about the struggle for freedom in India. Perhaps the best account of Motilal's conversion is given in Jawaharlal's *Autobiography,* which explains at some length the complex interplay of motives which led to this transformation. When the Mahatma gave his call for non-cooperation, Jawaharlal observes, Motilal took careful stock of the situation before he signified his support to the Mahatma. Indeed, he pondered over the question for a couple of months, before the special session of the Indian National Congress in Calcutta. That this should be so was hardly surprising. To respond positively to the Mahatma's call meant giving up, at the age of fifty-nine, the social, professional and intellectual commitments of three decades and more. "But . . . (Motilal's) reason, his strong sense of self-respect, and his pride, all led him step by step to throw in his lot wholeheartedly with the new movement. The accumulated anger with which a series of events, culminating in the Punjab tragedy and its aftermath filled him; the sense of utter wrong-doing and injustice, the bitterness of national humiliation, had to find some way out. But he was not to be sucked away by a wave of enthusiasm. *It was only when his reason, backed by the trained mind of a lawyer, had weighed all the pros and cons that he took the final decision and joined Gandhiji in his campaign.*"[28] (Emphasis not in original).

The decision to participate in the non-cooperation movement brought about a radical change in the style of life of Motilal and the members of his family. Almost overnight Motilal ceased leading the life, sartorially speaking, of an upper class Englishman; and under the influence of the Mahatma, he commenced wearing the simple khadi clothes which became the uniform of Gandhian nationalism in India. The sartorial transformation held a symbolic significance which needs to be emphasised in this context. Unlike the nationalism which flourished in India prior to the First World War, the nationalism activated by Gandhi in the 1920s, rested upon a conscious quest for the political identity and the cultural roots of India. The adoption of an indigenous style of dress, fabricated out of khadi, with the spinning wheel or *charkha* as the symbol of a resurgent India, represented an important facet of this quest for identity and cultural roots. Indeed, life at Anand Bhavan changed in other respects, too, partly for reasons of economy, since Motilal as a non-cooperator no longer accepted legal briefs, but more importantly, because he was consciously reaching out to the Indian past, at the same time as he identified himself with the militant yet non-violent politics of the Mahatma. Describing the changes which had transformed Anand Bhavan, as well as the members of the Nehru family, in a letter to Gandhi, Motilal observed: "What a fall, my countrymen! but, really, I have never enjoyed life better".[29]

When the Indian National Congress met at a special session in Calcutta in September 1920, Motilal was one of the few established leaders who voted for the adoption of non-cooperation. His enthusiastic support of the Gandhian programme earned him a place in the sub-committee which was appointed to work out a detailed programme of action for the attainment of swaraj within an year. He was, at the same time, elevated to membership of the Congress Working Committee, and appointed General Secretary to the organisation. So prominent was the position which Motilal acquired in the nationalist scheme of things, that Anand Bhavan, his residence, virtually became the headquarters of the freedom struggle in the United Provinces. The erstwhile setting of innumerable gatherings of high society in Allahabad now became "a caravanserai frequented by humble looking folk clad in homespun—party members sojourning or passing through Allahabad."[30]

The round of political activities which focused upon Motilal, Jawaharlal, and other members of the Nehru family, gained in intensity after the annual session of the Indian National Congress in December 1920 at Nagpur. The new year witnessed the unfolding, in Allahabad as well as in the surrounding rural districts, of the programme of non-cooperation which Motilal and other nationalist leaders had hammered out under the watchful eye of the Mahatma. This programme, which involved in the initial stages withdrawal from British created institutions of education, justice and administration, was designed to climax in a movement of civil disobedience which would involve the people in the non-payment of taxes to the Government of India. As the temper of the people rose to a high pitch of excitement, in anticipation of a "do or die!" struggle with the British Government, the Mahatma was asked time and again by the Congress leadership to give the green signal for a "no-tax" campaign. But he held his hand, at least partly because of a suspicion that the masses were insufficiently schooled in the technique of satyagraha to be drawn into a large scale non-violent struggle with the British Government.

In the meanwhile, the Government of United Provinces decided to put an end to the freedom of action enjoyed by two of the most distinguished exponents of Gandhian nationalism in the region. On 6 December 1921, a visibly nervous police officer arrested Motilal Nehru and Jawaharlal Nehru at Anand Bhavan. Next day, father and son were produced before a magistrate, and sentenced to a term of imprisonment for six months, to serve which term they were taken to the district jail at Lucknow. Here they anxiously awaited a call for civil disobedience from the Mahatma to the country at large. Instead came the decision to suspend the nationalist struggle. This call was issued by Gandhi after a violent confrontation between the police and a crowd of rural non-co-operators at Chauri Chaura, a remote village in the eastern United Provinces. In his prison at Lucknow, where Motilal resided along with his son, he received the news of this decision, and was aghast at the step taken by the Mahatma in calling off a countrywide movement of protest because of the loss of a few lives. For Motilal, as indeed for others who had accepted Gandhi's lead, the struggle upon which they had embarked was to result in swaraj. Instead, they found themselves suddenly in a situation where a countrywide agitation had been called off for what, in the first instance, appeared to be very trivial reasons.

VII

When Motilal was released from prison in 1922, he discerned that the nationalist movement of such monumental proportions, organised by the Mahatma barely two years ago, had become a fragmented and disorganised force. That things had come to such a pass was the reverse of surprising. For the sudden suspension of civil disobedience, after the Chauri Chaura incident, came as a great shock to the leadership of the Congress as well as to the people of India. In this climate of despondency, the All India Congress Committee appointed a committee to review the events of the past two years, and to recommend an appropriate course of action. This committee, on completing its task, found it difficult to recommend a clear-cut course of action. Some of its members—the so-called 'no-changers'—saw no reason whatsoever to modify the programme adopted by the Indian National Congress in September 1920. Others, Motilal prominent amongst them, were of the view that the struggle for freedom should next be taken up in the legislative councils, both in the provinces and at the centre, which had been created by the Act of 1919. Motilal's advocacy of a change of tactics received powerful support from C.R. Das, another very influential figure in nationalist politics, who was looked upon as the uncrowned king of Bengal; and the two were jointly able to win over to their position important leaders from the Presidency of Bombay, the Central Provinces, the Presidency of Madras and the Punjab.

The logic of Motilal's position in 1922, after the virtual collapse of the non-cooperation movement, and the arrest of the Mahatma, needs to be carefully examined at this juncture. The people of the country, Hindus and Muslims, rich and poor, urban and rural folk, so Motilal believed, had demonstrated an extraordinary solidarity, and a remarkable capacity for self-sacrifice, in response to the Mahatma's call for a non-violent struggle against the British Government. However, when the people were all set for a decisive trial of strength, Gandhi, for reasons which may have been perfectly legitimate in themselves, had suddenly called off the movement for civil disobedience. The powerful sentiment for freedom in various classes and communities, which had been so skilfully evoked by the prophet of non-violence, urgently called for a creative outlet; an outlet, moreover, that would help attain the objective of swaraj which had eluded the Mahatma in 1921. What could be more appropriate than transferring the nationalist struggle onto the arena of the new legislatures created by the Act of 1919? The essence of Motilal's strategy lay in capturing the reformed legislatures, and then utilizing them to put an end to British rule over India. The battle for swaraj had been fought earlier through a non-violent confrontation between satyagrahis and the British Government of India; this epic struggle was now to be taken up in the central legislature in New Delhi, as well as in the various provincial legislatures. The British Government had undoubtedly created these legislatures, with their "special" constituencies and their limited franchise, in order to dampen the fires of nationalism in India. But Motilal sought to transform the legislatures into instruments of the national will, which had been aroused to a level of political consciousness that had never been attained before, by the skilful leadership of the Mahatma, in the immediate post-war years.

Whatever be the validity of Motilal's perception of politics in 1922, he was unable to win over to his stance a majority of the leaders who had responded to the Mahatma's call for non-cooperation in 1920. When Motilal and C.R. Das spelt out their strategy at the Gaya session of Indian National Congress in December 1922, they made very little impression on the Gandhian loyalists who still dominated the councils of the organisation. As a result, they created a new organisation called the "Congress Khilafat Swaraj Party", which had Das as its President, and

Motilal as its General Secretary. The Swaraj Party, as it came to be called, proclaimed its overall loyalty to the creed of the Mahatma. But instead of seeking swaraj through the weapon of satyagraha, it sought to undermine the British Raj through obstructing the conduct of business in the new legislatures which had come into existence as a result of the Reforms of 1919.

Although C.R. Das was the President of the swarajists, he was so deeply involved in the politics of Bengal, that the affairs of the party at the national level were left largely in the hands of Motilal. The election manifesto of the new party, issued on 14 October 1923, described the swarajists as "a party within the Congress, and as such an integral part of the Congress."[31] The swarajists were equally committed, through their manifesto, to the cause of India's freedom, but they sought to secure this objective through means different from those adopted by Gandhi. Instead of relying on non-cooperation, the swarajists proposed to carry the struggle "into the enemy's camp by entering the councils."[32] Motilal's vigorous election campaign, and the logical strength of his position, were eloquently reflected in the creditable performance of the Swaraj Party at the polls. In the Central Legislative Assembly, the swarajists won an impressive 42 out of 101 elective seats. They faired equally well in the Provincial Assemblies in the United Provinces, Assam and Bengal; and in the case of the Central Provinces, they secured an outright majority.

As the leader of the Swaraj Party in the Central Legislative Assembly, Motilal rose to new heights of eloquence, and skill in political manoeuvre against the British Government of India. Indeed, his was the towering personality in an assembly which could boast of a host of outstanding figures, like M.A. Jinnah, or Lajpat Rai, or Madan Mohan Malaviya, or Sir Purshotamdas Thakurdas, or Sir Malcolm Hailey, or Sir Alexander Muddiman. Motilal secured a victory of very considerable proportions, at the very outset, when he was able to draw the Muslim and the moderate members of the assembly into a loose alliance with the Swaraj Party. The resulting coalition, the so-called Nationalist Party, possessed the strength in numbers to outvote the official members and their creatures in the Central Legislature, and this placed in the hands of Motilal a most formidable weapon, in his determination to wreck the reformed constitution from within the councils.

The strength of the Nationalist Party, under the leadership of Motilal, made itself felt at the very commencement of the new session of the Central Legislative Assembly. The constellation of political groups, which had been brought together by his adroit leadership, embarked upon a forceful campaign to wrest political concessions from the British Government. The opening shot in the campaign was fired by a private member, who moved a resolution demanding the appointment of a Royal Commission to review the Constitution of 1919, in such a manner as to secure for India the status of a self-governing dominion within the British Empire. Immediately thereafter, Motilal presented an amendment to this resolution, proposing that the new constitution be framed by a round table conference, drawing upon leaders who represented different strands of political opinion in India. Not surprisingly, this demand was rejected by Sir Malcolm Hailey, as a spokesman of the Government of India, who argued that the Constitution of 1919 had provided for a machinery of review after the lapse of a decade, that is, after 1929. But Motilal would have nothing to do with assurances that amounted to acts of grace on the part of the British Government. Moreover, he was of the view that the Constitution of 1919, upon which Hailey had taken his stand, was a piece of legislation designed with the sole purpose of thwarting the aspirations of the people of India for freedom. If the British Government could see its way to satisfying these aspirations, then the swarajists and their allies would extend a hand of cooperation to the alien rulers of the land. But if it took a contrary position, then (Motilal observed) "we shall, like men stand upon our rights and continue to be non-cooperators."[33]

That the British Government of India should reject the demand for political consultations leading to dominion status for India surprised no one, least of all Motilal and his followers in the Central Legislative Assembly. But the nationalists were able to score a tremendous moral victory over their opponents when 76 members of the Assembly voted in favour of Motilal's amendment, and only 48 voted against it. From this triumph Motilal went on to defeat the Government on a number of issues: for instance, the first four budgetary demands were rejected in their entirety; and a finance bill, too, was thrown out on its introduction. However, the Constitution of 1919 conferred on the Viceroy the power to veto the decisions of the legislature. As a result of this, Motilal's victories were not consequential of any practical effect, since the Viceroy, on each occasion when the Government was defeated, took recourse to the special powers with which he had been invested by the constitution. Nevertheless, as we have suggested above, the moral effect of these victories, which were proclaimed throughout the land by a jubilant nationalist press, was tremendous, and made the British Government look extremely ridiculous in the eyes of the educated classes of India.

With the legislative victories which he scored over the British Government in 1924, Motilal's stock stood extremely high in nationalist circles. Consequently, he made a bid to win over the Mahatma to his viewpoint towards the middle of the year. However, for the Mahatma non-violence was a philosophical creed, and the strategy and the tactics of non-cooperation were inextricably linked up to his overall view of the human condition. Motilal's argument that the events of 1922—the incident at Chauri Chaura, and the consequent suspension of civil disobedience—called for a new look at the political situation, indeed, for a change of tactics in the struggle against imperialism, failed to convince the Mahatma. Yet the Mahatma was not blind to the fact that the differences which had surfaced in the nationalist leadership worked entirely to the advantage of the British Government. Later in the year, therefore, he reached an agreement with the swarajist leaders, Motilal and C.R. Das, whereby their party became an integral part of the Indian National Congress. This agreement, which signified the closing of the nationalist ranks, was formally ratified at the Belgaum Session of the Indian National Congress in December 1924, which was held under the presidentship of Gandhi.

Notwithstanding the distinguished leadership which Motilal provided to the Swaraj Party in the Central Legislative Assembly during 1924-25, he presided over a very fragile constellation of political groups at this juncture. The nationalist coalition in the Central Assembly included moderate and Muslim members who were by no means fully committed to the policy of the Swaraj Party of undermining the constitution. Indeed, the provincial leaders who had gathered under Motilal's banner in the Bombay Presidency, and in the Central Provinces, resented the constraints which the strategy of wrecking the councils from within imposed upon them. These provincial leaders—M.R. Jayakar, or N.C.

Kelkar, or B.S. Moonje, among others—were men who had taken to politics under the aegis of the great Tilak; and although they had accepted the swarajist label in 1922, they were actually "responsivists", who believed in working the political system which had been created in 1919, even though their strategic objectives were no different from those of Motilal or the Mahatma. The constitutional prerogatives enjoyed by the Viceroy and the Provincial Governors greatly heightened such dissensions within the nationalist ranks, for even though Motilal and his followers succeeded in defeating crucial bills in the legislatures, the use of the veto by the Viceroy, and by the Governors, robbed their victories of any practical significance. The dissidence of the erstwhile Tilakites assumed the form of an open revolt when S.B. Tambe, the swarajist President of the Legislative Assembly in the Central Provinces, accepted membership of the Executive Council of the Governor. What the 'no-changers' had foreseen in 1922 thus actually came to pass. Men who had fought elections and entered the assemblies, presumably in order to wreck them, found the temptations of high office irresistible, and jettisoned the objective which had inspired them to enter into a constitutional "dialogue" with the British Government, at the central as well as at the provincial levels. However, Motilal was quick to read the writing on the wall. He realised that unless the rot was stemmed in time, the whole edifice which he had so carefully erected, stood in danger of crumbling into the dust. On 8 March 1926, therefore, he led the Swaraj Party out of the Central Legislative Assembly, in order to demonstrate beyond the shadow of doubt, his firm resolution to have nothing to do with a government which was so insensitive to the popular desire for swaraj.

VIII

Motilal's superb sense of timing in abandoning, in 1926, the stance which he had adopted after the suspension of non-cooperation in 1922, bears eloquent witness to the sensitivity of his political perception. For a change in the climate of politics was already making itself felt in the country, as the swarajists walked out of the legislature in New Delhi, and in the various provincial capitals, in a gesture of defiance against the British Government. The interlude between 1922 to 1926 was, in a manner of speaking, a difficult interlude for nationalists of different persuasions in the country. Not only had the countrywide agitation launched by the Mahatma come to an abrupt end in 1922, but deep cleavages between different religious communities, as well as between different generations of nationalists. had become manifest in the body politic.

The most alarming development of the period under review was the breakdown of the Hindu-Muslim entente, which the Mahatma had so skilfully conjured into existence during the heroic days of non-cooperation. This development, in striking contrast to the vindication of the nationalist position by Motilal and the swarajists in the legislatures, ensured that Hindus and Muslims spoke with discordant voices on the crucial political issues of the day, thereby seriously weakening the challenge which they could jointly mount against the British rulers of the land. Nor was the communal problem the only problem which confronted Motilal and the leaders of his generation. They further sensed that a younger generation of nationalists—represented best of all by a social democrat like Jawaharlal Nehru—was becoming increasingly critical of their strategy and tactics. This generation of nationalists wanted to launch a frontal attack on the British Government, and secure for the country *purna swaraj*, or complete independence. Over and above this, Jawaharlal and the younger generation of political activists also sought to transform nationalism from a purely political into a social and an economic question. They believed that the resolution of India's political bondage, as well as of her poverty, could best be achieved by reorganising the national polity on socialist principles, whereby the wealth of the country would be socially owned, and the rewards of labour equitably distributed between different social classes.

It was in this context that the British Government appointed a Commission, the so-called Simon Commission, with a membership drawn exclusively from the British Parliament, to review the political progress made by India since the enactment of the Reforms of 1919. That the British Government did not think it fit to associate even a single citizen of India with the Simon Commission, at a point in time when nationalism had become so powerful a force in the country, gives us a rare insight into the lofty arrogance of the imperial psyche. However, this arrogance was a blessing in disguise for nationalism in India. Practically all classes and communities in the country came together in their hostility to the

Simon Commission, and when the members of this ill-assorted group toured the length and breadth of the land, in order to exchange views with political leaders of differing persuasions in different regions, they were greeted everywhere by hostile crowds, which in their numerical strength no less than in their social composition, recalled the popular enthusiasm against the British Raj in the tumultuous years of non-cooperation.

At the same time as he appointed the Simon Commission, Lord Birkenhead, the Secretary of State, threw an open challenge to the nationalist leadership to devise a constitution for India that would be acceptable to all classes and communities in the country. Behind this challenge lay the arrogant assumption that the people of India had still to acquire a consciousness of nationhood; that the great religious minorities, the Muslim community in particular, would not agree to make common cause with the Hindus in presenting a charter of constitutional demands to the British Government; and finally, that Princely India remained largely untouched by the forces that were at work in the provinces of British India. Birkenhead's challenge was too arrogant a challenge to be overlooked by the nationalist leaders of India. Consequently, a decision was taken at the Madras session of the Indian National Congress, in 1927, to draft a constitution for an independent India, in association with other organised political groups in the country. In pursuit of this decision, an All Parties Conference met under the presidentship of M.A. Ansari, the distinguished Muslim leader, to devise a constitutional framework for an independent India. At this conference, a Sub-Committee with Motilal Nehru as its Chairman, and the distinguished liberal, Sir Tej Bahadur Sapru, as one of its members, was created to draft such a constitution.

The Nehru Report, as the constitution drafted by Motilal, with the assistance of Sapru, came to be known, was a document which was destined to play an important role in the political destiny of India. In drafting this constitution, Motilal had to resolve two basic problems. First, he had to devise a political system that would be acceptable to the leaders of the two major religious communities, namely, the Hindus and the Muslims. Secondly, he had to take into consideration the sentiments of the younger generation of nationalist leaders, men like Jawaharlal, who were pressing for a radicalisation of the national movement, and who had adopted as an immediate objective the attainment of *purna swaraj* by India.

Motilal's attitude to the communal problem which plagued the Indian polity, at this juncture, combined strategic firmness with tactical flexibility in finely balanced proportions. In the long run, so Motilal believed, the communal problem would of its own accord cease to loom so menacingly on the political scene. "We are certain that, as soon as India is free and can face her problems unhampered by alien authority and intervention, the minds of our people will turn to the vital questions of the day . . . parties will be formed in the country and in the legislatures on entirely other grounds, chiefly economic, we presume."[34] Yet whatever be the strategic prospect, it was clear to Motilal that, in the immediate future, some tangible assurances would have to be held out to the Muslims, if they were to join hands with the Hindus in presenting common political demands to the British Government. To this end, Motilal made a number of recommendations: first, he suggested that a declaration of rights, assuring religious and personal liberty to all citizens of India, should be inserted in the constitution; secondly, he recommended the creation of two new provinces, namely, the North-West Frontier Province and Sind, where the Muslims would constitute a majority of the population; and finally, although he recommended the abrogation of communal electorates, he sweetened the pill (so far as the Muslims were concerned) by the prescription that seats be reserved for Muslims, in the central as well as in the provincial legislatures.

As we have already mentioned, at the time when Motilal drafted his constitutional proposals, the radical temper of the younger generation of nationalists was also a matter of serious concern to him. Indeed, it was clear to Motilal, that in the political climate of 1928, the erstwhile formula of *swaraj*, which Gandhi had utilised earlier to attract different classes and communities to the standard of non-cooperation, could hardly be expected to meet the approval of these radical young men. However, Motilal believed that to opt for *purna swaraj*, or complete independence, would also be premature at this point in time. The constitution devised by him, therefore, stipulated that the status of India within the British Empire should be identical with the status of self-governing colonies like Canada or Australia. In formal terms, Motilal proposed that India be granted Dominion Status rather than complete independence.

Although Motilal produced in the Nehru Report a constitutional blue-print which dealt with the crucial issues in Indian politics with vision and sympathy, his proposals were unable to secure the approval of some significant sections of society in India. Soon after the Report was issued, the Congress leadership assembled at Calcutta, in December 1928, to discuss the constitutional proposals of Motilal. The Muslim leaders at the Calcutta Congress felt that, in view of the plural character of society in India, some of the recommendations of the Nehru Report—particularly the emphasis on a unitary constitution, and the abrogation of communal electorates—would not meet the wishes of their constituents. In a conference held slightly later, in March 1929, the Muslim leaders presented a radically different prescription for the constitutional future of India. They envisaged the political future of India in terms of a federal polity, wherein the minorities, particularly the Muslim community, would protect their interests through the mechanism of separate electorates.

In view of the leading role which he had played in drafting a constitution for India, Motilal was an obvious choice for the presidency of the Indian National Congress in 1928. As the time approached for the annual session at Calcutta, Motilal sensed the opposition which had crystallised to the constitutional future which he envisaged for the country. We have already dwelt upon the reaction of the Muslim leadership to the Nehru Report. Even more alarming than the Muslim response, were the differences which emerged between Motilal and the senior generation of nationalists, on the one hand, and the younger and radical nationalists, led by Jawaharlal and Subhas Chandra Bose, on the other. To Jawaharlal the adoption of Dominion Status as the objective of the Indian National Congress seemed a retrogressive and not a progressive step, and he questioned the sagacity of the position adopted by his father. Once more, as in 1920, the atmosphere at Anand Bhavan became electrified as Motilal and Jawaharlal sorted out the differing views which they held on the crucial issues of the day. "Father and son are atilt," Motilal confessed to a kinsman, not altogether without pride in the patriotic fervour of his son, "but Jawaharlal would not be my son if he did not stick to his guns."[35] Behind the differences between Motilal and Jawaharlal stood the revolt of a younger generation of nationalists, impatient of the relatively moderate stance of their elders. Here was a cleavage in the nationalist ranks, which was even more disturbing than the differences that had arisen between the Hindu and the Muslim leadership on the constitutional future of the country. Since he was confronted with a crisis of the most alarming character, Motilal turned to the Mahatma for support. How crucial was Gandhi's role in bringing about unity within the Congress, at this juncture, is vividly reflected in the proceedings of the annual session at Calcutta. In the Subjects Committee, where various issues were debated before they were taken up in the open session, the question whether the Nehru Report was to be adopted in its entirety, and Dominion Status accepted as the national objective, became a subject of heated discussion. The younger members of the Subjects Committee were insistent in their demand for complete independence. Indeed, but for the Mahatma's presence, and his healing touch, it is doubtful whether the revolt of the young could have been controlled by the older generation of leaders. As it was, what emerged in the Subjects Committee was in the nature of a compromise. The Nehru Report was accepted in its entirety, but on the crucial issue of Dominion Status, the Congress leadership decided that if the British Government did not concede this minimum demand within the span of a year, then they would initiate a movement of civil disobedience to win *purna swaraj* for the country. The compromise adopted in the Subjects Committee was then approved in the open session of the Congress.

Motilal's presidential address at Calcutta was, in the main, a stirring call for unity among different nationalist groups committed to securing political freedom for India. The constitutional provisions embodied in the Nehru Report, Motilal observed, whether they touched upon the vexed question of the political links between Great Britain and India, or whether they related to the communal question, represented a consensus which had been reached, after prolonged debate and discussion, at the All Parties Conference. The Report represented, in other words, the common ground between different strands of political opinion in the country. It was both legitimate and natural for members of the Indian National Congress to entertain more radical views on nationalist objectives, as they pertained to the communal question, or to the issue of Dominion Status versus *purna swaraj*. At the same time, the leaders of the Congress could not absolve themselves of the moral responsibility to carry different schools of thought along with them in their confrontation with British imperialism. "The position," Motilal observed, "as I view it, is this. Here is a constitution agreed upon by the various parties invited by the Congress to frame it. These parties know that the goal of the Congress is complete independence. They do not ask the Congress to change its goal, but present to it the result of their labours, such as it is, and say that they are prepared to go thus far and no further at present. They offered their cooperation and demand that of the Congress. . . . Is this Congress going to refuse them this cooperation. . . ? If the Congress will do that, it will abdicate its proper function to guide the nation on its forward march. The action calls for skilful generalship, and not academic discussions which take us nowhere."[36]

The decisions taken by the Indian National Congress at Calcutta were as much of a triumph for Motilal and the senior generation of nationalist leaders, as they were a triumph for Jawaharlal and the young radicals within the nationalist ranks. An important by-product of the Calcutta Congress was the return of the Mahatma to "active" politics, after a period of three or four years, during which period he had engaged himself in constructive work in his ashram. As we have indicated earlier, the support which the Mahatma extended to Motilal at Calcutta was crucial for the acceptance, although in a modified form, of the clause of Dominion Status by the Congress, at least for the space of a year. Furthermore, it was now clear that the organised forces of nationalism in India were heading towards yet another trial of strength with the British Government, just as it was also clear that the Mahatma, with his moral authority over the people enormously enhanced during the years of constructive work in his ashram, would once again be called upon to lead his countrymen in a non-violent assault on the British Raj.

These developments within nationalist politics were followed with close interest by the Viceroy, Lord Irwin, a Tory who was not altogether insensitive to the winds of change that were blowing across India, Irwin had earlier committed a monumental blunder in approving the wholly British composition of the Simon Commission, which had been constituted to review the political progress of the subcontinent. However, as Irwin's perception of politics in India sharpened, he came to realise more and more the extent to which the desire for freedom had taken firm root among the common people of the country. "There is quite clearly a strong movement to the left among advanced Hindu political opinion. . . ,"[37] he wrote to the Secretary of State for India in January 1929. The Viceroy was also convinced that the situation called for a liberal gesture on the part of the Imperial Government; a gesture which would clear the climate of distrust and suspicion which had come to plague relations between the British leaders and the nationalist leadership of India. Irwin had since some time, partly as a result of consultations with moderate leaders, been toying with the idea of initiating a dialogue between responsible Indian leaders and a delegation of British parliamentarians. He further believed that it had become necessary to declare, in unambiguous terms, that the constitutional progress of India would over the years confer on her a status comparable to the status of the self-governing dominions of the British Empire. Irwin took the opportunity offered by a vacation in Great Britain, in the middle of 1929, to place his views before the British Government. As a result of these consultations, Irwin declared, on his return to India, that the British Government would soon call a round table conference to discuss the political future of India; and further, that "the natural issue of India's constitutional progress" was "the attainment of Dominion Status."[38]

Irwin's declaration of October 1929 obliged Gandhi, Motilal and other Congress leaders to re-examine the decision, taken at the Calcutta Congress, to throw a challenge to the British Government, if Dominion Status was not bestowed on India by the end of 1929. As a result of the ostensibly conciliatory gesture made by the Viceroy, the more important Congress leaders, and a few distinguished liberals, met in Delhi in the first week of November, to draft a formal response to the viceregal declaration. The matter was one of considerable delicacy, since Irwin's declaration was eminently capable of being subjected to conflicting interpretations. At the meeting of the Congress and the Liberal leaders held in Delhi, Jawaharlal and Subhas Bose, who represented the radical viewpoint, were in favour of an outright rejection of Irwin's declaration. But Gandhi, Motilal, and the majority decided in favour of a positive response to the Viceroy's gesture. The statement issued by these leaders, popularly known as the Delhi Manifesto, welcomed the decision to hold a round table conference of British and Indian leaders to discuss the future of India.

However, the manifesto made it clear that the Congress leaders interpreted the Viceroy's statement to mean that the "Conference is to meet not to discuss *when* Dominion Status is to be established, but to *frame* a scheme of Dominion Status."[39] (Emphasis not in original).

If Motilal and some of the Congress leaders entertained any doubts as to the intentions of the British Government, their doubts must have been set at rest by the debate which took place in the British Parliament over Irwin's declaration. To put matters briefly, all sections of opinion in Great Britain, within the Government as well as outside it, threw their weight against any sympathetic (to Indian aspirations) interpretation of Irwin's declaration of October 1929. Reading, whose views carried the authority of a former Viceroy, who was also a distinguished Liberal, looked upon the declaration as "something which reflected adversely upon the dignity of the Simon Commission." Baldwin, the Conservative leader, who had sent Irwin to India, refused to endorse the policies of his protege. David Lloyd George, the leader of Great Britain during the First World War, utilised the occasion to launch a ferocious attack upon the Labour Government in power. Even Wedgewood Benn, despite his sympathy for Indian aspirations, wilted under the ferocity of the joint Liberal and Conservative assault, and simply explained away the declaration as a reiteration of the Montagu Declaration of August 1917.

Motilal's reaction to Irwin's overture had not been completely hostile when the Delhi Manifesto was issued. But the debate in the British Parliament made it clear to him that the Viceroy's declaration had not made any substantive change in the attitude of the British Government towards the issue of constitutional progress in India. As a result of this, even though Motilal joined Gandhi and Sapru in a meeting with the Viceroy, on 23 December 1929, he had little reason to believe that anything would emerge out of such an exchange of views. The meeting between the Viceroy and the Indian leaders turned out to be completely abortive of results. The Mahatma was the principal spokesman from the Indian side, and he frankly told Irwin that the Congress would not participate in a round table conference, unless an assurance was given that the Conference was meeting to draft a constitution ensuring Dominion Status for India. The Mahatma's stand was reiterated by Motilal, who impressed upon the Viceroy that the political leaders of Great

Britain needlessly "exaggerated the difficulties in the way of Dominion Status for India."[40] Irwin, on his part, made it clear that the terms of reference of the round table conference could not be redrawn to the satisfaction of the Congress leaders, although "it (the Conference) would have the fullest opportunity to discuss any proposals before it. . . ."[41]

The meeting between Irwin and the Congress leaders had a distinct air of unreality about it. For despite the momentary hopes aroused by the viceregal declaration, it was clear to all perceptive observers, that the real decisions about India's future would be taken at the annual session of the Indian National Congress, which was due to meet in Lahore in the last week of December. The nature of these decisions had been largely foreshadowed by the deliberations in Calcutta, roughly a year earlier; and even more so by the election, at the initiative of the Mahatma and Motilal, of the youthful Jawaharlal as President of the Congress. Jawaharlal arrived at Lahore on 29 December, to preside over this crucial session, and as Motilal handed over charge to his son, he recited a Persian couplet—*Herche ke pidar natawanad, pesar tamam kunad* (what the father is unable to accomplish, the son achieves)—which turned out to be prophetic. Predictably, with Jawaharlal in charge, the Congress solemnly resolved to fight for *purna swaraj,* and the Mahatma was given overall control of the movement through which this nationalist objective was to be achieved. In supporting Jawaharlal and the younger generation of Congress leaders at Lahore, Motilal had finally rejected the view that the objectives of the struggle of freedom could be achieved through a political dialogue with the British Government. "I hope you will give me the credit of fully realising what it means to me and mine to throw my lot . . . in the coming struggle," he wrote to the Muslim leader, M.A. Ansari. "Nothing but a deep conviction that the time for the greatest effort and the greatest sacrifice has come would have induced me to expose myself at my age and with my physical disabilities, and with my family obligations to the tremendous risk I am incurring. I hear the clarion call of the country and I obey."[42] The reference to his physical disabilities was not without significance. For although Motilal plunged into the fray with his customary enthusiasm, his health was fast giving way, under the stresses and strains of a busy public life.

Shortly after the Lahore Congress, in March 1930, when the

Mahatma decided to initiate civil disobedience through the Dandi March, Motilal and Jawaharlal travelled to the village of Jambosar in Gujarat, which was one of the intermediate stages of the march, to demonstrate their moral support for the salt satyagraha. On his return from Jambosar, Motilal had a medical check-up by Ansari, who was a very eminent physician. The results of this check-up were very alarming, and Ansari felt obliged to report the state of Motilal's health to the Mahatma. "I found Panditji's health in a very unsatisfactory condition this time. The continuous anxiety and strain which he has recently gone through, and his visit to you . . . had placed a further strain on his dilated heart . . . .(But) he has not been sparing himself and is determined not to spare himself in future. . . . "[43]

However, as anticipated by Ansari, Motilal was disinclined to let the state of his health become an issue at a time when the people of India, under the leadership of Gandhi, were engaged in a desperate struggle for freedom. All over the country, in cities, in towns and in the larger villages, the nationwide organisation of the Congress initiated a popular movement for civil disobedience, the like of which had not been seen before in the subcontinent. Along with the rest of the nation, the members of the Nehru household, too, were drawn into the activity of manufacturing salt and disobeying non-violently the laws of a Government which had lost all moral authority to rule over the country.

When the British Government was faced with the defiance of an entire nation under the leadership of Gandhi, and of the Nehrus, father and son, it lost little time in showing its repressive face to the people of India. The Mahatma was imprisoned on 5 May; and Jawaharlal, who had given a call to the rural masses of the United Provinces, was clamped into prison even earlier. Before his incarceration, Jawaharlal had appointed his father, frail in health, acting President of the Congress in his absence. He had also accepted from him Anand Bhawan, which was appropriately renamed Swaraj Bhawan, as a gift to the nation.

It, therefore, fell upon Motilal, as President of the Indian National Congress in the absence of his son, to lead the country in its grim battle against the British Government. Apart from directing political activities in Allahabad and in the United Provinces, Motilal was also involved in a number of organisations at the national level, of which the most important was the Boycott

Committee, which made arrangements with the textile mill-owners of Bombay and Ahmedabad for the boycott of foreign cloth. Given the repressive temper of the Government of Lord Irwin, it was a matter of time before Motilal, too, found himself behind prison bars. On 30 June 1930, he was arrested at Allahabad and joined his son in Naini prison.

Motilal and Jawaharlal found in prison life an ideal opportunity to come close to each other. Jawaharlal was disturbed to see how much his father had deteriorated in health, and nursed him with a degree of affection and care which deeply moved Motilal. "Hari (my personal servant) could well take a leaf out of Jawaharlal's book in the matter of serving me. From early morning tea to the time I retire for the night, I find everything I need in its proper place. . . . Jawaharlal anticipates everything and leaves nothing for me to do. I wish there were many fathers to boast of such sons,"[44] Motilal wrote at this time. Indeed, life in prison was a touching period of discovery for father and son, since within the walls of prison they could share experiences, and understand each other's point of view, in a manner which the demands of a busy public life had made it difficult earlier.

The community of feeling between Motilal and Jawaharlal is reflected most clearly of all in the extent to which the father shared, at this juncture, the political perception of his son. As we have indicated earlier, Motilal had hitherto believed that it was possible to work out a satisfactory arrangement of the political future of India with the British Government. But he now accepted Jawaharlal's position, namely, that freedom would come to India only through a bitter struggle with the British Government. The ambiguous phrasing of the Irwin Declaration of October 1929, and the position taken by the Viceroy in his meeting with the Indian leaders on the eve of the Lahore Congress, had finally persuaded Motilal that Jawaharlal's appraisal of the situation was much more realistic than the optimistic view which he had formerly taken of British motives. The hardening of Motilal's stance is clearly reflected in the outcome of the initiative taken by the Liberal leaders, Sapru and Jayakar, with encouragement from Irwin, to persuade the Congress leaders to make peace with the British Government. Both Motilal and Jawaharlal looked upon this move with considerable suspicion, and their attitude was instrumental in persuading the Mahatma, too, to take a tough line. As Jayakar, one of the mediators, recalled about the negotiations: "They (the Nehrus) practically said that they were the belligerent power which had very nearly succeeded in bending the British Government, and as such, all talk of a compromise must be with them directly, and on all essential points, leaving the R.T.C.(Round Table Conference) to regularise their decisions."[45]

Motilal, however, was not destined to struggle much longer for India's freedom. The serious state of his health became obvious even to the British, and he was released from prison on 11 September 1930 on grounds of ill-health. Immediately, thereafter, he travelled to the hill resort of Mussourrie in a bid to recover his strength. However, the strains and stresses of a busy public life had exacted a terrible toll. Motilal had always suffered from asthma, but his system was now plagued by a variety of ailments. In the middle of November, he went to Calcutta to take advantage of the medical facilities which were available there. An examination of his condition revealed the extent to which his system had been damaged by a combination of ailments. "The X-rays have revealed that the heart, the lungs and liver are all affected,"[46] he wrote to Allahabad. When Jawaharlal was released from prison in January 1931, he rushed to his ailing father's bedside, and was deeply shocked by his physical condition. "There he sat like an old lion mortally wounded and with his physical strength almost gone, but still very leonine and kingly . . . he was evidently often struggling with himself, trying to keep a grip of things which threatened to slip away from his grasp,"[47] he states in his *Autobiography*. Yet even then Jawaharlal did not sense the full seriousness of the situation. Motilal, however, had a premonition of what was to come. "I am going soon Mahatmaji," he told Gandhi, "and I shall not be there to see Swaraj. But I know that you have won it and shall soon have it."[48] Prophetic words! For not very long after Motilal had uttered them, on 6 February 1931, after a restless night during which Swarup Rani and Jawaharlal sat by his bedside, he breathed his last. His story of earthly achievements was over.

VIII

How can one sum up a life so full of achievement, so rich in the range of its experiences, as the life of Motilal? Perhaps the best way to do so is to briefly recapitulate the three distinct phases of

Motilal's career: first, as a lawyer of distinction; secondly, as a moderate nationalist engaged in a constitutional dialogue with the British rulers of India; and finally, as a militant nationalist, who followed the Mahatma as a principal lieutenant in those epic struggles of the 1920s, and the 1930s, which shook the edifice of the British Raj to its very foundations.

Motilal belonged to a scholarly family hailing from Kashmir which had settled in Delhi at a time when the Mughal Empire had entered a phase of decline. Notwithstanding the declining fortunes of their patrons, the ancestors of Motilal held offices of distinction at the Mughal Court, and were rewarded with a substantial *jagir* for their services. The acquisition of jagirdari status by the literati was not unusual in this period, though what may have marked out the Nehrus was the intellectual stature of the family, reflected most clearly of all in the scholarly eminence of Raj Kaul, the ancestor who had been persuaded by the Emperor Farrukhsiyar to migrate to Delhi.

The Uprising of 1857 was as much of a traumatic experience for the Nehrus as it was for the people of north India as a whole. However, what may have heightened the trauma for the Nehrus was the death of Gangadhar, the head of the family, at the relatively young age of thirty-four. Yet such moments of adversity often bring out the best in individuals whose moral fibre combines resilience with strength. The Nehrus, headed by a woman of great courage, stood the test of adversity exceedingly well, and they were able to re-establish themselves, first in Agra, where they had migrated immediately after 1857, then in Khetri, and finally in Allahabad.

An important feature about the Nehrus, at this juncture, was the transition which the family underwent from a traditional to a western culture. The story of Motilal's youth, his career as a student in Allahabad, and his professional life thereafter, bears witness to the success with which this transition was accomplished. Motilal acquired professional skills in law, and these skills enabled him to carve out a career of distinction for himself as a lawyer. Law, as we have indicated earlier, was a profession in which it was possible for young Indians of ability to make their mark in life. For the British had created a structure of government and property in the United Provinces, which offered opportunities to brilliant men in the legal profession to earn distinction for themselves. However, although Motilal's rise to success was facilitated by a favourable milieu, this should not blind us to the quality of his achievement in climbing to the very top of the legal profession. Apart from a favourable milieu, it was the incisive quality of Motilal's intellect, as well as his capacity for sheer hard work, which enabled him to gain recognition as a leading member of his profession in the country.

The transition, from a legal to a political career, came easily to men of distinction in Indian society in the closing decades of the nineteenth century. Motilal was for a while fully engaged in making a success of his professional career. But when he had climbed to the very top of the legal profession, he turned to public activity, initially in the domain of civic politics, and then in provincial politics, and finally in national politics.

Motilal's political views at this juncture were those of a nationalist who was also a moderate. Perhaps the climate in which these views were shaped needs a little elaboration. The British had created a political system in India which rested, on the one hand, upon modern bureaucratic and judicial institutions, and on the other, upon private property in land. Men like Motilal, with their deep knowledge of law and the principles of constitutional politics, were very well-equipped to understand the nature of these institutions, as well as the values which sustained them. Their legal training created in their consciousness a deep respect for the laws and institutions of a liberal and property owning society. As a result of all this, Motilal, when he initially turned to public activity, was not altogether without sympathy for the British Raj. He believed that the British were seeking to conjure into existence a liberal polity in India, and he, therefore, assumed that they would respond sympathetically to the growing consciousness of nationhood in the country.

However, Motilal's experience of the representative institutions created by the British, in 1909, proved to be quite different from what he had expected of a sensitive imperial system. Behind the rhetoric of liberalism, the British Raj emerged as a rigid system, clinging blindly to a position of privilege so far as imperial interests were concerned, and ready to take recourse to repressive policies in order to undermine the growing strength of nationalism in India. Motilal's alienation from the Raj, an alienation stemming from his changing perception of its character, is clearly reflected in the political stance which he adopted in the years after the First World War. By 1918, Motilal had grasped the exploitative character of British imperialism, and he parted company from his moderate friends, to join the rank of those nationalist leaders who were willing to wage a militant struggle against the British Government of India. The "frightfulness" of the massacre at Jallianwala Bagh, in 1919, merely heightened the perception which Motilal had already acquired of the character of British imperialism in India.

Motilal's decision to reject the moderate stance in politics did not automatically lead him to extend support to the Mahatma and the non-cooperation movement. The change from a radical nationalist, who had no illusions about the British Raj in India, to a satyagrahi, who actively dissociated himself from British institutions in pursuit of the Gandhian path to swaraj, was by no means an easy change for Motilal, since he was deeply influenced by the liberal political culture of Great Britain. This is a subject on which scholars have given us differing, if not conflicting, interpretations of Motilal's political behaviour. Our own assessment coincides with the assessment voiced by Jawaharlal in his *Autobiography*. For Motilal (as, indeed, for Jawaharlal), the only authentic expression of militant nationalism in India was the Gandhian weapon of satyagraha. No one, apart from the Mahatma, had shown how swaraj could be won. No other leader had achieved the same rapport with the rural masses which the Mahatma had achieved in a remarkably short span of time. Such considerations persuaded Motilal, despite the reservations which he may have entertained about the politics of satyagraha, that it was morally incumbent upon him to participate in the non-cooperation movement, and through such participation, seek to liberate India from foreign rule.

Yet Motilal's acceptance of the Mahatma, in 1920, was in all probability not as wholehearted as Jawaharlal's acceptance of this prophet of non-violence. Nothing reveals this as clearly as the alacrity with which Motilal took once again to legislative politics, after the collapse of non-cooperation in 1922, even if he did so to destroy the British Raj. The swarajist interlude is an episode to which historical scholarship has paid insufficient attention. However, this interlude constitutes a crucial chapter in the history of our struggle for freedom, for the swarajists made a valuable contribution to the nationalist cause. The suspension of civil disobedience, in 1922, by the Mahatma had left the nation in a very frustrated mood. The decision to do so came as an anti-climax to the heightening desire for freedom which had grown up between 1919 and 1922. Motilal drew into the Swarajist Party the growing sense of nationhood, which the Mahatma had conjured into existence during the non-cooperation movement. Even more, he was able to impart a new vitality to this consciousness, at a time when its frustration could have undone what had been achieved, at great sacrifice, in the preceding years. In the Central Legislature in New Delhi, as well as in the provincial legislatures, the Swaraj Party offered determined resistance to the British Government, and made it clear to them, that it was only a matter of time before the powerful impulse for freedom in the country would oblige them to quit India. Over and above all this, the leaders of the Swaraj Party learnt the art of parliamentary politics, in a manner which was to stand them in good stead later; in 1937, when the Congress participated in the provincial elections held under the Act of 1935, as well as in the decades after the attainment of independence in 1947.

Whatever be the achievements of the Swaraj Party, Motilal was quick to discern a decisive change in the popular mood towards the close of the 1920s. This change came about through a variety of reasons: through the resentment caused by the appointment of the Simon Commission; through the growing disaffection of the intelligentsia; and finally, through the discontent which the approach of a worldwide economic crisis spread through the cities as well as the villages of the subcontinent. It was clear to Motilal, that the militant mood of the people called for a renewed assault on British imperialism in India. In 1928, as in 1920, Motilal differed from Jawaharlal, as to the manner in which the popular mood could be harnessed to serve the cause of freedom. He looked upon the achievement of Dominion Status by India as a consummation which would safeguard her political and economic interests. In the constitution which Motilal devised about this time, he therefore recommended that the objective of Dominion Status be endorsed by all those who were involved in the struggle for freedom. However, when the younger generation of nationalists, led by Jawaharlal, made it clear to Motilal that they had set their hearts on complete independence, he had no hesitation in accepting a compromise, whereby the British Government was given the grace period of a year to confer Dominion Status on India, failing which a struggle for *purna swaraj* would be launched by the Congress. Indeed, as Motilal came to appreciate the growing strength of radical nationalism in India, he drew closer to Jawaharlal in his assessment of the political situation. This is clearly reflected in his stance towards the Irwin Declaration of October 1929; as it is also reflected in his role during the negotiations with Irwin, on the eve of the Lahore Congress, in December 1929. Indeed, in the closing years of his life, the conviction grew on Motilal that the British Government would not loosen its grip over India, unless it was compelled to do so by the organised strength of militant nationalism in the country. The support which Motilal extended to the demand for *purna swaraj* at the Lahore Congress, as well as the enthusiasm with which he participated in civil disobedience in 1930, bear witness to the extent to which he shared, at this juncture, the radical perception of British imperialism.

Motilal did not live to see the day when India became free. But the leading role which he played in politics, in the decade and slightly more after the First World War, ensured that British rule over India would be destroyed before long. That an individual who grew up as an admirer of British values and institutions, should have become an adversary of the Raj, speaks volumes of its exploitative character in India. It speaks equally forcefully of Motilal's love for his country; of his ability to outgrow the milieu in which he had achieved intellectual maturity and professional success; that he plunged into the struggle for freedom with a rare sense of commitment, and sacrificed everything which belonged to him in this struggle. When men like Motilal, who were so deeply influenced by the liberal political culture of Great Britain, turned against the British Raj, then its days in India were, indeed, numbered. For this reason, and also because of the distinguished leadership which he provided to the nationalist cause, Motilal occupies a position of lonely eminence in the history of the struggle for freedom in India.

NOTES

1. Jawaharlal Nehru, *An Autobiography* (London, 1936), p. 1.

2. Mirza Asadullah Khan Ghalib, *Dastanbuy: A Diary of the Indian Revolt of 1857*, trans. by K.A. Faruqi (Bombay, 1971), pp. 40-41.
3. B.R. Nanda, "Motilal Nehru" in B.R. Nanda, *Gokhale, Gandhi and the Nehrus: Studies in Indian Nationalism* (London, 1974), p. 86.
4. The North-Western Provinces became the United Provinces in 1901, and Uttar Pradesh after India became independent.
5. Sir Harcourt Butler, quoted in D.A. Low (ed.), *Soundings in Modern South Asian History* (Berkeley, 1968), p. 8.
6. Amarnath Jha, "Muir Central College: The Foundations" in *The Allahabad University Magazine,* Vol.LIII, June 1975.
7. Sir Sunderlal did not normally use his surname Dave.
8. K.N. Katju, quoted in B.R. Nanda, *The Nehrus: Motilal and Jawaharlal* (London, 1962), p. 27
9. *Pandit Motilal Nehru: A Great Patriot* (New Delhi, 1976), p. 27.
10. Ibid., p. 50.
11. Ibid., p. 176.
12. Nanda, op. cit. (n. 8), p. 24.
13. *An Autobiography,* p. 8.
14. Nanda, op. cit. (n. 8), p. 39.
15. *Motilal Nehru Papers, Nehru Memorial Museum & Library* (hereinafter referred to as *MN Papers*). Motilal to Prithinath Chak, dated 22 December 1899.
16. *Jawaharlal Nehru Papers, Nehru Memorial Museum & Library* (hereinafter referred to as *JN Papers* Motilal to Jawaharlal, dated 19 October 1905.
17. C.A. Bayly, *The Local Roots of Indian Politics: Allahabad 1880-1920* (Oxford, 1975).
18. Speech by Motilal at the First Provincial Conference of the United Provinces *dated 29 March 1907.*
19. Ibid.
20. *JN Papers,* Motilal to Jawaharlal, dated 30 August 1909.
21. *JN Papers,* Motilal to Jawaharlal, dated 29 April 1910.
22. Nanda, op. cit. (n. 8), p. 126.
23. Nanda, op. cit. (n. 8), p. 136.
24. Nanda, op. cit. (n. 8), p. 148.
25. *An Autobiography,* p. 41.
26. "Responsible Self-government", Presidential Address of Motilal Nehru delivered at the thirty-fourth annual session of the Indian National Congress, dated 27 December 1919, at Amritsar.
27. Nanda, op. cit. (n. 8), p. 175.
28. *An Autobiography,* p. 65.
29. *MN Papers*, Motilal to Gandhi, dated 1921.
30. Nanda, op. cit. (n. 8), p. 185.
31. Election Manifesto of the Swaraj Party dated 14 October 1923 quoted in Nanda, op. cit. (n. 8), p. 207.
32. Ibid.
33. *The Legislative Assembly Debates* (Official Report), *Vol. IV, Part I,* (Delhi, 1924), p. 370.
34. Quotation from *Nehru Report* in R. Coupland, *The Indian Problem 1833-1935* (Oxford, 1943), p. 89.

35. Nanda, op. cit. (n. 8), p. 303.
36. "Dominion Status or Independence", Presidential Address of Motilal Nehru delivered at the forty-third session of the Indian National Congress, dated 29 December 1928, at Calcutta.
37. Irwin to Wedgewood Benn, dated 17 January 1929; quoted in *The Earl of Birkenhead, Halifax: The Life of Lord Halifax* (London, 1965), p. 263.
38. Quoted in J.M. Brown, *Gandhi and Civil Disobedience* (Cambridge, 1977), p. 62.
39. All-Parties Leaders' Joint Statement dated 2 November, 1929: *The Collected Works of Mahatma Gandhi,* Vol. XLII.
40. *Record of a meeting held at the Viceroy's House on December 28, 1929:* made by Cunningham, P.S. to Lord Irwin, *Sapru Papers.*
41. Ibid.
42. *MN Papers,* Motilal to Ansari dated 7 February 1930.
43. Ansari to Gandhi dated 30 March 1930 quoted in Nanda, op. cit. (n. 8), p. 329.
44. Nanda op. cit. (n. 8), p. 332.
45. Quoted in J. Brown, *Gandhi and Civil Disobedience* (Cambridge, 1977), p. 166.
46. Nanda, op. cit. (n. 8), p. 337.
47. *An Autobiography,* p. 246.
48. *MN Papers,* Motilal to Gandhi dated January 1931.

4

Gandhi, Ambedkar and the Poona Pact, 1932*

As the struggle between Nationalism and Imperialism gathered momentum within India in the first half of the 20th century, the social cleavages which characterised the subcontinent—cleavages of religion, of community and of class—became a matter of serious concern to the participants in this grand confrontation. British statesmen who framed imperial policy and British civil servants who presided over its implementation, spent considerable time in locating these cleavages and in drawing them into the constitutional reforms which they devised in response to the growing sentiment of nationalism. As against this, the leaders of the nationalist movement attempted to highlight, historically as well as contemporaneously, the overarching solidarities within India, which held together different constituents of society, and offered the basis of nationhood to a civilisation which was as complex in its social configuration as it was monumental in its demographic proportions.

The differences between the several religious communities of India have, for reasons which are obvious, been a matter of very considerable historiographical debate over the past few decades. Such differences spring into bold relief the moment we explore the

*I am deeply obliged to my colleague, Dr. Hari Dev Sharma, for the help he has given me in writing this essay. His knowledge of the sources as well as the events associated with this period have made my task much easier than it would have been otherwise. However, any shortcomings in interpretation and analysis are to be attributed exclusively to the author.

texture of consciousness and the structure of identity within Indian society; and they constitute the motivators of social loyalty and political action in communities whose outlook is moulded substantially by elite or populist religious beliefs. So far as the British Government was concerned, these differences formed an essential ingredient of the constitutions which it devised for the governance of India; constitutions which sought to appease growing nationalist sentiment through allocating new resources of power to the colonial society. However, for the nationalist leaders, prominent among them Mahatma Gandhi, these very cleavages posed a challenge to be surmounted before the transformation of a civilisation of antiquity into a modern Nation was achieved. With respect to the Muslims, historians have focused upon Gandhi's inability to integrate this community within the framework of Indian nationalism as his greatest failure. Yet the Hindu-Muslim divide was not the only one with which the Mahatma had to reckon as the leader of a nationalist movement embracing an entire subcontinent. Within Hindu society, there were a number of social divisions which threatened to erupt into the open, at certain critical junctures, with consequences that could be disastrous for the cultural and political unity of the subcontinent. None of these cleavages held the dangerous possibilities which were presented by the divide between the caste Hindus, on the one hand, and the Untouchable communities, which stood outside the system of *varna,* on the other. Yet if Gandhi failed in healing the cleavages between Hinduism and Islam within the subcontinent, he was remarkably successful in preventing the emergence of a fatal divide between the caste Hindus and the Untouchable communities. Relations between these two constituents of Hindu society came to a head during the constitutional deliberations of 1932, not wholly without gentle prodding from the British Government, and it took a "fast unto death" by the Mahatma to heal a breach pregnant with the most disastrous possibilities.

In this essay, I propose to explore the constitutional crisis which obliged the Mahatma to embark upon a "fast unto death" in September 1932. What was Gandhi's vision of Hindu society and how did he seek to ameliorate the conditions of its Untouchable members? How did the leaders of the Untouchables react to the centuries of humiliation which Hinduism had heaped upon their followers? In what manner did the British Government prepare the ground for the battle royal between the caste Hindus, on the one hand, and the Untouchable communities, on the other, during the course of the deliberations leading to the Constitutional Act of 1935? What was the manner in which Gandhi met this challenge, and what were the resources of moral persuasion and political power which were available to him at this juncture? How was an agreement brought about between the two constituents of Hinduism under consideration? And finally, what was the impact of this agreement upon relations between the caste Hindus and the Untouchables; as well as upon the place which the Untouchables occupied within the world of Hinduism? These are some of the questions to which I shall seek answers in the rest of this essay.

I

To appreciate Gandhi's perception of Hindu society, and of the social divisions within Hinduism, it is necessary to commence with a brief review of his political activity in South Africa, during the decade and a half in which he founded the Natal Indian Congress and developed Satyagraha as an ideology and a mode of political action. The Indian community with which Mahatma Gandhi dealt in South Africa was atypical of indigenous society within the subcontinent of India. Gandhi had been invited to South Africa on legal business, by a Gujarati Muslim merchant, who formed a part of a mercantile class which had established itself with conspicuous success in South Africa. Yet the majority of Indians in South Africa were drawn from the lowly rural proletariat of the Presidency of Madras; and they provided labour for the farms and plantations owned by the British and the Boers, mainly the latter, in the countryside. Gandhi's achievement lay in forging these two distinctive constituents of Indian society into a formidable force, through the ideological weapon of Satyagraha and through the party which he conjured into existence. The success with which he handled the African situation is admirably reflected in the sentiments voiced by General Smuts, his adversary within the South African Government, when he learnt that the Mahatma was on his way to India in 1915: "The saint has left our shores", observed Smuts, "I sincerely hope for ever."[1]

Despite the limited range of the Indian community in South

Africa which Gandhi shaped into a cohesive political force, he became fully conscious, at this juncture, of the social divisions which had plagued Hinduism since times immemorial. As a social reformer, Gandhi was comparable to distinguished co-religionists like Bankim Chandra Chatterjee and Swami Vivekananda, who devoted their lives to the moral and material transformation of Hinduism.[2] Both Bankim and Vivekananda recognised caste as a social institution which stood in the way of a revitalisation of Hindu society and its ability to effectively face the western challenge. Both these reformers (and Gandhi shared their views) realised that prior to the 19th century, Hinduism was innocent of any notion like the *'umma'* in Islam; or the 'community' in Christianity; which could form the basis of a cohesive social formation geared to purposeful spiritual activity and secular endeavour. Hence they attempted to stimulate within Hindu society a sense of community comparable to the sense of community within Islam or Christianity. For such a consciousness to strike root, the division of Hindu society into castes and subcastes, had to yield to an entirely new social configuration, in which the differentiated constituents of Hinduism had been transformed into a homogenised social mass. Both in their writings and in their speeches, therefore, reformers like Bankim, Vivekananda and Gandhi spoke repeatedly of the necessity of a cohesive Hindu social order; just as they attacked those distinctions of caste and sect within Hinduism which undermined its capacity to act as a unified social entity.

Perhaps the transformation which Gandhi sought to bring about within Hindu society was first tried out by him in his ashram on the banks of the Sabarmati, near Ahmedabad. Sensing the schism between the caste Hindus and the Untouchables as the most fatal schism within Hindu society, Gandhi tried to introduce within the social community of Sabarmati Ashram, Untouchables who were to live with other ashramites on terms of equality and dignity. This revolutionary attempt at turning the (Hindu) 'world upside down', within the microcosm of the ashram, revealed to the Mahatma the full force of orthodoxy within Hinduism. Even his devoted wife Kasturba, who had thus far accepted his moral and social experimentation without demur, protested vehemently at the prospect of having to tolerate within the Ashram, as free and equal members, individuals drawn from the Untouchable castes.

Gandhi's views on caste and the social configuration of Hinduism underwent a subtle change around this period.[3] As he organised populist agitations of elemental power in Champaran, or in Kheda, or within the country as a whole, he became acutely conscious, on the one hand, of the indissoluble links which tied the Untouchables to the caste Hindus in relations of subordination and superordination; and on the other, of the necessity of an indirect rather than a direct attack upon caste, if success was to be achieved in any movement of social reform. At this juncture, therefore, Gandhi commenced speaking of a distinction between *varnashramadharma* as a prescriptive value, and caste as an existential reality. The former, so the Mahatma argued, was a philosophical ideal of classical origin which legitimised differential modes of economic activity in order to facilitate the cycle of productivity necessary to maintain the social order. There was nothing exploitative about the *varna* system as it was conceived. Nor did this system allocate to different castes positions of superiority or inferiority within the framework of Hindu society. As against the classical theory of *varna* organisation, caste as an existential reality reflected the degeneration of Hindu society over the centuries. This fall from a morally unexceptionable state had to be reversed if Hinduism was to regain its creative capacity in the 20th century. As the Mahatma observed:

> When we. . . have cleansed ourselves, we may have the four *varnas* according to the way in which we can express the best in us. But *varna* then will invest one with higher responsibility and duties. Those who will impart knowledge in a spirit of service will be called Brahmanas. They will assume no superior airs but will be true servants of society. When inequality of status or rights is ended, everyone of us will be equal.[4]
>
> Fight, by all means, the monster that passes for *varnashrama* today, and you will find me working side by side with you. My *varnashrama* accommodates many Panchama families with whom I dine with the greatest pleasure—to dine with whom is a privilege. My *varnashrama* refuses to bow the head before the greatest potentate on earth, but my *varnashrama* compels me to bow down my head in all humility before knowledge, before purity, before every person, where I see God face to face.[5]

Such a social vision enabled the Mahatma to face the British

Government of India with very considerable confidence, in the demands he put forth on behalf of Hindu society as a whole, not excluding the Untouchables, for *Swaraj*.[6] It was not as if there were no social divisions within Hindu society. Yet caste, as it existed contemporaneously, represented the vulgarisation of social institutions, which had been created in the remote past, to meet the requirements of an agricultural civilisation possessed of considerable moral stature and material creativity. Nevertheless, the relationship between the caste Hindus and the Untouchables was a very basic relationship within Hindu society, the erosion of which would cause the Hindu social order to disintegrate into chaos. It was the responsibility of morally sensitive Hindus to rectify the shortcomings of caste society and to face the 20th century with the vitality of their community fully restored. Yet any attempt from without at transforming the position of the Untouchables within Hinduism was doomed to failure; and it would cause as much social agony to the Untouchables as it would cause to the caste Hindus.

II

Gandhi's perception of Hindu society, and his prescription for its reform, stood wholly at variance with those of B.R. Ambedkar, the most distinguished thinker and political activist thrown up by the Untouchables in the 20th century. Here, it is appropriate to spell out, in very brief, a life sketch of Ambedkar, in order to appreciate his outlook as well as his opposition to the strategy of transforming Hindu society advocated by Mahatma Gandhi.[7] Ambedkar was born in the Mahar community of western India, which community, although untouchable in status, held a position of some importance in rural society in Maharashtra. His father had achieved the rank of a non-commissioned officer in the Indian Army; so that Ambedkar belonged to a family of some substance, and a community of some standing, notwithstanding the lowliness of his position in the scale of caste. Equally important was the fact that Ambedkar possessed an intellect which combined brilliance and incisiveness in finely balanced proportions. He was also fortunate in being supported by the Princely Ruler of Baroda for studies at Columbia University, in the U.S.A.; and thereafter, he spent some time at the London School of Economics. Though

Ambedkar formally studied law and economics, he had a broad interest in politics and sociology. This enabled him to arrive at a sensitive understanding of the place occupied by the Untouchables within Hinduism, and the social action which could ensure their uplift within the framework of Indian society.

Although Ambedkar occupied the position of Professor of Economics at one of the premier educational institutions of Bombay, he was also very active in public life, with the specific objective of promoting the welfare of his caste fellows. To this end he started an organisation called the *Bahishkrit Hitkarani Sabha*, as well as a fortnightly paper entitled the *Bahishkrit Bharat*. Besides, Ambedkar also conducted some agitations in Maharashtra having as their objective the removal of the indignities suffered by the Mahars and other Untouchables.

Ambedkar directed his formidable intellectual powers to a critical understanding of the social structure of Hindu society, with the objective of utilising this understanding for the purpose of social reform and political action. In an essay entitled "Castes in India", Ambedkar put before the Untouchables as well as the caste Hindus, one of the most perceptive critiques of Hindu society.[8] The basic characteristic of Hindu society, so Ambedkar argued, was that castes were not distinct entities by themselves, like social groups defined by terms like class and tribe. Castes constituted the organic constituents of a larger whole, wherein the relations of superiority and inferiority between different units were controlled by those who occupied the apex of society, namely, the upper castes; and who had, over the centuries, succeeded in generating a culture of dominance which obliged the inferior castes to accept their lowly position no less readily than the superior castes accepted their superior status. Although ostensibly such a social hierarchy drew sustenance from the philosophical framework of brahmanical Hinduism, in reality the various castes and subcastes had come into being through very different social processes. Some of the castes originated as tribal social formations; others were created through migrations and inter-marriage; others, yet again, owed their genesis to the rise of new sectarian movements. Yet whatever be their origin, the various castes and subcastes looked upon themselves as the primary constituents of Hindu society, and the social consciousness of their members was restricted to the spatial distribution of their fellows. The bedrock of the Hindu social order was provided by the rules of matrimony and kinship; and these rules, remarkable for their sharpness of definition, had enabled caste society to survive, with its basic features unaltered, over two millennia.

Not only did Ambedkar regard the relationship of superiority and inferiority between the different castes as basic to Hinduism, but he also believed that it was incapable of being transformed into an egalitarian social bond. Indeed, in speculating about the possibilities of reform within Hindu society, Ambedkar observed that since the caste order was underpinned and legitimised by the Shastric literature of Hinduism, it was virtually impossible to conceive of a situation where Hindus would cut themselves adrift from their spiritual heritage, and reshape their society into one sustained by the liberal principles of the 20th century. The Mahatma's attempt at widening the moral horizons of Hinduism and obliging orthodox Hindus to adopt a new social outlook was, according to Ambedkar, doomed to failure. This was so because Hindu philosophy and Hindu social thought rested upon the belief that men were inherently unequal; and that they ought to seek satisfaction in the different vocations and social hierarchies wherein they had been located through the workings of their *karma*. As Ambedkar observed in his essay entitled "Annihilation of Caste":

> Unlike the Mahatma there are Hindu leaders who are not content merely to believe and follow. . . . Yet how many Brahmins who break Caste every day will preach against Caste and against the Shastras? For one honest Brahmin preaching against Caste and *Shastras* because his practical instinct and moral conscience cannot support a conviction in them, there are hundreds who break Caste and trample upon the *Shastras* every day but who are the most fanatic upholders of the theory of Caste and the sanctity of the *Shastras*. Why this duplicity? Because they feel that if the masses are emancipated from the yoke of Caste they would be a menace to the power and prestige of the Brahmins as a class. The dishonesty of this intellectual class who would deny the masses the fruits of their thinking is a most disgraceful phenomenon.
>
> The Hindus in the words of Mathew Arnold are "wandering between two worlds, one dead, the other powerless to be born". What are they to do? The Mahatma to whom they appeal for guidance does not believe in thinking and can therefore give no guidance which can be

> said to stand the test of experience. The intellectual classes to whom the masses look for guidance are either too dishonest or too indifferent to educate them in the right direction. We are indeed witnesses to a great tragedy. In the face of this targedy all one can do is to lament and say—such be thy Leaders, O! Hindus.[9]

Ambedkar's perception of Hindu society, and of the values which informed its Brahmanical leadership, made it obvious to him that it would be impossible for the Untouchables to seek redemption *within* a social framework which condemned them to so lowly a position. In the evidence which he gave before the Southborough Committee in 1919, he advanced the view, that (like Muslims and Sikhs and Christians) the Untouchables, too, should be treated as a distinctive community in any future constitutional arrangements for the subcontinent. Indeed, to enable the Untouchables to exercise an effective voice in the representative councils being created at various levels in the polity, they should be given the right to vote in separate electorates. If the Untouchables were denied such a right; if they were given nothing more substantial than reserved seats in Hindu constituencies; then they would be unable to elect representatives who could voice their true interests. A leadership created through the provision of reserved seats in Hindu constituencies would be so much under the influence of the dominant upper castes, that it would be unable to perform the task of speaking for the Untouchables.[10]

Ambedkar further argued that since the Untouchables were a deprived community, educationally as well as in their access to economic resources, the conditions of franchise for them should be different from those of caste Hindus and others. Untouchables with relatively small holdings in property; or with relatively modest educational credentials; ought to be given the right to vote in order to enfranchise a sufficiently large number of such lowly individuals. Thus, by the second decade of the 20th century, Ambedkar had developed a very distinctive view of the place which the Untouchables should hold in any constitutional arrangements in India; and his view of what was appropriate for the Untouchables in a free polity stood at complete variance with the views entertained by Gandhi on this crucial aspect of national regeneration.

III

The conflicting views of Gandhi and Ambedkar on the possibility of transforming Hindu society from within created a major crisis during the political deliberations which preceded the Government of India Act of 1935.[11] As is well-known, at the First Round Table Conference convened to discuss the future constitution of India, notwithstanding the absence of any leader from the Indian National Congress, the assembled delegates from British India as well as from Princely India, took the momentous decision that the growth of nationalism in the subcontinent necessitated the creation of an all-India federal government free of British control. The assembled delegates also took the view that the provinces of British India, as well as the Princely States, should seek membership of such a federal polity as its autonomous constituents; and that the various minorities—particularly the great Muslim community—should extend their loyalty to the federal polity in return for constitutional guarantees and prerogatives of franchise that would safeguard their political interests as well as their cultural identity. Yet while it was relatively easy to secure a consensus on the desirability of a federal form of governance for India, the minority problem posed insurmountable difficulties, which proved difficult of resolution during the course of the Conference.

In the meanwhile, the Viceroy, Lord Irwin, took the initiative in persuading the leaders of the Indian National Congress, who were engaged in a movement of civil disobedience against the British Government, to participate in the Second Round Table Conference, which was due to assemble in London towards the close of 1931. The ground for such participation was prepared through a series of meetings between the Mahatma and the Viceroy. As a result of this summitry, Gandhi called off the civil disobedience movement; and he indicated his willingness to participate in the constitutional deliberations, after consulting his colleagues within the Congress. Immediately after the conclusion of the Gandhi-Irwin Pact, as it is termed, the Mahatma attended the Karachi session of the Indian National Congress. In Karachi his understanding with the Viceroy was endorsed; and he was chosen as the sole representative of the Congress to the Second Round Table Conference. However, this responsibility was bestowed on Gandhi on the understanding that he would work for a constitution wherein the minorities—Muslims, Sikhs and Christians—were assured that they would be consulted on *every* issue affecting their material and cultural interests; at the same time as the provision of separate communal electorates, which had created so much tension and strife in the political system, would stand cancelled.

Gandhi attended the Second Round Table Conference in London as the most outstanding political leader from India. Pitted against the Mahatma, in this Conference, were numerous British leaders of distinction, as well as fellow Indians, handpicked by the Imperial authorities, to represent these counterpoised (to nationalism) constituencies of class, community and religion, upon whom the British relied to retard the constitutional progress of India. In a memorable speech before the Federal Structure Committee, Gandhi spelt out the substantive issues facing the assembled delegates, British and Indian, in terms which admitted of very little ambiguity. The Indian National Congress which he represented was "if I am not mistaken, the oldest political organisation we have in India. . . it is what it means—national. It represents no particular community, no particular class, no particular interest. It claims to represent all Indian interests and classes. . . . [Above] all the Congress represents, in its essence, the dumb semi-starved millions scattered over the length and breadth of the land in its 700,000 villages, no matter whether they come from what is called British India or what is called Indian India."[12] Given so powerful a support base among the people, Gandhi argued, the demand of the Congress for *Purna Swaraj*, or complete independence, was the only legitimate solution of the Indian problem. Moreover, the Congress could be trusted to protect the interest of all classes and communities in the country; just as it could also be relied upon to sustain, as the spokesman of an independent polity, a relationship of equality between Great Britain and India within the framework of the British Empire. If a firm undertaking on the fundamental issue of freedom was forthcoming from His Majesty's Government, Gandhi argued, other questions—of relations between the federal polity and its constituent members; or the manner in which the rights of minorities would be protected—could be resolved without much difficulty.

The British Government, needless, to say, entertained a very different view of the manner in which the Round Table Conference could proceed to the business of framing a new constitution for India. As Ramsay MacDonald, the Prime Minister, told the assembled delegates, the real challenge before them lay in devising a system of representation whereby power could be equitably shared by different classes, communities and religious groups, before the shape of an independent all-India polity was hammered out.[13] The Prime Minister's statement immediately prompted Ambedkar to put before the Minorities Committee a document setting out the quantum of representation that was fair and equitable for the Untouchables in different popularly elected legislatures. In doing so, Ambedkar also challenged the Mahatma's assertion that the Congress represented all classes and communities in India, not excluding the Untouchables. Yet at this juncture there was no mention of separate electorates for the Untouchables by Ambedkar.[14]

However, when the members of the Minorities Committee took a decision slightly later, to resolve the vexed question of minority participation in any future system of representative government, through informal discussion between themselves, the problem became an extremely complicated one. The representatives of the Muslims, the Indian Christians, the Anglo-Indians, the Europeans and the Untouchables now put before the Prime Minister a joint proposal, not only setting out the quantum of representation adequate for their constituents in different legislatures: but also demanding on their behalf the right to elect their spokesmen through the agency of separate electorates.[15] In communicating the so-called Minorities Pact to the members of the Minorities Committee, Ramsay MacDonald observed that in the absence of any agreement between the representatives of different minorities, on the one hand, and the spokesman of the Congress, on the other, he would be obliged to take note of its provisions in any decision which His Majesty's Government took regarding the constitutional future of India.[16] Gandhi saw in Ramsay MacDonald's declaration a clear reflection of the "Divide and Rule" policy which apparently guided His Majesty's Government in its relations with the nationalist movement in India. The very composition of the Indian delegation to the Round Table Conference, whose members were nominated by the British Government, Gandhi observed, assured that no agreement would be reached. The solution, according to the Mahatma, lay in hammering out the fundamentals of a new constitution expeditiously without letting the deadlock in the Minorities Committee paralyse the work of the Conference as a whole. The policy of permitting "special interests" within Indian society, whether they were Muslims, or Sikhs, or other minorities, to hold back the progress of the entire country could hardly be looked upon as an equitable policy. Above all, it was the possibility of creating separate electorates for the Untouchables—a demand voiced in the minorities Pact, that Ramsay MacDonald had apparently endorsed—which pained the Mahatma most of all. Such a provision could only be advocated by those, so Gandhi observed, who were ignorant of social conditions in India or ill-disposed towards the country:

> Let this Committee and let the whole world know that today there is a body of Hindu reformers who are pledged to remove this blot of untouchability [stated the Mahatma in ringing tones]. We do not want on our register and on our census untouchables classified as a separate class. Sikhs may remain as such in perpetuity, so may Mohamedans, so may Europeans. Will untouchables remain untouchables in perpetuity? I would far rather that Hinduism died than that untouchability lived . . . . I don't mind untouchables if they so desire, being converted to Islam or Christianity. I should tolerate that, but I cannot possibly tolerate what is in store for Hinduism if there are two divisions set forth in the villages. Those who speak of the political rights of the untouchables don't know their India, don't know how Indian society is today constituted, and therefore I want to say with all the emphasis that I can command that if I was the only person to resist this thing I would resist it with my life.[17]

That Gandhi's emotively charged declaration reflected his determination to resist at all costs the delinking of the Untouchables from the mainstream of Hindu society was not uttered lightly, became apparent before long to all concerned. On his return to India from the Second Round Table Conference, the Mahatma was promptly put behind bars. From his prison cell in Yeravada, Pune, the fate of the Untouchables, whom he was soon going to rename the *Harijans* or the Children of God, continued to exercise his mind. In the spring of 1932, therefore, he addressed a communication to Sir Samuel Hoare, the Secretary of State for India, reiterating what he had said earlier before the Minorities Committee of the Second Round Table Conference; and formally recording his decision, as was his practice as a true *Satyagrahi*, to 'fast unto death' in the event of the creation of separate electorates for the Untouchables in any future constitution of India.[18]

The release by Ramsay MacDonald of the Communal Award on 16 August 1932, confirmed the worst fears of the Mahatma.[19] The constitution which the British Government proposed to create for India, observed the Prime Minister, could not turn a blind eye to the diversity of communities and the depth of social cleavages within the subcontinent. It was appropriate, in such a situation, to protect the interests of specific social groups through the device of separate electorates; and such a facility would henceforth also be extended to the Untouchables, in recognition of the demands put forward by their spokesmen. Besides conferring upon the Untouchables the right to vote with other members of the Hindu community in what were defined as general constituencies, the Prime Minister, therefore, also created "a number of special seats filled from Depressed Class electorates in the areas where these voters chiefly prevail".[20] The actual number of such seats created by the Award was 71. The only glimmer of hope lay in the assurance, also voiced by Ramsay MacDonald, that if the communities concerned came to an agreement between themselves, then the British Government would be prepared to substitute the terms and conditions of such an agreement for the terms and conditions spelt out in the Award. For the Mahatma, however, the die was cast. Soon after the announcement of the Communal Award, he formally communicated to the Prime Minister his decision to undertake, on 20 September 1932, a 'fast unto death', unless the provision of separate electorates for the Untouchables was cancelled before that date.[21]

IV

The publication on 13 September 1932 of the correspondence between Mahatma Gandhi, Ramsay MacDonald and Sir Samuel Hoare, precipitated a crisis of the most alarming proportions in India. "To find a parallel for (sic!) the anguish of September 1932 we have to go back to Athens twenty-three hundred years ago when the friends of Socrates surrounded him in prison and importuned him to escape from death,"[22] observed Chakravarti Rajagopalachari, a distinguished leader of the Congress very close to Gandhi. Yet it was not only in his immediate following that the prospect of the Mahatma, wasting away to an agonising death in his prison cell due to the sins of Hinduism and the indifference (or worse) of the British Government, shook men and women belonging to different classes, communities and religions to the very depth of their being.

Among the very first leaders to react to the threatened fast was the distinguished Liberal, Sir Tej Bahadur Sapru.[23] He pointed to the need for prompt action on the part of all parties, to save the Mahatma's life, and asked the Government of India, in particular, to release him from prison and restore to him freedom of movement and consultation. Sapru's plea was endorsed by G.D. Birla, the Marwari industrialist, who combined a freewheeling nationalist position with an intense personal admiration for the Mahatma.[24] Rajendra Prasad, one of the Congress leaders very close to Gandhi, came out with a similar statement of concern.[25] However, extremely significant, in the circumstances, was the reaction of Madan Mohan Malaviya, who spoke more authoritatively than any other leader for conservative and orthodox Hindu sentiment, whatever be its formal political colouring. Drawing attention to Gandhi's ceaseless endeavour for the uplift of the Untouchables, Malaviya appealed to their leaders as well as to the leaders of the caste Hindus to devise an agreement that would render it wholly unnecessary for Gandhi to undertake the projected 'fast unto death'. Malaviya also took the initiative in convening a meeting of caste Hindus and Untouchable leaders with the specific objective of hammering out an agreement that would oblige His Majesty's Government to amend the Communal Award.[26]

What was the response to the Mahatma's projected "fast unto death" among the Untouchable leaders? Predictably, Ambedkar's initial reaction was in keeping with his stance during the deliberations of the Second Round Table Conference. "I do not care for political stunts," he observed. "My decision stands. If Mr. Gandhi wants to fight with his life for the interests of the Hindu community the Depressed Classes will also be forced to fight for their lives to safeguard their interests."[27] Yet Ambedkar's views were not shared by all the leaders of the Untouchable community. Conspicuous among those who differed from Ambedkar was M.C. Rajah, an Untouchable leader from Tamil Nadu, a province with the dubious distinction of sheltering the highest proportion of "the wretched of Hindu society". Rajah, a member of the Central Legislative Assembly then in session at Simla, had a distinguished record of service for his community, and firmly believed that his caste fellows would have to organise themselves as an entity distinct from the upper castes to win for themselves a place of dignity within Hindu society. Indeed, even prior to the announcement of the Communal Award, Rajah had worked out in association with B.S. Moonje, a leader of the Hindu Mahasabha, a system of reservation of seats for the Untouchable community resting upon joint electorates. He now put forth his arrangement as the basis of a new accord; and simultaneously pointed out that the Communal Award was an attempt at transforming a community which was "socially untouchable" into one which would become "politically untouchable". Rajah also conveyed these sentiments to the Viceroy in the course of a long interview with him on 4 September.[28]

While the leaders representing different shades of Hindu opinion, orthodox, Gandhian and liberal, were on their way to Bombay in response to Malaviya's call, a Citizens Emergency Committee was constituted in that city, consisting, among others, of Mathuradas Khimji, Sir Purshotamdas Thakurdas, Sir Chunilal Mehta and G.D. Birla, with the objective of concerting measures to save the Mahatma's life. A meeting of this Committee was held on the 16th to plan an appropriate course of action. A decision was taken on the 16th to send a delegation to Poona, to ascertain, in discussion with the Mahatma, the possible conditions upon which an agreement could be framed. It was not clear to the mediators, at this juncture, whether Gandhi's objection to separate electorates for the Untouchables also extended to the reservation of seats for them. Of course, if the authorities had been a little less callous, and released for the public consumption a letter which Gandhi wrote to the Government of Bombay on 15 September, the members of the delegation would have found their task superfluous.[29] For Gandhi's position, as stated in this letter, was unambiguous. He was opposed to reservations since they would absolve caste Hindus of the moral responsibility of striving for the uplift of the Untouchables. Yet if the Untouchables so desired, the Mahatma would not oppose the reservation of seats for them. As was to be expected, the Mahatma reiterated this position before the leaders from Bombay who called upon him on 19 September.

No less reassuring than Gandhi's relatively flexible stance were developments within the Untouchable community during the crucial days preceding 20 September. It soon became obvious to the British Government as well as to the nationalist leadership that the Untouchables were quite literally split into two camps over the crucial issue put before them in so dramatic a form by the Mahatma. At public meetings of the Untouchables held in Nagpur, or Karachi, or Lucknow, or Lahore, their spokesmen voiced their confidence in the leadership of Gandhi; while the leaders of the community in Poona and Madras regarded the prospect of negotiations under intense moral pressure—that is, a "fast unto death"—as distasteful in the extreme.[30] Not surprisingly, the differences within his community obliged Ambedkar to soften his stance somewhat. On the eve of the Conference convened by Malaviya, he made it clear that he did not entirely rule out negotiations on the issue of joint electorates. "I desire to assure the public that . . . I am prepared to consider the proposals of Mr. Gandhi,"[31] he observed in a public statement. What may possibly have triggered off such a reconsideration on the part of Ambedkar was the likelihood of bloodshed in the country in the event of the Mahatma's martyrdom:

> I hope that Mr. Gandhi will desist from carrying out the extreme step contemplated by him [Ambedkar observed]. We mean no harm to Hindu society, when we demand separate electorates we do so in order to cancel total dependence on the sweet will of the caste Hindus in matters affecting our destiny. . . . Whether he knows it or not Mr. Gandhi's act will result in nothing but terrorism by his followers against the Depressed Classes all over the country. . . .
>
> It is still more important to note that Mr. Gandhi is releasing reactionary and uncontrollable forces and is fostering the spirit of hatred between the Hindu community and the Depressed Classes by resorting to this method and thereby widening the existing gulf between the two. . . .
>
> If Mr. Gandhi does not want all this to be repeated on a larger scale let him, for God's sake, reconsider his decision and avert the disastrous consequences. . . .[32]

Ambedkar's retreat from an earlier position of intransigence, and his realisation of the possibility of large scale violence if the Mahatma's call for a new relationship between the caste Hindus and the Untouchables went unheeded, constituted an appropriate backdrop to the Conference of Hindu and Untouchable leaders which opened in Bombay on 19 September. Prominent among the participants were Madan Mohan Malaviya (the convenor), Sir Tej Bahadur Sapru, M.R. Jayakar, Sir Chimanlal Setalvad, C. Rajagopalachari, Hridayanath Kunzru, B.S. Mooje and A.V. Thakkar, as representatives of the caste Hindus; and B.R. Ambedkar, M.C. Rajah and P. Baloo as representatives of the Untouchables. While the open sessions of the Conference were marked with a spirit of conciliation, the substantive negotiations were conducted at a closed meeting held on the 20th, between a few important Hindu leaders, on the one hand, and Ambedkar, on the other. The crucial breakthrough came as a result of a proposal mooted by Sapru, always the resourceful mediator. Sapru pleaded with Ambedkar to give up his insistence upon separate electorates; and proposed its substitution by a system of primary and secondary elections, which, while conforming to the principle of joint electorates, would in fact enable the Untouchables to chose their candidates. Ambedkar signalled his assent to the compromise formula advocated by Sapru, very much to the relief of all present on the occasion. It was agreed, therefore, that in regard to the 71 seats stipulated by the Communal Award, the Untouchable voters would, in the first instance, elect for each seat a panel of three or four candidates; which panel would then be put before the Untouchable and caste Hindu voters *jointly* for their choice. All that remained after this agreement was to persuade the Mahatma that it met his crucial requirement concerning the abolition of separate electorates for the Untouchables.[33]

At Yeravada Central Prison, Pune, in the meanwhile, on 20 September, the Mahatma was engaged in enacting a solemn ritual reflecting the profound moral crisis which had engulfed Hindu society.[34] He rose early in the day, and listened to his favourite hymn entitled "Vaishnava Jana", with the haunting refrain: "He alone is the true Vaishnava/Who knows and feels for another's woe," in the course of the morning prayer meeting. At 11.30 A.M. he had his 'last meal' prior to the 'fast unto death'. In its moral awesomeness and the lonely agony of a frail individual, the scene was reminiscent of a comparable scene enacted in Jerusalem two millennia ago. Around the Mahatma, anxious at heart, but calm in spirit and resigned of mood, stood a few faithful disciples like

Vallabhbhai Patel, Mahadev Desai, Pyarelal and Brijkishan, to be joined after a brief while by Kasturba and Sarojini Naidu. As the prison bell struck 12, at midday on the 20th, Gandhi's "tussle with God" commenced in right earnest. Shortly afterwards, the Mahatma spoke to newsmen within Yeravada Prison of the reasons which had obliged him to embark upon so extreme a step. Despite the gravity of the situation, he appeared the reverse of despondent. The Mahatma stated:

> I believe that if untouchability is rooted out, it will not only purge Hinduism of a terrible blight but its repercussions will be world-wide. My fight against untouchability is a fight against the impure in humanity. . . . You will, therefore, see that my fast is based first of all in faith in my cause, faith in the Hindu community, faith in human nature itself and faith even in the official world. My cry will rise to the throne of the Almighty God.[35]

On the second day of the fast, a deputation from the Bombay Conference consisting of Sapru, Chakravarty Rajagopalachari, Rajendra Prasad, Jayakar, Birla and Devadas Gandhi called upon the Mahatma to put before him, for his approval, the agreement which had been hammered out earlier with Ambedkar. Gandhi's initial response was favourable. But he asked for some time to consider the proposal in full. He also indicated a desire for a face-to-face dialogue with his principal adversary, Ambedkar.

While Ambedkar was on his way to Pune in response to the Mahatma's request, Gandhi continued his consultations with Sapru and his associates. To their surprise, he proposed an agreement even more generous than the Bombay Agreement, by suggesting that the provision of primary and secondary elections be extended to all the seats reserved for the Untouchables, instead of being applied only to the 71 seats mentioned in the Ramsay MacDonald Award. Gandhi also discussed his proposal with M.C. Rajah and P. Baloo, who, needless to say, had no hesitation at all in supporting his liberal initiative.

The meeting between Gandhi and Ambedkar, which was crucial to a successful resolution of the crisis, took place on the evening of the 23rd. The Untouchable leader, though somewhat subdued, was in no mood to surrender. At the very outset he told Gandhi: "Mahatmaji you have been very unfair to us."[36] Yet Gandhi was determined to charm his opponent into a conciliatory frame of mind. Referring to the system of primary and secondary elections which Ambedkar had accepted during the consultations at Bombay, he repeated what he had told Sapru and Rajah earlier. Why not extend such a system of election to *all* the seats reserved for the Untouchables? Ambedkar was overwhelmed by the liberality of the Mahatma's offer. Gandhi had thus achieved what, as a true Satyagrahi, he always strove for: He had won his opponent's heart! A mellowed Ambedkar confessed to the Mahatma: "I have made my concession, Mahatmaji, by accepting joint electorates. Your offer to accept primary elections for all the seats is very kind."[37] The differences between the two leaders, one an untouchable by birth; the other an untouchable by volition; were thus healed.

Although the meeting of the 23rd between Gandhi and Ambedkar did not bring matters to an instant conclusion, it made the task of the caste Hindus and the Untouchable leaders who met on the 24th relatively easy of accomplishment. The leading spokesman for the caste Hindus were Sapru, Jayakar, Birla and Rajagopalachari, while Ambedkar dominated the Untouchable delegation. A number of precise questions were thrashed out between the two sides; and the formal solutions to these questions were embodied in an agreement, which has come down to history as the Poona Pact. The draft of this agreement was sent across to the British Government, which, after carefully examining its provisions, set aside the sections of the Communal Award pertaining to the Untouchables. Once this happy state of affairs was achieved, the Mahatma was able to break his fast on 26 Setpember 1932.

V

What, we may ask in conclusion, were the enduring consequences of the Poona Pact? Was Gandhi's perception of the nexus between the caste Hindus and the Untouchables a valid perception? How real were the fears which he entertained regarding the consequences of providing separate electorates for the Untouchables? Would such a constitutional provision have created an unbridgeable gulf between the caste Hindus and the Untouchables, with disastrous consequences for both? And last but not the least: What did the caste Hindus gain through the Poona Pact? What were the tangible benefits which it conferred upon the Untouchables?

There can, of course, be no simple answers to such complex questions. Yet Gandhi's perception of Hindu society, and of the ties which bound the caste Hindus to the Untouchables, possessed a validity which scholars have come to appreciate more and more with the passage of time. Nor did Ambedkar differ very much from the Mahatma in his understanding of the structure of Hindu society. Where Ambedkar differed radically from Gandhi, was in his firm conviction, that the salvation of the Untouchables lay in shaping for themselves a new religious identity. Be that as it may, repeatedly, in the letters which he wrote to Ramsay MacDonald and Samuel Hoare, Gandhi stressed that the upper caste and the Untouchable communities, distributed in each one of half a million villages, were tied to each other through such intimate social and economic bonds, that their severence would cause an upheaval of disastrous proportions within the macrocosm no less than the microcosm of Hinduism. He also stressed the fact that no external agency, howsoever well intentioned it may be, could succeed in the liberation of the Untouchables. The solution had to come, so the Mahatma believed, from within Hindu society; and the solution was tied (in Gandhian language) to a "change of heart" among the caste Hindus, who presided over a system of social exploitation that was centuries old.

If Gandhi's perception of Hindu society was valid, then his fears about the possible consequences of separate electorates were probably equally valid. The provision of such a system of representation for the Muslims had demonstrated that separate electorates created more problems than it solved. Besides, the position of the Untouchables was radically different from that of the Muslims. Unlike the latter, the Untouchables constituted an organic part of Hindu society, howsoever lowly be the position which they occupied within it. To confer upon them the dubious privilege of separate electorates was to condemn them for ever to the status of Untouchables. As Gandhi put it: Should Untouchables be regarded as such for eternity? Or in the words of Rajah: The Communal Award would have the effect of transforming "social" into "political" Untouchables! Moreover, the constitutional engineering contemplated by the British Government carried the risk of exposing of millions of small communities of Untouchables, located in remote rural settlements, to harassment and worse at the hands of the caste Hindus. Gandhi was aware of such a possibility from the very outset. This realisation gradually dawned upon Ambedkar, too, in the course of the crisis.

The benefits which accrued to the Untouchables from the Poona Pact were, therefore, in the first instance, negative benefits. If the Communal Award had not been redrawn in the sections pertaining to the Untouchables, it is likely that an unlovely civil war would have erupted in Hindu society. In every village and hamlet of the land, caste Hindus would have utilised their local power to break up the Untouchables as a separate political formation. To prevent reform of the caste system from triggering off such a crisis, Gandhi stressed the need for a fundamental change in the social attitudes and the moral outlook of the upper castes—through persuasion and example—as an essential prerequisite for the liberation of the Untouchables. The Mahatma was determined to save Hindu society from caste warfare of the most monumental proportions; and to the extent the Untouchables were a part of Hindu society; to save them, too, from social annihilation. The results of the Poona Pact were, therefore, of the most profound significance for Hinduism. The agreement between the Mahatma and Ambedkar saved a society from turning upon itself and committing collective suicide. Indeed, the Poona Pact was a victory won by Gandhi in the course of a struggle seeking to liberate Hindu society from a dangerous malformation lodged in the very core of its social being. It was, perhaps, the Mahatma's finest hour.

NOTES

1. This quotation is taken from W.K. Hancock, *Smuts. The Sanguine Years*, (Cambridge, 1962), vol. I, p. 345. The three best sources for Gandhi's political activity in South Africa are: R.A. Huttenback, *Gandhi in South Africa, British Imperialism and the Indian Question, 1860-1914*, (London, 1971); M.K. Gandhi, *Satyagraha in South Africa*, Revised 2nd Edition, (Ahmedabad, 1961) and Pyarelal, *Mahatma Gandhi: The Early Phase*, Vols. I & II (Ahmedabad, 1965).
2. The two comprehensive studies on this theme are: C.H. Heimsath, *Indian Nationalism and Hindu Social Reform* (Bombay, 1964), and N.S. Bose, *The Indian Awakening & Bengal* (Calcutta, 1960).
3. See Dennis Dalton, "The Gandhian View of Caste and Caste After Gandhi"

Philip Mason, *India and Ceylon: Unity and Diversity* (London, 1967), pp. 159-181.

4. M.K. Gandhi, *Harijan,* 9 April 1936.
5. M.K. Gandhi, *Young India,* 22 September 1927.
6. See in this connection, L.I. & S.H. Rudolph, *The Modernity of Tradition, Political Development in India* (London, 1967) and my essay entitled "Class, Community or Nation". R. Kumar, *Essays in the Social History of Modern India* (Oxford, 1984), pp. 47-68.
7. See Dhananjay Keer, *Dr. Ambedkar, Life and Mission* (Bombay, 1962).
8. B.R. Ambedkar, "Castes in India", *Indian Antiquary,* Vol. XLI, May 1917.
9. Ambedkar's essay entitled "Annihilation of Caste" has a very curious history. It was initially written as an address before the *Jat-Pat-Todak Mandal* of Lahore, a body created under the auspices of the Arya Samaj, to reform Hindu society. However, when his hosts saw the draft of Ambedkar's address, their enthusiasm disappeared, and they postponed the meeting. Ambedkar, however, published the essay as a brochure. It is reproduced in *Baba Sabeb Ambedkar: Writings and Speeches* (Bombay 1979), Vol. I, pp. 22-96.
10. Evidence Before the Southborough Committee on Franchise: *Baba Saheb Ambedkar: Writings and Speeches* (Bombay, 1979), Vol. I, pp. 246-276.
11. The constitutional debate which led to the Government of India Act of 1935 is dealt with in a number of studies. Especially relevant here are the following (1) R.J. Moore, *The Crisis of Indian Unity 1917-1940* (Delhi, 1979), particularly chapters 3, 4, & 5; (2) J.M. Brown, *Gandhi and Civil Disobedience, The Mahatma in Indian Politics (1928-1934),* (Cambridge, 1972), particularly chapters 4, 5 & 6; Halifax, *Fulness of Days* (London, 1977); Viscount Simon, *Retrospect* (London, 1952).
12. *Indian Round Table Conference* (Second session) 7 September 1931 to 1 December 1931, *Proceedings of Federal Structure Committee and Minorities Committee,* Vol. I (Calcutta, 1932), p. 43, hereinafter cited as *IRTC.*
13. *IRTC,* Vol. III, See Speech by Ramsay MacDonald, pp. 1334-1336.
14. *IRTC,* Vol. III, Speeches by B.R. Ambedkar pp. 1337-38; 1341-42; 1336; and 1356-58.
15. *IRTC,* Vol. III For Text of the agreement, also called the Minorities Pact, see Appendix II, pp. 1394-1398.
16. *IRTC,* Vol. III, Speech by Ramsay MacDonald, pp. 1385-86.
17. *IRTC,* Vol. III, p. 1385.
18. M.K. Gandhi to Sir Samuel Hoare dated 11 March 1932: reproduced in Pyarelal, *The Epic Fast* (Ahmedabad, 1932), pp. 99-103. I have drawn extensively from this work of Pyarelal, and it is hereinafter cited as *The Epic Fast.*
19. The Communal Award by His Majesty's Government dated 16 August 1932: *Command Paper 4147 of 1932.*
20. Statement issued by Ramsay MacDonald on 16 August 1932, on the occasion of the Publication of the Communal Award: *See Command Paper 4147 of 1932.*
21. M.K. Gandhi to Ramsay MacDonald dated 18 August 1932, *The Epic Fast,* pp. 104-106.
22. See *The Epic Fast,* p. vii.
23. *Times of India,* 14 September 1932, p. 9.
24. *Times of India,* 14 September 1932, p. 10.

25. *Times of India*, 15 September 1932, p. 10.
26. *Times of India*, 15 September 1932, p. 9.
27. *Times of India*, 14 September 1932, p. 9.
28. *Times of India*, 14 September 1932, p.9.
29. M.K. Gandhi to the Government of Bombay, dated 15 September 1932, *The Epic Fast*, pp. 111-117.
30. For account of meetings of Untouchables in the main cities of India see *Times of India*, 19 September 1932, p. 12.
31. Interview with *Times of India*, 17 September 1932, p. 11.
32. Statement by B.R. Ambedkar, *Times of India*, 19 September 1932, p. 12.
33. *The Epic Fast*, pp. 51-52.
34. *The Epic Fast*, pp. 40-41 gives a moving account of the occasion.
35. *Times of India*, 21 September 1932, p. 11.
36. *The Epic Fast*, p. 59. It may be noted that Mahadev Desai and Pyarelal kept extensive notes of various interviews and meetings which Gandhi held during the course of the fast. Pyarelal has drawn extensively from these notes in writing *The Epic Fast;* and I have, in turn, utilised his account of the interviews and discussions.
37. Ibid., p. 61.

5

The Role of Urban Society in Nationalist Politics

Over the past two decades there has emerged a substantial corpus of historical literature on the rural classes which were drawn into the nationalist movement of the late 19th and 20th centuries. To an extent the agrarian bias of historical inquiry into the nationalist movement is an understandable bias. India was and very largely remains an agricultural society, and no political phenomenon in the subcontinent can be termed truly significant unless it also reaches out to the social classes which reside in the villages. The British Government, too, knew full well that whomsoever controlled the villages controlled India; and it was only when the nationalist movement, in the decades after 1920, drew increasingly upon the rural social classes that the Government yielded political control over India to the nationalist leaders.

Yet in all this the role of cities and of the urban classes remained a pivotal role, whose exploration is likely to add substantially to our understanding of nationalist politics in the subcontinent. That nationalism as an ideology first transformed the consciousness of certain urban social classes—particularly the urban notables and professional men; that the first organised expressions of nationalism found root in the cities, and from there spread to the towns and *qasbas* (of which we shall have more to say later); that the artisan classes of the traditional cities as well as the working classes of the new industrial cities made a very substantial contribution to the nationalist struggle; all these are phenomena that are well known to historians of modern India. However, what we lack is an integrated view of the place of cities and urban society in the structure and dynamics of nationalist politics. What was the structure of British authority over India? How did this structure relate to the web of urban society? How was British authority challenged by those classes within the urban realm which participated in the nationalist struggle? These are some of the questions to which the historian of modern India can profitably address himself in order to discern the role played by the urban classes in the struggle for political independence.

I

Before we examine the structure of British authority over India, particularly as it related to urban society, it may be profitable to analyse the spatial distribution and the social configuration of cities in the subcontinent as they were linked to each other and to rural society.

In a recent essay on this theme, I have referred to three inter-linked varieties of urban settlements in the country.[1] Urban society, at the basal level, was made up of petite settlements called *qasbas,* which were the market centres for small groups of villages whose consumer needs were partially met by these markets, and whose surplus produce was syphoned off by them to larger markets within the country and overseas. Above the *qasbas* and linked to them were towns of intermediate size which provided administrative, commercial and political coherence to a number of *qasbas* and their rural hinter-land. Superior still to such towns in their population and social complexity were urban settlements which we can describe as cities, and which presided over the constituents of urban society in a region. This three-tiered pyramid of urban society rested upon tens of thousands of villages whose agricultural activity sustained the economy of the region as a whole.

Our portrayal of the fabric of urban society, with the three tiers of the city, the town and the *qasba,* is brief to the point of caricature. But it is essential to convey some idea of the structure of this society if we are to explore the part played by its constituent classes in nationalist politics. The social ecology of urban settlements in the coastal region, particularly in the late 19th and early

20th centuries (which is the period with which we are concerned here), was different from those of urban settlements in the interior, and this difference related to the distinct economic roles which these settlements performed in the larger context of the social order. The coastal cities were industrial centres, as well as the ports of entry for industrial products from overseas, and ports of exit for the agricultural produce of the country to markets across the seas. In these cities, therefore, resided substantial elements of an industrial proletariat, drawn from the rural areas, and involved in the production of goods under the control of private owners of factories. The industrial bourgeoisie was the next most significant class in these cities, a class bearing a position in urban society out of proportion to its numbers, but linked to the concentration of economic power in its hands. Between the owners of industry, on the one hand, and the working classes, on the other, stood powerful communities of merchants as well as the professional bourgeoisie, whose education and culture, over and above their material interests, conferred on them a seminal role in the development of the nationalist struggle in India.

The urban settlements of the interior had a different structure than similar settlements of the coastal region. The cities of the interior lacked centres of industrial activity within their social matrix. The predominant economic activity in such settlements was of a mercantile character; and this activity related to the distribution of consumer goods, which entered the country through the port-cities, or were fabricated through indigenous industrial enterprise. Again, such urban settlements could also act as conduits for the transmission of the surplus agrarian produce to overseas markets through the mediation of the port-cities. Quite often, also, the cities of the interior housed substantial artisan classes, whose craft activity met the consumer requirements of the regions in which they were located. Over and above this, the cities of the interior also housed substantial professional classes—men employed in the civil service, or in vocations like law, medicine, journalism and teaching—though it is important to remember that the professional classes of the interior lacked that access to western ideas that shaped the worldview of their peers in the coastal cities.

As the literature on colonial society in modern India reveals, there were two parallel and mutually reinforcing channels which upheld the authority of British Government over India. At one level, the British Government had built a system of informal alliances with certain classes in society—the most obvious examples being the landed magnates in rural society and the urban notables who performed a variety of roles in the cities—which extended powerful support to the British Raj in return for the protection of their special interests.[2] This system of informal alliances was backed by a military presence, which ensured that any challenge to imperial authority would be crushed expeditiously. The spatial distribution of military power, as the supportive constituent of a system of class collaboration, to which we have already referred, broadly followed the spatial structure of urban society, to which we have also referred earlier. Most of the important cities were not only centres of administrative, industrial and commercial power, but they also housed very substantial cantonments or military stations, discreetly set apart from the rest of the city, yet present as a grim reminder of the ultimate sanction behind British rule over India. The administrative and judicial institutions of British rule fanned out from the cities, through towns of intermediate size. to the *qasbas,* and they were buttressed by a number of military stations, big and small, which ensured that all challenges to British authority would be effectively met very early in their career. Broadly speaking, the structure of military authority and its spatial distribution had taken firm shape by the first quarter of the 19th century, though the Uprising of 1857, on which we shall dwell briefly hereafter, encouraged the British Government to bring about some changes in the racial composition of the army in India and the military technology that was entrusted to native contingents of this army.

II

Even though the Uprising of 1857 does not form a part of the nationalist movement, as defined for the purposes of the present essay, we can gain an appreciation of the texture of British military authority, its distribution in space as well as its linkage with urban society, if we explore the mechanisms by which British power collapsed in the Gangetic plain, in the space of a few weeks, in the summer of 1857. The "mutiny" broke out initially in the cantonment city of Meerut, which was located in close proximity to the former imperial capital of Delhi. From Meerut the "mutiny" spread to Delhi, and it was the revolting sepoy regiments of Meerut who marched to the erstwhile Mughal capital and persuaded their fellows in Delhi to rise against authority and confer upon the ageing Mughal Emperor the shadow of imperial authority over the country as a whole. From Delhi the seeds of disaffected rural notables and downwardly mobile landed which housed the administration (executive and judicial) of the district officers, in addition to modest contingents of the British army. The initiative in staging an uprising was in each case taken by the sepoys stationed in the district towns, who attacked administrative and judicial offices after eliminating their British officers. In the next stage, the revolting sepoys were joined by substantial sections of the urban population, often led by dispossessed and disaffected rural notables and down wardly mobile landed magnates resident in the city. It was only in the final stage that revolt against the imperial authority spread out to the villages, affecting, as some detailed studies have shown, different classes of rural society, some of which were wholly or partially stripped of their possessions under British Raj while others perceived in its institutional and legal framework a threat to their social identity.[3]

The mechanisms of revolt which we have sketched above for the Delhi-Meerut region, urban and rural, also indicate how British authority crumbled in 1857 throughout the Gangetic plain. In the North-Western Provinces, as they were then constituted, cities like Bareilly and Aligarh were the regional centres of revolt. In Avadh, which stood apart from provinces which had experienced direct British rule for substantial periods, the pattern of revolt was basically similar. The same was true of Bihar, where Patna and some other urban centres, which were equally the basis of military and administrative power, were the first to witness localised uprisings, and it was only thereafter that the social classes of the smaller towns, and of the villages, raised the banner of revolt against the British Government.

A portrayal of the manner in which British authority over the Gangetic plain crumbled in 1857 substantiates our contention that urban settlements, big and small, were the true bases of British military authority over India. It is equally true, as we have suggested earlier, that this authority provided the underpinning to the informal political alliances which the British Government had contracted with powerful sections of Indian society, like the landed gentry and the urban notables, to mention only two. Here it needs to be stressed that the political alliances which sustained British rule were very fragile alliances, at least in the first half of the 19th century, and it was only because they were backed by military power, distributed through an intricate network of cantonments and military stations over the subcontinent, that British authority appeared so formidable. The moment British military power disintegrated through the tensions which had accumulated within the army over half a century, the Raj stood exposed as a paper tiger, with little capacity to survive as a purely political phenomenon.[4]

III

The manner in which the British Government in India rebuilt its military and administrative infrastructure after 1857 has been spelt out in a number of scholarly studies.[5] Here we can do no more than to refer in passing to the findings of such studies before we resume our analysis of the role of the urban classes in the national movement. At the political level, the system of alliance which the British Government had attempted to build even earlier, with important classes within Indian society, was reinforced through extending concessions to the ruling princes and the landed magnates, on the one hand, and the peasant proprietors, adversely affected by the market economy introduced under colonial aegis, on the other. Besides, for the first time the British Government tried to set up, at the imperial level in Calcutta, as well as at the provincial levels, mechanisms for consultation in the form of embryonic legislative institutions, through the induction of individuals drawn from the landed classes, who were regarded as the natural leaders of the people. Over and above this, the British Government also attempted to create within the cities centres of civic and municipal activity, which would draw the rapidly growing educated and professional classes into a framework of politics that would link them in bonds of sympathy to British rule over India. Such changes in political strategy were accompanied by a radical overhaul of the military system in India. This overhaul was directed much more at the ethnic composition of the army than it was directed at its spatial distribution, in contingents big and small, in the urban network to which we have referred earlier. Briefly speaking, the British component of the army was reinforced in a substantial way. In addition to this, the recruitment base for Indian soldiers was completely transformed, particularly so far as the Gangetic plain was concerned. The pre-1857 armies had been largely drawn from the upper caste village zamindars, thakurs, brahmans and bhumiyars, of the middle regions of the Gangetic plain. Thereafter, the Indian army was predominantly recruited from the more modest peasant proprietary classes of the Punjab and the border regions. Finally, the artillery units were made an exclusive preserve of British officers and men. Through such a strategy, which, on the one hand, reinforced British military power over India, and on the other, established a new framework of consultation between the colonial state and powerful classes within Indian society, the British attempted to place their domination over the subcontinent on a firm and enduring basis.

IV

Our examination of the part played by the urban classes in the nationalist movement, which became so significant a political phenomenon in India towards the closing decades of the 19th century, can best be conducted in the context of the bases of British military and political power which we have sketched above.

Although the professional classes in the cities had been allocated a role of considerable significance in the political system which the British Government conjured into existence after 1857, it would be a mistake to imagine that their newly awakened political consciousness, a consciousness which encouraged them to redefine the political identity of India in terms of a "Nation-State" on the Western model, was contained within the framework devised by the British Raj. Even the sectional interests of the professional bourgeoisie could not be fully satisfied by the structure of politics which the British Government had created in the closing decades of the 19th century. However, a number of scholarly works reveal that the professional classes looked upon themselves as a supra-class social category exercising responsibility for the "Nation" as a whole; although this national interest was perceived within the frawework of the market economy and the capitalist order.[6] Within the confines of a vision shaped by such a social system, the educated classes, particularly those based in the cities of Calcutta, Bombay and Madras, expressed themselves through a politics which refused to acquiesce in a role strategically subordinate to that of the British Government over India. Within a few decades of the Uprising of 1857, therefore, the professional classes within the urban realm were able to create for themselves political institutions which articulated their newly discovered consciousness, and they conceived in the Indian National Congress an organised movement for the realisation of the destiny of the "Indian Nation".

Although the political strategy of the professional classes was never clearly spelt out in the first few decades after 1857, it is clear that their leaders (a) looked upon institutions like the Indian National Congress as an embryonic parliament of the people of India, and (b) gradually envisaged the transfer of political power from British into Indian hands. In spelling out such a strategy, the educated classes seemed to believe that the destiny of the Indian Nation, as they conceived it, could be decided by them, in a dialogue with the British Government, without reference to the social classes residing in the villages. This was so despite the fact that some leaders of the Indian National Congress tried to reach out to the peasantry, or the tenantry (depending upon whether they were located in a ryotwari or a zamindari region), and relate their grievances as well as their social activism to the nationalist struggle.[7]

Although the social base of organised nationalism in the 19th century was confined to the professional classes within the cities, the strategy of political action outlined above did not exhaust the ideological resources of these classes. We are referring here to the revolutionary movement of the first two decades of the twentieth century, which sought to overthrow the edifice of empire through militant action, of a terrorist variety, rather than through constitutional means. In the first instance, it is important to remember that, with the possible exception of the Punjab, the revolutionary movement were drawn from a lower strata of the educated classes. These social groups rejected the constitutional strategy held out by their peers in the Indian National Congress, and sought to overthrow British authority through violent means. We have little reason to believe that the urban classes dedicated to the violent overthrow of British rule had any links with the rural classes in their respective regions. Despite the absence of such a link, however, their theory of revolutionary action envisaged a scenario in which they would, through heroic acts of terror (like the assassination of key British officers) destroy the psychological hold of the British Government over the people of India, and encourage them to rise in an insurrection against their alien rulers. This was a theory of political action which had found formal expression in 19th century Tzarist Russia, where the intelligentsia not only dreamt of triggering off a successful revolution through acts of violence, but backed their strategy by "going out to the rural people" in a bid to raise their level of political consciousness.

V

When Gandhi entered nationalist politics in the second decade of the twentieth century, the political consciousness of the urban classes—professional, petty bourgeois and working—acquired a new militancy in the context of the dialogue between nationalism and imperialism within the subcontinent. Gandhi applied to nationalist politics the strategy of militant non-violence, as a strategy particularly well-suited to the needs of the anti-imperialist struggle in India. In the first instance, it is important to remember, the organisational instruments which Gandhi created (the Satyagraha Sabhas) or usurped (the Home Rule Leagues) for the promotion of his movements were largely urban in social character.[8] As a scholarly survey conducted recently indicates, the Rowlatt Satyagraha, the first nationwide agitation to be launched under the aegis of Gandhi, was mainly confined to the cities and towns, big and small, in the subcontinent. Here, too, the intensity of the agitation against the Rowlatt Act varied greatly from region to region, and city to city, depending upon the character of the local discontents which Gandhi was able to draw into his moral crusade.[9] However, the scale of the agitation, as well as the manner in which it sought to paralyse the Imperial Government were novel, and it was this combination of scale and novelty (of agitational technique), which provoked the authorities into brutal acts of repression, more particularly in the province of the Punjab and in the city of Amritsar.

When we look at the non-cooperation movement of 1920-22,

which Gandhi launched close on the heels of the Rowlatt Satyagraha, then the role of the urban classes in the new style of nationalist politics introduced by Gandhi becomes even more crucial than before. The tactics adopted by Gandhi were designed to paralyse, through militant yet non-violent action, some of the key institutions of British rule over the country, namely, those of the administration, the judiciary and education. The professional and commercial classes were destined to play a key role in the paralysis of such institutions, as well as in the paralysis of British commerce in India. Gandhi hoped to draw the urban classes solidly into his agitations, and he believed that if they refused to extend cooperation to British imperialism in India, then the British Raj would collapse like a house of cards.[10] Only in the final stages of the onslaught were the rural classes to be drawn into the fray, through their refusal to pay to the British Government the taxes which were due to it. For reasons connected with facility of organisation and political education, the Gandhian programme, so far as it concerned the urban classes, and the institutions of government resting within the cities, was set in motion with devastating consequences for British rule in 1920 and 1921. Gandhi thus largely depended on the urban classes, in the first instance, to win the battle which he was waging against the British Empire. While it is true that the message of the Mahatma went beyond the cities and towns, big and small, to transform the consciousness of the rural classes, it is also true that Gandhi was extremely cautious about drawing such classes into the nationalist struggle. So far as the ryotwari regions were concerned, the position was a relatively straightforward one, since the peasant-proprietors in such regions were involved in a direct economic relationship with the British Government. But in the zamindari areas, the rural social structure was more complex, and there was every "danger" of a no-tax campaign being transformed into a no-rent campaign, thus triggering of a species of class warfare which Gandhi was anxious above everything else to avoid. Paradoxically, therefore, although Gandhi has gone down in the history of the freedom struggle as the leader who took the struggle against the British Government from the cities to the villages, it is also true that the danger of class warfare in rural society prevented Gandhi from making use of the rural classes, in the anti-imperialist struggle, in the same manner in which he made use of the urban classes.[11]

Even within urban society, the Gandhian agitations against the British Government were mounted with great caution and restraint. Thus although Gandhi had acquired considerable experience as a proletarian leader, in the course of the Ahmedabad textile workers' strike, and although he had propounded a full-blown theory of Capital-Labour relations, as the basis of non-violent action by the working classes, it is beyond dispute that the working classes were not drawn in any significant measure into the non-cooperation movement of the 1920s, or even the campaign for civil disobedience which he waged in the 1930s.[12] Why this was so is not difficult to discern. Gandhi knew full well that individuals, no less than social classes, needed a substantial measure of education before they could be drawn into the satyagraha mode of political action. Apart from the workers residing in Ahmedabad, Gandhi had not been able to influence their fellows in any significant measure with his political ideology, in contrast to the influence he exercised over the commercial classes, the professional classes and the petty bourgeois in the cities of India. Because of this, Gandhi was reluctant to draw a volatile class, acutely conscious of its organised power, into a nationalist struggle which could very easily transform itself into class warfare within Indian society. We have reason to believe that the working classes were involved to a certain limited extent in movements like the non-cooperation campaign of 1920-22, but such participation came about under the influence of Khilafat leaders, or "socialist" leaders, who took the initiative in joining the nationalist struggle in the hope of securing through such participation sectarian or class objectives.

It would, in this context, be a mistake to imagine that the classes politicised by Gandhi exhausted the list of those who participated in the nationalist struggle so far as urban society was concerned. In the decade after World War I, the working classes in industrial centres like Bombay, Ahmedabad, and Calcutta (among others) were organised in a powerful trade union movement, which was as conscious of the conflict between nationalism and imperialism as it was conscious of its class interests. This movement had three ideological facets: the workers of Ahmedabad had organised themselves along Gandhian lines, though they were unique in this respect. In Bombay, in Calcutta and in other industrial centres, the trade union movement was either dominated by a socialist leadership, which sought to radicalise nationalist politics, or it was controlled by a liberal leadership, which believed that the working class should keep away from the political struggles that characterised the contemporary scene.[13] During the nationalist movement of 1920-22, working class organisation was at a relatively undeveloped stage, and the members of this class did not feature very significantly in the agitations of these years. However, within a decade, the working class movement had acquired considerable organisational strength and political consciousness, largely under socialist leadership. When the leadership of the Indian National Congress, under Gandhi, sought to launch a campaign of civil disobedience against the British, the organised working class seemed capable, jointly with other classes, urban and rural, of delivering a death-blow to British rule over India. The reaction of the British Government to the threat of united action on the part of the professional and the working classes is revealing. We have spoken earlier of the manner in which the informal alliances which the British Government had contracted with certain social classes were backed by the military power of the garrisons and cantonments distributed in the cities and towns of the subcontinent. In the case of any renewed nationalist assault on British institutions, comparable to the assault launched in 1920-22, the British were confident of their capacity to frustrate the designs of Gandhi and the leadership of the Indian National Congress. However, this confidence rested upon the assumption that the nationalists would be unable to destroy the communication system which linked the principal cities of the subcontinent to each other, and also linked each city to the townships and *qasbas* within a region. The prospect of a non-violent struggle, that would not only paralyse institutions like the administration, the judiciary, and schools and colleges, but would also undermine the communication system (since the railway workers had been unionised under radical premises) greatly alarmed the British Government. Such a fusion of bourgeois and radical nationalism within urban society, even if it did not reach out to the villages, could spell the end of British rule over India. Hence, in the late 1920s the British Government struck with great force at the socialist movement in India, which controlled a substantial proportion of the workers in the factories as well as in the railway system, by incarcerating the leaders of this movement in the remote city of Meerut.[14] With the Marxist leaders removed from the scene of action, British officials in Delhi as well as in the provincial capitals were confident that they would be able to defeat the Gandhian movement, whose lineaments they had come to recognise so well through the encounters of 1920-22.

It would be interesting to speculate as to whether a paralysis of the institutions of government in the cities could by itself have destroyed British rule over India. It is difficult to make any categorical assertion in this regard, because the Gandhian campaigns of the 1920s and the 1930s rested upon social support from urban society which varied greatly from region to region and from city to city. The historical literature on nationalism assumes that the participation of the rural classes was essential to the success of the nationalist cause. It would be difficult to wholly reject this perception. Yet it would also be difficult to deny that a paralysis of the institutions of urban society, particularly if accompanied by a breakdown of communications between different regions, and within different regions, could seriously endanger imperial authority over India. Perhaps the erosion of imperial authority in the cities by *itself* was insufficient to deliver the *coup de grace* to the British Government. At the same time an urban uprising was an *essential* pre-condition to such a consummation, if only for the reason that the institutions, civil and military, through which the British Government could re-establish its hold over rural society were largely located in the cities. All this is exemplified by the Uprising of 1857, to which we have already referred. It is also exemplified by the Uprising of 1942, when the breakdown of British authority in the cities, towns and *qasbas,* within the Gangetic valley (and in some regions outside the Gangetic valley) was as striking a phenomena as it was in 1857. Perhaps the role of the urban classes in the nationalist movement, as we have sketched it out, was crucial in two respects. In any attempt at revolutionary change, the initial responsibility for organisation and politicisation inevitably falls upon the urban classes. The participation of the urban classes is also necessary to ensure the success of a revolutionary movement. Yet by themselves, both these pre-conditions may not suffice in bringing about a revolutionary transformation. Over and above what men, and social classes, can do in the cities, they need the cooperation of their fellows in the villages, before they can mount a successful attack on established authority within a political system.

NOTES

1. R. Kumar, "The Changing Structure of Urban Society in Colonial India," *Indian Historical Review,* Vol. V. No. 1-2.
2. This view has been expressed in a number of scholarly studies. The two classic statements of this position from the "elite" and the "class" view, respectively, are: (a) A. Seal, *The Emergence of Indian Nationalism* (Cambridge, 1968) and (b) A.R. Desai, *The Social Background of Indian Nationalism* (Bombay, 1959).
3. See, for instance, the essays on this theme in E. Stokes, *The Peasant and the Raj* (Cambridge, 1978).
4. The best factual account of the Uprising of 1857, which spells out clearly the mechanisms of the upsurge, still remains S.N. Sen's *Eighteen Fifty-seven* (New Delhi, 1957).
5. For changes in civil and military policy after 1857 see: T.R. Metcalf, *The Aftermath of Revolt: India, 1857-1870* (Princeton, 1965) and H.L. Singh, *Problems and Policies of the British in India (1859-1898),* (Bombay, 1963).
6. The argument that the intelligentsia sought to articulate the interests of the "Nation" as a whole is succinctly put forward by B. Chandra, *The Rise and Growth of Economic Nationalism in India* (New Delhi, 1966).
7. For an attempt on the part of the Poona intelligentsia to reach out to the ryots of western India, see R. Kumar, *Western India in the Nineteenth Century* (London, 1968), pp. 174-175. For similar attempts by the Bengali intelligentsia around this time, see Seal op. cit., pp. 222-224.
8. See H. Owen, "Organising for the Rowlatt Satyagraha of 1919" in R. Kumar (ed.), *Essays on Gandhian Politics* (Oxford, 1971).
9. See "Introduction" by R. Kumar in *Essays on Gandhian Politics* (Oxford, 1971).
10. See *Collected Works of Mahatma Gandhi,* Vol. XXI for Gandhi's position in this regard.
11. See, for this view, the concluding chapter of Kapil Kumar, *Peasants in Revolt* (New Delhi, 1984).
12. Vide R. Kumar, "Nationalist Politics in the City of Bombay, 1920-32", in D.A. Low, *Congress and the Raj* (New Delhi, 1977).
13. R.K. Newman, 'Labour Organisation in the Bombay Cotton Mills, 1918-1929' (University of Sussex Ph.D. Thesis, 1980).
14. *NAI (National Archives of India)* See Note Section of File No. Home Political 18/XXVI of 1928.

6

The Secular Culture of India

The transformation of India from a classical civilisation to a national polity, simultaneously undergoing a change in the means whereby material life is sustained through social production, poses several questions to scholars in the social sciences. Some of these questions pertain to the character of the traditional social order; others relate to the nature of the transformation which the subcontinent has undergone, in the political no less than in the economic domain, over the past two centuries; others, yet again, touch upon the texture of the cultural values which need sustenance if the vision of a creative society, resting upon a modicum of material affluence; upon social and economic equity; and, last but not the least, upon catholicity of outlook and social tolerance, is to be realised in the years which lie ahead.

In this essay, I propose to explore some of the issues raised above, partly to gain an insight into the character of Indian civilisation; and partly also to illumine the structure of the political society which is crystallising contemporaneously in our midst. For this purpose I shall, in the first instance, dwell upon the social and intellectual texture of traditional society in India. Next, I shall focus upon the changes which British imperial domination induced in the subcontinent; and the response of the people of India to the imperial presence. The last section of the essay shall be devoted to an examination of contemporary reality and potentialities. Therein, I shall dwell upon the ideological trends which define political society in India; and suggest a prescriptive worldview which can, so I believe, constitute the basis of an enduring and liberal social democracy in the country.

I

It is for our purposes important to look at the moral and material characteristics of Indian civilisation, as it crystallised over the centuries, before we proceed to survey the contemporary scene. Perhaps the very use of the term civilisation has a significance which needs to be highlighted in this context. It implies the primacy of social institutions; the primacy also of cultural and religious values; as the basis of the social order. That India has a history which goes back to three millennia and more is something upon which there is a consensus amongst scholars. Yet the continuity of Indian civilisation rests not so much upon political institutions as it rests upon social institutions and the dissemination of a corpus of religious values among different classes and communities in the subcontinent. The civilisation of India was also geared to a cycle of agricultural activity, to support material life, and this activity very substantially determined the total ordering of society. Hence the fact that the great epicentres of Indian civilisation were located in the plains of the Indus and the Ganga in the north; and those of the Mahanadi, the Godavari, the Krishna and the Cauvery in the south. Over the centuries, the people living in these riverine regions had conjured into existence a round of economic activity, and a set of social institutions (of which more later), which were designed to produce the agricultural wealth which sustained material life. Indeed, the structure of rural society, with a central place occupied by the cultivating classes, which were linked by ties of patronage and prescription to numerous artisanal and menial groups; and the fabric of caste society, with the interlocking institutions of varna and jati; has to be looked upon as the praxiological answer of the Indian genius to the needs of sustaining production in an agricultural society. The striking feature of this social organisation was the premium which it put on self-sufficiency and survival without necessarily achieving a high level of productivity. This is not to reactivate the myth of an unchanging rural society which featured so prominently in our historical perception of the past till very recently. This is merely to emphasise the fact that substantially self-regulating village communities, scattered over the face of the subcontinent, and characterised by relatively weak economic and cultural interaction with one another, constituted the distinctive feature of rural society over the centuries. Hence the vision of a timeless and static world which surfaces again and again in the historical literature on Indian civilisation. The classic formulation of this vision is to be found in the memoranda penned by British civilians of the 19th century, who, while they overstated the case for changelessness, nevertheless grasped an essential truth about the structure and configuration of rural society in India:[1]

> The Village Communities are little Republics, having nearly everything they want within themselves, and almost independent of any foreign relations [observed Sir Charles Metcalfe]. They seem to last where nothing else lasts. Dynasty after dynasty tumbles down; revolution succeeds to revolution; Hindu, Pathan, Mughul, Mahratta, Sikh, English, are masters in turn; but the village communities remain the same. In times of trouble they arm and fortify themselves; a hostile army passes through the country; the Village Community collect their cattle within their walls, and let the army pass unprovoked; if plunder the devastation be directed against themselves and the force employed be irresistible, they flee to friendly villages at a distance, but when the storm has passed over they return and resume their occupation.

Although the social characteristics of Indian civilisation can be related to the needs of an agricultural order, this does not mean that such material factors in themselves explain everything about structure and values in Indian society. Indeed, a given material base offers a variety of praxiological possibilities to the creative psyche, so far as the fabrication of social institutions and religious worldviews is concerned. The actual delineation of the social institutions and religious worldviews of India is a matter of empirical inquiry; and illustrates how the collective genius of India responded to the challenge of creating a viable and enduring civilisation in the subcontinent. It is, indeed, instructive to look at the ideological as well as the structural configuration of Hindu society from such a perspective. To start with, the definition of Hinduism is a task so beset with difficulties that it baffles even the classical scholar. Yet for our purposes it would suffice to look upon this religion as constituted of a loose constellation of values and beliefs articulated in a social order characterised by a distinctive structural identity. The seminal constituents of Hindu religion are to be found in a few texts like the Upanishads, the Bhagavad Gita and the Vedanta Sutras. Yet the intellectual notions informing these texts find reflection in a wide range of philosophical trends, sectarian movements, devotional orders and folk cults which are located in different sectors of the social order. Indeed, this luxuriant growth of spiritual subsystems makes it obvious that the unifying principle of Hinduism lies in social structure rather than in doctrinal identity. Hindu society, in other words, is made up of a large number of endogamous units called *jatis;* each one of which rests upon well defined rules of social conduct and social interaction. More likely than not, the members of a *jati* originally enjoyed a localised distribution in geographical space; and different *jatis* were related to each other through a scheme of hierarchical organisation known as the system of *varna.* The diverse forms of belief and allegiance that taken altogether aggregated into the Hindu religious worldview, were lodged in one or the other of the *jatis* which went into the making of the Hindu social universe. But as already emphasised, social control in Hinduism—unlike social control in religions like Judaism, Islam or Christianity with a sharp doctrinal focus—lay much more in the normative structure of the *jatis* than in allegiance to any one of the cults, denominations and sectarian movements which proliferated in the subcontinent.

The assertion that the material creativity and the intellectual values of Hindu society flowed from an agricultural civilisation should not be taken too literally. For evidence about the past makes it clear that the existence of urban settlements; and the existence also of artisanal and commercial productivity; was very much a part of the social order since, at the very latest, the times of the Buddha. Indeed, any survey of Indian civilisation over the past two and a half millennia cannot overlook the place of urban society and craft productivity and commercial activity in the social economy. There were periods in the history of India—the middle of the first millennium B.C.; or the first few centuries of the Christian era; or the 16th and 17th centuries, among others—when cities, big and small, and craft production or trade appeared to be a fairly important facet of social activity; just as there were periods when a breakdown of the urban order and a ruralisation of society appears to have taken place. Yet once we have taken note of the presence of an urban culture, it remains to be emphasised that the major influences, material or intellectual, which went into the making of Indian civilisation related to the round of secular and spiritual activity in rural rather than in urban society.

II

Any portrayal of the moral and material texture of Indian civilisation which focuses exclusively upon the religious worldview and the social institutions of Hinduism would be untrue to the complexity of the social order in the subcontinent. Indeed, even during the centuries when Hindu society was crystallising in the valleys of the Indus and the Ganga, new tribal and warrior communities from Central or West Asia poured into the region, bringing with them alien worldviews and modalities of corporate life. However, most of these warrior communities, with their exotic gods and novel social institutions, were slowly but surely absorbed within the Hindu fold. The resilience of the institution of *varna;* which could accommodate a new clan or tribal community within the Hindu social constellation as yet another *jati;* and the catholicity of Hindu religious belief; wherein strange gods could readily fuse into existing gods; greatly facilitated the absorption of such social groups into Hindu society.

However, towards the end of the first millennium A.D., a new religion, resting upon a clearly articulated ideology, made its appearance in the north-western regions of India. The religion of Islam, which Hinduism encountered as the vibrant faith of tribal warrior communities from West or Central Asia, was qualitatively different from the spiritual worldviews which it had earlier so successfully absorbed in its amorphous matrix. To start with, these warrior communities probably possessed a military technology and a political system which was superior in its ability to generate power than the indigenous military technology or the Hindu polity. Over and above such secular differences, Islam rested upon the concept, theoretically if not existentially, of the *umma* or a cohesive community which linked all who subscribed to this religion in bonds of loyalty to God. This was probably the first historical encounter between Hinduism and a system of religious belief resting upon the notion of a community held together in allegiance to an all-powerful God. Small wonder, then, that Hindu society was unable to absorb the warrior communities of Islam in the resilient social and spiritual domain in which so many warrior communities which had come to India earlier, from Central or West Asia, had discovered an appropriate niche for themselves.

Perhaps a brief reference to the spatial distribution of Muslim communities within medieval India would be appropriate at this juncture. The most significant concentration of Muslims was located in the north-western region of India, partly as a numerically small yet socially powerful aristocracy and gentry; but largely as a peasantry which had over the centuries embraced the religion of Islam. East of this region, in the plains of the Ganga and its tributaries, the lower and intermediate classes in rural society retained their allegiance to Hindu Gods; yet a Muslim aristocracy and gentry, a substantial proportion of which was constituted of outsiders, established itself as a superior ruling class. In the extreme north-east of India, through social processes of which we have inadequate understanding, not only the rural elite, but large sections of the peasantry, too, were drawn into the embrace of Islam. When we look at other regions of India, the map of religious affiliation is somewhat different from the picture we have drawn of the plains of the Indus and the Ganga. In such regions, Muslim communities were more often than not confined to coastal settlements and port-cities; and they were largely constituted of commercial castes, originally Hindu, and engaged in commerce with their peers in West Asia and East Africa. The only exception to this picture lay in the province of Kerala, where apart from the commercial classes, a large segment of the peasantry, too, had adopted Islam. The sociology of religious conversion in medieval India is a theme on which researches are still in a state of infancy. However, there is reason to believe that the proselytising activity of the Sufi saints, of whom more later, played a significant part in attracting substantial numbers to the religion of Islam.

Perhaps it is necessary, in this context, to speculate briefly about the quality of secular and spiritual interaction between Islamic and Hindu communities in medieval (or late medieval) society in India, particularly because of the misunderstandings which prevail in this domain. In the first place, instead of referring to the community of Islam, or the community of Hinduism, in the singular, as is done so often, we should, more accurately, refer to such communities in the plural. So far as Islam was concerned, we have drawn attention to the notion of the *umma*, or the cohesive brotherhood held together in allegiance to Allah, which constituted the very basis of this religion. Nevertheless, the existential reality of Islam in India, or elsewhere, was strikingly different from the social ideal held out by the Prophet Mohammad. In medieval India, for instance, it is clear that Muslim society was divided into a number of social groups, which differed in their enjoyment of social status and economic power, and which sported very different styles of life. The dominant class in Muslim society was the aristocracy and the gentry, that was distributed as a thin stratum in the plains of the Indus and the Ganga, and was made up, particularly in the latter region, of the warrior elements which had migrated from Central or West Asia to India.

Totally different from the aristocracy or the gentry, both in their access to resources and in the status which they enjoyed, were the indigenous peasant communities, often tribal in structure, which had been attracted to Islam. These peasant communities drawn into Islam were concentrated, first, in the north-west of India, in the valley of the Indus and its tributaries; and secondly, in the north-east of the subcontinent, in the delta region of the Ganga, or in the valley of the Brahmaputra, in both of which areas Hinduism had apparently not reached out to the median and lowermost rural classes. Apart from the rural classes, rich and poor, of the Indo-Gangetic plain, the religion of Islam had also transformed the consciousness of urban social groups in considerable numbers, both within this region as well as without it. Thus the cities and towns of the Gangetic valley contained substantial artisan communities, whose labour provided goods for conspicuous consumption by the aristocratic classes, and who often subscribed to heterodox movements within Islam. Similarly, the western coast of India was dotted by a number of coastal settlements, which were the bases of mercantile classes trading with West Asia and East Africa, some of which embraced the religion of Islam. In the south-west of India, in the region of Kerala, Islam spilled beyond the mercantile communities to embrace the peasantry, the so-called Moplahs, whose devotion to Islam found reflection periodically in millenarian movements of great moment.

It need hardly be observed, at this juncture, that different Muslim classes and communities in India subscribed to radically different interpretations of the message set out in the Koran. Perhaps the aristocracy and the gentry, largely of alien origin, whose members were distributed over the Indo-Gangetic plain, and formed the social base of the Delhi Sultanate, from the 12th to the 15th centuries; and the Mughal Empire, for the next three centuries, were closest to orthodox Islam in their religious outlook. However, the worldview of the peasant communities was quite different from the worldview of the ruling elite, more particularly in regard to questions of the transcendence or immanence of Allah; the observance of ritual; and faith in popular deities whose magical powers had been sanctified by custom and tradition. Here it is important to remember that these rural communities were drawn to Islam largely through the proselytising activity of Sufi saints, whose hospices dotted the countryside, along the major routes of trade and commerce, or wherever social activity created urban settlements.[2] It is also important to remember, that the outlook of the sufis was quite different from the outlook of the *ulemas*, particularly with reference to the seminal concepts of *Sulah-i-kul* and *wahdat-al-wajud*, whereby the *sufis* sought "peace with all" and advocated the view that Allah in his immanence bestowed grace upon everyone, irrespective of their formal allegiance to Islam.[3] Over and above matters of doctrine, the rural communities in India which subscribed to the religion of Islam, shared a large number of folk deities and myths and sacral memories with the Hindu peasants with whom they co-existed in the same physical space. This is eloquently reflected in the literature on the quality of popular religious consciousness in high and late medieval society. As a distinguished scholar of Islam observes in describing one Muslim tribal community in India:[4]

> In the south-western direction from Delhi, in the native states of Alwar and Bharatpur, lived the Mēōs and the Mīnās. They had purely Hindu names or tagged on *Khan* to a Hindu name. They celebrated not only *Divali* and *Dasehra* which, though Hindu festivals, had acquired something of a national character, but also *Janam-asthami,* the birthday of Shri Krishna, and on the day preceding Amavas, the night when there is no moon, ceased, like the Hindus, from all labour. . . . Few could recite the *kalimah*. . . . However, it was Salar Masud Ghazi, believed to be a son of one of the generals of Sultan Mahmud of Ghazni, Madar Sahib, an equally mythical figure, and Khwajah Sahib, (Shaikh Muinuddin Chishti) of Ajmer whose heroic or semi-divine personalities loomed largest in the religious consciousness of the Mēōs.

No less heterodox in their religious outlook than the rural communities which had embraced Islam were the artisans who pursued their humble vocation in the cities and towns of the Indo-Gangetic valley. Perhaps the most outstanding example of such heterodoxy is to be found in the worldview of Kabir and the Kabirpanthis; who represented a remarkable spiritual development in one of the core regions of the Gangetic valley, the region around the sacred city of Varanasi, in the late 15th and early 16th centuries. Indeed, Kabir was at the very centre of a powerful movement among the lowly classes wherein Hinduism and Islam achieved a coming together that made it difficult to distinguish one religion from the other. As a verse created by Kabir puts it:[5]

> O servant, where dost thou seek me?
> Lo! I am beside thee.
> I am neither in temple nor in mosque:
> I am neither in Kaaba nor in Kailash:
> Neither am I in rites and ceremonies,
> Nor in Yoga and renunciation.
> If thou art a true seeker, thou shalt at
> once see Me; thou shalt meet Me
> in a moment of time.
> Kabir says, O Sadhu! God is the breath
> of all breath.

The possibility of a spiritual synthesis between Hinduism and Islam was explored, in the medieval centuries, not only at the popular level but also at the elite level. The initiative among the elite was taken by men like the Emperor Akbar, whose religious eclecticism, witness the welcome which he afforded to learned scholars of diverse persuasions at his court, was to find expression in a new worldview, called the *Din-i-Illahi,* which sought to locate in his person the sanction for spiritual as well as secular power within the Mughal Empire. That this new religious worldview, with the Emperor as its apex, failed to attract any social class, other than the nobles who adorned the Imperial Court, merely reflects the fact that the great traditions of Hinduism and Islam articulated very different sensibilities and very different perceptions of the sacred no less than the profane. Perhaps much more serious in intention were attempts like those of Dara Shikoh, the Emperor Shahjahan's unfortunate Crown Prince, who patronised explorations in the comparative frame of the religious philosophies of Hinduism and Islam, with the objective of creating bonds of understanding between the religious and the secular intelligentsia of the two communities. Despite such attempts, however, the spiritual dialogue between Hindu and Muslim elites never achieved that community of sentiment which characterised popular religion among the lowly classes from these two religions. Yet differences in religious belief did not prevent political alliances and secular cooperation between the Hindu and Muslim ruling classes with the objective of creating a stable political system in the subcontinent.

Before concluding this survey of the structure and content of Indian civilisation in the medieval centuries, a few observations are appropriate about the nature of secular interaction within as well as between Islamic and Hindu communities. To portray this elusive theme it is important to emphasise that agriculture for subsistence was the principal activity of rural society; although production for the market; for consumption in cities and towns; and for payment of taxes to the ruling classes; necessitated the generation of substantial surpluses. All this meant that relations of exchange and market interaction between different individuals and social groups, whether they subscribed to Hinduism or to Islam, were relatively weakly articulated in this period. Indeed, the picture of Indian civilisation as a vast honeycomb, in which small, fragmented communities made up the individual cells of the honeycomb, largely isolated from one another, yet drawn into an organic entity, is a fairly accurate illustration of the social organism as a whole, although recent research has clarified the extent to which the cleavated units of the social organism actually stood in isolation from each other. However, what needs to be emphasised is the overall authenticity of this portrayal; just as it is also important to remember that in pre-capitalist societies individuals and social groups do not interact with each other with the frequency and intensity with which they interact with each other in capitalist societies.

III

The establishment of British dominion over India, by the first quarter of the 19th century, brought about certain seminal changes in the political economy, the social structure and the intellectual values which sustained Indian civilisation; and we shall now briefly consider these changes with a view to capturing their overall impact.

In the first instance, we should stress that British rule was established over India with the objective of extracting material resources from the subordinate economy for the benefit of the dominant economy. As a perceptive scholar has pointed out, a host of rationalisations were advanced to explain British dominion over India. The civilising spirit of Christianity; the Benthamite view of utility as the most rational basis of the social order; the romantic perception of a classical civilisation which needed the guiding hand of a younger and more vigorous society to flower afresh in the 19th century; and last but not least, the worldview of social drawinism, according to which the struggle for existence between diverse racial and political communities inevitably resulted in the domination of the stronger and the more evolved societies over the weak and the disorganised; were some of the justifications of this act of conquest and subsequent exploitation. Yet such ideologies were little more than smokescreens to mask the relationship of subordination and superordination between Great Britain and India in the 19th century.

To extract tribute from her vast colony, the British Government created an altogether new corpus of laws and institutions of administration; just as it also attempted to transform the values, social and political, of the subject classes. Not surprisingly, these attempts at social engineering triggered off complex changes within Indian society, some of which were anticipated and others anticipated not at all. Perhaps a brief review of these changes—and the instruments; social, economic and intellectual, which initiated them—is necessary before we can assess how they transformed Indian society, and what was the indigenous response to such a transformation.

Any review of the changes which the British Government wrought in India needs to dwell, in the first instance, upon the institutions of governance created to facilitate the transfer of surpluses in the economy from India to Great Britain. The initial steps taken by the British Government, therefore, sought to fashion a system of administration designed to appropriate a substantial proportion of the surplus generated in rural society, in the form of a tax on the land. To start with, in the provinces of Bengal, the system of tribute extraction rested upon an all-powerful Collector in each district, who conducted his business with the assistance of the territorial aristocrats created by the Permanent Settlement of 1793. As British dominion spread into the southern, the western and the northern provinces of India, during the first half of the 19th century, the colonial civil servants acquired the self-confidence and the institutional means to eliminate the aristocracy and the gentry, and strike contact with petite landlords and peasant-proprietors within villages, for purposes of surplus extraction. Such a system of extraction had numerous advantages, from the British standpoint, over the system established in the provinces of Bengal. First, it prevented the leakage of resources to intermediaries like the landed magnates created by the Permanent Settlement, who, so British civil servants argued, performed no role in the rural economy, whatever be their political utility as a collaborating class within the imperial system. Secondly, such a mechanism of extraction linked the Colonial State to the self-interest of hundreds upon thousands of small owners of property in the villages, whose acquisitiveness and productive labour could provide the basis for economic growth in rural society.

The system of extraction outlined above called for the creation of entirely new infrastructures in the territories controlled by the British Government. Throughout the 19th century, therefore, this government strove to build up communication and market linkages between cities, towns and villages, which were designed to break down the isolation of rural communities in a way it had never been broken down before; although such linkages were not altogether absent earlier. The results of such a transformation are reflected in the literature about agrarian society generated by colonial administrators in the 19th century and social scientists contemporaneously. This literature speaks eloquently of the opening up of rural society, if only to facilitate the extraction of rural surpluses and the marketing of the consumer products generated by British industry. From the great ports of Calcutta, Madras, Bombay and Karachi, rail and road networks reached out to the cities of the interior; and from such cities, to the district towns and the *kasbas,* or rural townships, which served as market centres for clusters of villages. This enormous network of communication, which took almost a century to establish, served as a conduit for a two-way process of exchange which underpinned the colonial economy. From the village settlements the products of agriculture reached out, through the *kasbas,* towns and cities, to the ports; from where they were drawn into the economy of the metropolitan heart of the Empire. Conversely, through this very conduit the industrial products of Great Britain, and other European societies, with a high level of technological development, flowed into the Indian economy and served the consumer needs of the traditionally affluent, or the newly enriched, social classes in India. This process, whereby the far-flung rural communities of India were drawn into subordinate relationship with the capitalist society of western Europe, has been graphically described in the writings of neo-marxist scholars who subscribe to the theory of the "world system"; although the development of the Indian economy during the colonial era does not necessarily sustain the thesis, that the cooption of the pre-capitalist into the capitalist societies necessarily brings about the "development of under-development".

The social and intellectual consequences of the transformation described above were no less momentous than their economic consequences. It should be obvious from our account of the colonial era that some of the traditional solidarities and cleavages of Indian society were undermined and recast along novel lines in the period under consideration. This is reflected in the widening horizons of caste institutions; just as it is also reflected in the crystallisation of new social relationships within the communities of Hinduism as well as of Islam. We have touched earlier upon the existence of small, fragmented social units, each trapped in a distinctive world of consciousness and economic relationships, which made it difficult for larger solidarities to emerge within the framework of Indian civilisation. Indeed, to illustrate the structure of traditional society in India, we have drawn upon the analogy of the honeycomb; with the comb representing the configuration of the total social order; and the cells within it depicting distinctive social units like *jatis* and village communities. While it is difficult to spell out the rate at which the honeycomb structure gave way to an associational configuration of classes and communities, such a process was very much in evidence in the closing decades of the 19th or the opening decades of the 20th century.

Nothing reflects the emergence of new social and class solidarities within Indian society more sensitively than the novel systems of religious belief and social action which were active within Hinduism and Islam in the decades under review. This is hardly

the occasion to dwell upon the movements of religious and social reform, as such developments are conventionally described, which characterised Indian society during the second half of the 19th century. Here we can do no more than focus attention upon the salient features of these movements, which sought to shape anew the consciousness of those who subscribed to the spiritual world-views which had moulded Indian civilisation over the centuries. Some of these movements of reform were revivalist in character, and sought to reactivate systems of belief which had ostensibly flourished since classical times. Others were daring attempts at a synthesis between indigenous and western traditions. Others, yet again, sought to reject the Indian heritage, and to recreate systems of belief and social action which owed their origin wholly to the western intellect. Yet whatever be the content and configuration of such movements, they were the products of the colonial dispensation, and sought to conjure into existence novel modalities of social action; novel forms of social consciousness; and a novel awareness of solidarities and cleavages within Indian society. The overall result of this moral and material transformation was to create a social order in which a market economy, albeit under the domination of Great Britain, not only created new relations of production and exchange, but also paved the way for the generation of new values within the matrix of Indian civilisation.

IV

The growth of a national movement, which in its wider connotation pertained as much to the social and economic domain as it pertained to the political and intellectual domain, played a crucial role in the transformation of India from a medieval civilisation to a modern political society. In the sphere of social production, the advocates of nationalism sought to fashion within India an industrial society resting upon the capitalist mode of generating material wealth and upon a national market with well articulated linkages between urban and rural society; just as in the social and political spheres, they envisaged a cohesive polity: characterised by popular participation in politics; by representative institutions as the basis of the social order; and by political formations and movements of the intellect which would mediate between the citizen and the State and thereby lay the basis for the "good society".

While we do not propose to explore the manner in which the people of India liberated themselves from colonial bondage, it is necessary to examine briefly the different worldviews which sought to provide the basis for nationhood in India. From the very outset, it was clear to the founding fathers of the national movement in India, that the instruments of social cohesion which had sustained Indian civilisation over the centuries would be inadequate to the purposes of holding together a society characterised by the industrial mode of production; and characterised also by representative institutions; by political parties; and by popular participation in politics. The founding fathers were also conscious of the fact that in a pre-industrial society, the intensity and frequency of social interaction, among individuals no less than among collectivities, was of a relatively modest order; thereby enabling the values of popular religion, despite their weak articulation in the social system, to hold together different constituents of society in an amorphous nevertheless distinctive civilisation.

The leaders of the national movement in fact believed that the social identity of India had to be defined in a novel fashion if the old agricultural order was to be gradually displayed by a new industrial order. Hence the stress on nationhood as the new basis of the Indian identity, which would hold together an industrial society characterised by considerable social plurality in bonds of loyalty to a Nation State. Among the leaders who sought to generate national consciousness in India, there was a consensus that an enduring society would have to ensure equity to all citizens, irrespective of their religious beliefs and irrespective also of their status in the hierarchy of society. Nevertheless, the advocates of different schools of nationalist thought were not necessarily in agreement upon the strategy whereby such a state of affairs could be achieved.

A critical appraisal of the systems of belief and action which were articulated within the framework of the national movement reveals three ideologies, each one of which reflected a distinctive view of the basis whereby the "good society" could be conjured into existence within India. Yet before these three ideologies are spelt out, a few brief observations may be appropriate. As already emphasised, the leaders of the national movement, whatever be their position on questions of intellectual belief and social action, were convinced that the traditional values of popular religion would no longer suffice to socially integrate different classes and communities in a modern society. Nevertheless, such a belief did not lead the nationalist leaders of India to the conclusion, so widely shared by European (particularly French) leaders of thought, that religious values had to be purged altogether from popular consciousness, if only as a concession to the fact that in India such values were organically lodged in the social order. To this extent, therefore, the nationalism which gained momentum in India during the closing decades of the 19th century, did not acquire the characteristics of nationalism in Europe, where it strove to drive religious consciousness out of the social domain. Instead, the tremendous strength of religious consciousness among the popular classes was recognised, explicitly or implicitly, by all schools of nationalist opinion in India. Where these schools differed from each other, and we shall dwell upon these differences later, was in the role they accorded to popular religion in the political arena.

The first school of nationalist thought to which reference is necessary is the school of liberal and secular nationalists, who believed that the most creative domain for the play of religious consciousness was the private rather than the public domain. They further believed that the loyalty of the individual to the Nation rested upon his moral and material self-interest, as a constituent of a political community devoted to the welfare of its members. Although there is no necessary or logical relationship here, liberal and secular nationalists linked such a notion of political society to the private ownership of the means of generating wealth in society, just as they also related it to the market economy; though their perception of the backwardness of the Indian economy led them to advocate "protectionism" as the necessary precondition of industrial growth in the subcontinent. The liberal and secular advocates of nationalism placed an integrated and rational vision of India's future before their countrymen. Yet their success in propagating their worldview was limited, particularly when we consider social groups other than the middle classes which had benefited from the system of education created by the British Government. A number of factors contributed to the limited success achieved by nationalists of the liberal and secular school. It is likely that the idiom in which they articulated their worldview was unrelated to the culture of large sections of Indian society. Moreover, in a community characterised by such an adverse relationship between demographic numbers, on the one hand, and the social product available for consumption, on the other, the notion of a property owning capitalist society could hardly be expected to arouse much enthusiasm among the popular classes, whose life-style vested upon economic scarcity and social deprivation.

The second school of nationalism, also 'secular' as this term is understood in contemporary Indian society, can be described as the sarvodaya school of secular nationalism. The advocates of this school—the towering figure among them was Mahatma Gandhi—had an altogether different (from the liberals) view of the role of popular religion in the generation of national consciousness in India. Like other nationalists, the advocates of sarvodaya recognised that the traditional religious values of India did not offer the basis for creating national unity and loyalty to a Nation State. However, these leaders believed that a transformed religious consciousness, among the Hindus no less than among the Muslims and the followers of other religions in India, could offer the basis for such a development. The transformation which the sarvodaya leaders sought to induce within traditional religions is reflected best of all in the reforming activity of Gandhi; who attempted to sharpen as well as to widen the moral sensibility of Hindu society; just as he also sought, at least in the final decades of his life, to break up the institution of caste in order to create a single cohesive Hindu community.

The economic vision of the sarvodaya leaders was an uneasy mixture of liberal individualism and traditional collectivism. Men like Gandhi did not look upon private property and control over the means of producing agricultural or industrial wealth as morally reprehensible or socially parasitic, provided the landed or the industrial magnates were guided by the principle of trusteeship. According to this principle, property and productive wealth could be held by individuals only in trust for the community. Such property and wealth ought, therefore, to be utilised for the good of the community as a whole rather than be expended to satisfy the conspicuous needs of wealthy owners.

The sarvodaya version of secularism was immensely popular with the rich as well as the poor, partly because of its reliance on traditional religious values, albeit transformed to suit the needs of the 20th century; and partly also because it drew upon the concept of trusteeship of wealth, which was more than reassuring to the propertied classes. Indeed, sarvodaya secularism virtually became the basis of a pluralistic national identity for different social classes and religious communities in the subcontinent. It would be pertinent to ask why this version of secularism gained so much popularity during the decades when the people of India were engaged in a struggle against the British Raj. Apart from the charismatic personality of Gandhi; and the moral influence which he exercised over different classes and communities; two factors probably contributed to the success of this ideology. First, and this is crucial, any concept of national identity and national regeneration articulated through a religious imagery—through notions like *Swaraj* or *Rama Rajya*—was bound to exercise great popular appeal. Here it is important to remember that new forms of consciousness can be disseminated in a political community only through an already existing corpus of culture. The propagators of sarvodaya recognised this cardinal truth. They, therefore, spoke of nationhood and self-determination through symbols, myths and images, which had been engrained in the popular psyche, over the centuries, by the folk saints of India. Neither the advocates of liberal secularism, nor those of radical secularism (as we shall presently see), could draw upon a similar cultural heritage in their attempts to shape a new political identity for India.

Notwithstanding the cultural sensitivity of the sarvodaya leaders, it would be a mistake to overlook the role played by their economic beliefs in popularising their worldview. Howsoever Gandhi and his disciples may have interpreted the concept of trusteeship of wealth, the propertied classes probably accepted this ideal for very different reasons. Indeed, given the scarcity of resources in India, the democratisation of nationalist politics carried with it the very real threat of the socialisation of property and productive wealth. The concept of trusteeship, married as it was in the worldview of Gandhi to popular religious values, offered the prospect, to men of property, of a state of society in which no harm would befall their material interests. Small wonder, then, that the more discerning landed and industrial magnates threw their support squarely behind the Mahatma, even though their perception of sarvodaya and of trusteeship bore no relationship to the moral grandeur of the Gandhian vision.

The third variety of secular nationalism which featured on the political stage of India was the school of radical secularism. The advocates of this view shared some of the beliefs of liberal secularists, who had initiated the growth of national consciousness in India in the closing decades of the 19th century. The radicals—their most distinguished representative was Jawaharlal Nehru—were firmly of the view that popular religion could play no creative role in the political affairs of a modern society. Indeed, they argued, to drag religion in the political domain was likely to reinforce conservative and reactionary interests in the social order. Hence, they further argued, the language of popular religion and moral regeneration should be displaced by the language of class and social equity in the vocabulary of Indian politics. Otherwise, the landed and the industrial magnates would capture the national movement; and ensure that the liberation of India would serve their interests, as a whole. Such nationalists, who believed that religion ought to play a role only in the domain of private belief, also adopted a radical position on the ownership of property and the means of production in society. Indeed, their stance on such crucial issues were of a piece with their stance on the induction of popular religion, albeit in a transformed manifestation, for the purposes of mass politics.

The sarvodaya and the radical visions of a secular society co-exist in creative tension with each other in contemporary India. Indeed, it is even possible to discern, on occasions, a blurring of the distinction between the two ideologies on the political stage of India, before 1947, or after the attainment of independence. Nevertheless, the dialectical relationship between these two systems of belief and social action provides the basis for which engages the intelligentsia. The rational resolution of which debate is inextricably linked with the emergence of a modern industrial society in India.

NOTES

1. Minute by Sir Charles Metcalfe dated 17 November 1830; cited in P. Spear, *Twilight of The Mughals* (Cambridge, 1951), p. 117.
2. Asim Roy, *The Islamic Syncretistic Tradition in Bengal* (Princeton, 1983). Particularly see chapter entitled: "Social Origins of Muslims in Bengal" and "The Emergence of the Bengal Muslim Cultural Mediators". Also see the following two works: (i) G.A. Oddie, *Religion in South Asia: Religious Con-*

version and Revival Movements in South Asia in Medieval and Modern Times (New Delhi, 1977). (ii) Aziz Ahmad, *Studies in Islamic Culture in the Indian Environment* (Oxford, 1964).
3. A. Ahmad, *Studies in Islamic Culture in the Indian Environment* (Oxford, 1964) Chapters IV, VI and VIII.
4. M. Mujeeb, *The Indian Muslims* (London, 1968), pp. 10-11.
5. *One Hundred Poems of Kabir* (Trans.). Rabindranath Tagore (London, 1943), ps. 1.

7

The Past as a Mirror of the Future

It is a common fallacy to look upon the study of the past—the principle concern of the historian—as an exercise in antiquarianism. It is a fallacy to do so partly because of the causal links which relate the past to the present; and partly also because of the seminal role of history in an understanding of the present no less than in the "construction" of the future of human society. Paradoxically, therefore, the most vital input in a sensitive understanding of the present; and the construction of the future; is a rigorous perception of the past.

In the light of such philosophical assumptions about history and its place in praxis, I propose (in the course of this essay) to examine the legacy of the nationalist movement in India and to dwell upon the possibilities which this movement has opened up before the people of the country. To this end, I shall first examine the historical roots of Indian society. Thereafter, I shall reflect upon the character of the nationalist movement and finally touch briefly upon the possible "future" of the country.

I

An examination of nationalism in India as a phenomenon affecting all facets of life, reveals certain striking features which are highly relevant to us today. To appreciate this, it is necessary to recapitulate briefly the evolution of society in India. Since the first millennium B.C., when India underwent a transformation from a pastoral to an agricultural society, the economy of the country has been determined by a way of life in which the productive activity of hundreds upon thousands of peasant households, located in villages scattered over the face of the subcontinent, has been the central feature of our social existence.[1] This agricultural economy was largely subsistence in character; and the small surplus that it generated sustained a religious intelligentsia and a ruling class, which jointly established a precarious political authority over civic society. Linked to the agricultural economy was a craft economy and a mercantile economy, which created pockets of urbanisation in what was essentially an agrarian world. Further, there is reason to believe that the relative, as well as the absolute, magnitude of the urban sector in relation to the rural sector varied over the centuries, depending upon the level of economic productivity and political cohesion that was achieved by society as a whole.

The different constituents of this society were held together by bonding materials made up of two elements. These elements can be characterised as structural and ideational. Over the centuries, the peasant communities—as well as the artisan and the mercantile communities—were drawn together into a social fabric underpinned by the institution of caste. Also over the centuries, a metaphysical worldview, reflected in the formal schools of Hindu philosophy, permeated this social fabric and endowed it with a cultural unity which was as remarkable for its vitality as it was remarkable for its capacity to survive. Initially, the worldview of Hinduism was reflected largely in the moral vision of the religious intelligentsia and the ruling classes. But at the beginning of the second millennium A.D., there arose in India a powerful current of popular religion which was able to disseminate the moral outlook of the religious intelligentsia to the peasant and the artisan communities. The dissemination of the classical worldview of Hinduism to the lowly classes was a very significant achievement. It created a shared world of values encompassing both the elites and the lowly classes and it was one of the factors responsible for the remarkable survival of Hindu society over time.[2]

When we refer to the cultural and structural unity of India since medieval times, we have to keep in view two relevant social phenomena. First, we have to take into consideration the rural economy, resting upon substantially self-sufficient peasant households which were located in villages scattered over the face of the country. Such an agrarian economy gave rise to a social order in which interaction between individuals and social classes, to the extent such interaction is governed by relations of economic exchange, was of a very low order. Secondly, we have to remember that, since the first millennium A.D., substantial sections of the peasantry, and the artisans, were drawn within the embrace of Islam. It could be argued that the peasant classes, or the artisan classes, which turned to Islam for spiritual sustenance, were inspired by a worldview which had nothing in common with the worldview of Hinduism. However, this would be a mistaken understanding of the texture of popular Islam, as distinct from the Islam of the upper classes, in the Indo-Gangetic plain. Although our understanding of Islam as a popular religion in medieval society is still limited, there is reason to believe that the Muslim peasant classes were linked to the Hindu peasant classes, living close to them, through allegiance to shared rituals as well as shared concepts of the sacred and the profane worlds. We must, therefore, realise that the advent of Islam did not necessarily bring about any sharp cleavages in cultural unity at the popular level. Such cultural cleavages as appeared at this juncture, pertained much more to the elite classes in Hindu and Muslim society; though even among the elites there existed, by the end of the 16th century, something close to a distinctive Indian view of the world and a distinctive Indian culture.[3]

II

The cultural unity which characterised society in India, historically speaking, and the economic order which underscored this unity, give us some idea of the task confronting those nationalist leaders who sought to introduce a material transformation and a cultural renaissance within India in the 20th century. It is important to remember that such leaders had before them not only a political objective—namely, the liberation of India from British bondage—but they also envisaged a programme of social and economic reconstruction of India. Thus, to gain a true measure of nationalism in India, we have to focus just as much on the wider societal objectives of this process, as we have to focus on its political objectives. With the exception of Gandhi, and those loyal to his views, the leaders who were committed to bringing about a national revival in India in the 20th century, were as much concerned with ensuring her transformation into a modern industrial society, enjoying a material culture comparable to the material culture of western societies, as they were interested in waging a political struggle designed to destroy British imperialism.

It is crucial to emphasise the wider objectives of nationalism in India because the search for a new political order was inextricably linked with the search for a new social and economic order.[4] It was abundantly clear to the men who were seeking to shape the destiny of India at this juncture that the cultural cement which had held together different constituents of society over the ages, namely, the fabric of popular Hinduism and the values which it shared with popular Islam, would no longer provide the basis for social unity in the future. This was so because the nationalist leaders envisaged a major transformation in the rural no less than in the urban way of life. The relative autonomy of hundreds upon thousands of peasant households, producing for subsistence, would be substituted by the interdependence of small farming units, producing as much for the market as they produced for their own consumption. More importantly, the artisan in the urban domain would be drawn into a method of generating wealth in which sophisticated technology and new sources of power would multiply manifold the productive capacities of the individual. Both these transformations, that is, the emergence of commercial agriculture in the villages and the emergence also of the industrial mode of production in the cities, would come about within the matrix of an economic system that would ensure the free exchange of material values in a national market.

What was the cultural unity appropriate to the new scheme of things in India? This was the question faced by those engaged in liberating the country from the bonds of imperialism and, at the same time, shaping a new economic order for its citizens. While it was difficult to provide any clear answer to this question, it was obvious that the values which had held together society in India over the ages, would no longer suffice to provide the basis for unity in modern India. The needs of the hour were different; India required a moral vision and a political system which could reflect the aspirations of her diverse classes and communities, within the framework of a market society characterised by the industrial mode of generating wealth.

It was clear, at this juncture, that a new political unity, and a new consciousness of this unity, had to be forged between different classes and communities within Indian society, in response to the needs of agricultural and industrial modernisation. The political ideology appropriate to the needs of society in India was the ideology of nationalism which, ever since the French Revolution in 1789, had powerfully influenced the destiny of Europe. Nationalism, as it manifested itself in the West, rested on a wide range of social, political, economic and intellectual phenomena. In the domain of the economy, it reflected the emergence of new classes in society, arising out of commercialised agriculture and the industrial mode of production. In the domain of politics, it reflected the emergence of liberal republics, or constitutional monarchies, which put an end to the segmented States of the feudal era and substituted in their place cohesively organised polities. Intellectually, these transformations were reflected in the concept of nationhood; a concept which incorporated the social and economic processes associated with the modernisation of political communities.

III

We must digress a little here to consider the concept of nationalism in detail. We have so far spoken of nationalism as a unitary concept. However, if we explore the European scene in the first quarter of the 19th century, two different varieties of nationalism become evident. The first variant may be called rational nationalism. This is reflected most clearly in the ideological articulation of the French Revolution of 1789. The revolution which took place in France sought to achieve many objectives; but above all it sought to link the people of France through formal ties to a centralised State which would accept reason as the great fly-wheel of the social order. Moreover, this rational nationalism sought to reshape French society according to a social vision which rested partly upon the principle of popular democracy and partly also upon the economic institutions of the bourgeois order.

The rational nationalism of the French Revolution was not the only variant available to those who addressed themselves to the problem of shaping a new political identity for India. The community of historians is all too familiar with the German response to the French Revolution of 1789. This response rested upon romantic premises, in the precise philosophical sense of this term. Instead of highlighting the primacy of reason in the organisation of political society, German nationalism focused upon the potential of folk culture and myth as creative social agencies. Under this influence, the German people were encouraged to reach out to their past—a mythical past—in order to conjure into existence a centralised polity that would sweep away the vestiges of feudal segmentation in their political system. Over and above this, the romantic nationalism which characterised German politics in the 19th century had ambiguous stance towards the economic transformation of the social order. It discerned in commercial agriculture, just as, it also discerned in the industrial mode of production, a means for the vitalisation of the polity. Yet, there was a reluctance on the part of the German nationalists to accept the social and economic consequences flowing from such a transformation. This may partly have been a consequence of the level of social development of German society, which was lower than the level of the social development of contemporary French society. It may also have been related to the different social structures of German and French societies: the feudal classes occupying a position of dominance in Germany which they did not in France. Be that as it may, it is a striking fact that the nationalist ideology which crystallised in Germany in the first half of the 19th century was qualitatively different from the nationalist ideology which took root in France after 1789.

IV

When we focus upon the quest of the political leadership in India for a new identity in the late 19th and early 20th centuries, we notice that the level of social development which characterised Indian society exercised a decisive influence upon the ideological texture of nationalist politics. Not surprisingly, the concept of nationalism which took root in India was the romantic concept, though it came to us through the mediation of Italian nationalism. Like its German counterpart, nationalism in India was shaped, from the outset, in an environment characterised by a low level of social and economic development. It was also shaped in a social context in which feudal reality, using the term in a loose sense, had a powerful hold over social, political and economic institutions as well as over the popular psyche. Small wonder, then, that under the spell of romantic nationalism, the people of India turned increasingly to a mythical past, at the regional level as well as at the subcontinental level, in order to create the basis of nationhood in the country.

The distinctive characteristics of nationalism in India, in the realm of social structure no less than in the realm of ideas, were reflected most cogently in the political tradition articulated by Mahatma Gandhi. The first and most striking feature of this tradition, as already emphasised, was to conceive of an Indian nation in the light of a mythical past in which, so it was assumed, the moral and material creativity of the people had flourished in a way it could not flourish under an alien dispensation. Gandhi described the social objective of nationalism in India as a recreation of "Ram Rajya"; and the symbolism upon which he drew secured for him the support of the Hindu rural classes. Yet it is important to remember that Gandhi owed his success as a popular leader as much to the invocation of a mythical past, as he owed it to the consummation of an alliance between different social classes and religious communities within India. The fact that different classes could come together on a nationalist platform did not imply the absence of social tensions within Indian society. What it did imply, however, was the absence of a heightened sense of class consciousness among the masses; and a careful attempt on the part of the leadership to avoid issues that would divide rather than unify the social order.[5]

Equally striking was the concept of a "secular" nation as defined by Gandhi. In the western context, secularism stood for social trends which undermined the hold of religion over the intellect. But the Gandhian variety of secularism merely emphasised an equality of status for all religions in the public domain. A crusade against religion, as a public no less than as a private ideology, was conspicuously absent in the Indian understanding of secularism.[6] This is reflected best in the political struggles which marked the nationalist movement in India in the first half of the 20th century. In the agitation conducted by Gandhi during the years 1920-22, for instance, Hindus, Muslims and Sikhs were encouraged, as members of distinctive religious communities, to join an anti-imperialist alliance against the British Government of India. Such a nationalist strategy, seeking to unite the rich and the poor, on the one hand, and members of different religious communities, on the other, was remarkably successful in mobilising the people of India in a crusade against the British Government. We shall return to this theme later; but here it is enough to say that this mobilisation was achieved without bringing about any qualitative transformation in the nature of popular consciousness. This is not to suggest that Gandhi had not aimed at any such transformation in the popular psyche. Indeed, he had explicitly assumed that the experience of participation in a common struggle against the British Government would forge the bonds of an overarching loyalty—to the Indian Nation—between different classes and religious communities in the country. Over and above this, the Gandhian programme of social action envisaged the elimination of poverty in the country; just as it also envisaged a more equitable distribution of material wealth between zamindars and kisans, on the one hand, and capitalists and the workers, on the other. However, the course of the freedom struggle in India suggests that Gandhi's success remained confined to the arena of mass mobilisation. By and large, he was unable to transform popular consciousness, let alone trigger off a revolution that would place the means of achieving material self-sufficiency within the reach of the poor in the cities or in the villages.

V

The manner in which freedom came to India in 1947, and the ideational and institutional constituents of nationalist politics, inevitably influenced the social and political development of the country in the decades after independence. I would like to suggest here that the Gandhian tradition of political action ceased to have much relevance for India after 1947. The Gandhian programme rested upon three important constituents. First, there was a mobilisation of different classes and communities in a nationalist and anti-imperialist struggle; secondly, the notion of nationhood was disseminated among those so mobilised; and thirdly, stress was laid on the desirability of bringing about, non-violently, a more equitable distribution of wealth among different social classes. Gandhi was successful only in the first objective: that of mobilisation. The partition of India in 1947 stands as tragic witness to the fact he failed to forge bonds of loyalty to nationhood between different religious communities. Finally, there is little evidence to suggest that the great vision of a non-violent revolution—a revolution that would persuade the capitalists in the cities and the zamindars in the village to share their material wealth with the lowly workers or the impoverished peasants—is anywhere near realisation in Indian society.

The strategy of social and economic development adopted after 1947, under the leadership of Jawaharlal Nehru, was shaped both by the successes and the failures of the Gandhian era. I would like to consider, in the first instance, two specific characteristics of the decades since 1947, about which there exists a substantial corpus of literature in the social sciences. We have referred earlier to the multi-class and multi-communitarian political alliance forged by Gandhi in the process of fighting British imperialism. This alliance was reflected in the structure and constitution of the Indian National Congress, as it was reorganised by Gandhi after 1920. There is every reason to believe that the multi-class and multi-communitarian character of the Congress remained unaltered under Jawaharlal Nehru in the decades after 1947. As before, the Congress remained primarily a party of the intelligentsia and the peasantry, though it also sought to incorporate in an electoral alliance, under the conditions of adult franchise, which obtained after 1951, the industrial working classes, the rural proletariat and other social groups. The multi-class character of the Congress after 1947 is fully recognised by those social scientists who seek to explain how it functioned as the dominant party in a democratic polity, in contrast to the breakdown of the liberal order in other societies of the Third World. However, the social classes enumerated above do not exhaust those which were drawn into a supportive relationship with the Congress. There is evidence to suggest that powerful sections of the industrial and commercial bourgeoisie occupied an important place within the Congress before and after 1947. It would be a caricature of reality, though, to suggest that through such a process of induction the Congress became a passive instrument of these classes.[7]

Be that as it may, the strategies of economic growth adopted by the Congress after 1947 were shaped, and circumscribed, by the interests of those social classes which extended political support to it. This is reflected most clearly in the development of planning in India.[8] When Jawaharlal Nehru turned his attention to the re-shaping of the Indian economy in the 1920s, he envisaged a social order in which the institution of private property, particularly as reflected in concentrations of industrial and agricultural wealth, would be conspicuous by its absence. This vision is expressed in his essay entitled "Whither India". The radicalism of Jawaharlal Nehru underwent a dilution when he sensed the constellation of conservative social forces which underpinned the nationalist move-ment, and more specifically, the Indian National Congress. The planning which he initiated in the late 1930s, therefore, departed substantially from his earlier formulation of India's future. Yet the concessions did not come exclusively from Nehru; the bourgeoisie, too, accepted the necessity for concessions which would enable a multi-class alliance to function within the Indian political system. This can be seen in the attempt of the leaders of the industrial bourgeoisie to formulate in the 1940s a blueprint for economic development wherein planning and state control of the economy featured in a prominent fashion.

When Jawaharlal Nehru assumed control over India in 1947, the policies adopted by him reflected the alliance which underpinned the political strength of the Congress. In the Industrial Policy Resolution of 1948, the private sector as well as the public sector were given appropriate places in the economy; furthermore, there was evident concern for the artisan classes whose political as well as economic stake in India was substantial, though the explicit recognition of this stake had to await the formulation of the Second Five-Year Plan. Over and above this, what has been insufficiently stressed in the literature of the social sciences is the extent to which the Congress was the great party of the peas-antry—a term which refers to owners of small rural property, who produced for subsistence, though it also includes a rural class whose agricultural activity was increasingly designed for the market. That the Congress was a party of the peasantry imposed its own constraints upon the policies which it adopted. The main thrust of the Congress, in the decades before 1947, was an anti-feudal thrust. Above everything else, the Congress reflected the interests of the landowning peasantry in the ryotwari regions, and the tenant-farmers in the zamindari areas, who had varying deg-rees of security of tenure. After 1947 a series of legislative and political steps were taken to break up the great concentrations of landed wealth in rural society and to transfer the ownership of land to those who cultivated it. At the same time, under the aegis of the State, a number of institutional reforms were initiated, which ensured the flow of fresh inputs into agriculture, and in doing so enabled the newly enfranchised peasant-proprietors to break through centuries of stagnation in rural production. These changes had nothing to do with socialism in the formal sense of the term. All they sought to ensure was that the peasant proprietor would own a secure title to land; and that he would have at his disposal the fiscal and technical resources whereby he could increase agricultural production. At Avadi, in 1955, Nehru attempted to introduce cooperative agriculture in a manner which would have diluted, marginally, the principle of private property in rural society at the level of the peasant-proprietors. This measure of reform remained wholly inoperative, largely because the Congress as a political organism was dependent upon tens upon millions of peasants who were deeply attached to the institution of private property, howsoever diminutive be their holdings in land.[9]

If the attempt to weaken the institution of petty property in land was unsuccessful, this does not imply that the fiscal and technical measures taken to stimulate agricultural productivity proved abortive. One of the striking developments in India contemporaneously is the manner in which agricultural production has increased in the decades between 1950 and 1980. Since the advent of agriculture in the riverine plains, increases in production in the rural domain had been achieved mainly through horizontal expansion in cultivation, although marginal improvements in yields were also brought about through irrigation and related measures. In the decades since 1950, however, while the area under cultivation has increased substantially, for the first time in the history of Indian agriculture, an increase in productivity per acre has been achieved through the promotion of high technology cultivation oriented for the market. This development was particularly marked after 1966; and it would be no exaggeration to state that Indian agriculture has, over the past thirty years, progressed in a manner to which our history offers no parallel. Such an achievement needs to be highlighted in any review of India's performance since 1950. This development, however, has also posed acute political problems to which we shall turn shortly.

The record of industrial growth, in the private no less than in the public realm, is in some respects comparable to the record of growth in the agricultural domain. As is well known, the State reserved to itself after 1947 control over the "commanding heights" of the economy. In other words, the State established its monopoly in the domain of heavy industry, and in related areas, leaving to private enterprise a fertile field of activity in the fabrication of goods for popular consumption. This division of labour between public and private economic activity also reflected a balance of political power between the industrial bourgeoisie, on the one hand, and the populist classes, on the other. Thus, a political no less than an economic balance was achieved in the blueprint for development that was drawn up in the 1950s. This notion of "balanced development" is further substantiated by the place accorded to artisan and craft activity in the growth of the economy; because here, too, we strike a social interest which needed to be accommodated within the framework of a strategy for growth.

VI

We do not propose to dwell any longer upon the growth of the industrial and agricultural sectors under the policies adopted in India after 1947. It is enough to emphasise that the developments outlined here yielded results unprecedented in India's historical experience, though the record is not wholly free of failures and distortions. The nature of these failures and distortions becomes clear when we examine the political problems posed by these decades of growth and development.

The first series of problems pertain to the rural domain. Because of the vertical as well as the horizontal expansion of agriculture over the past three decades, rural society in India is, today, characterised by a very substantial class of rich peasants, well-versed in high technology agriculture and fully alive to the requirements of a market economy. The emergence of this new class has created serious problems for rural society, locally, as well as for the wider polity, nationally. Locally, these affluent peasant-proprietors seek to extract more and more from those below them in the rural communities, whose labour they exploit in the capacity of a docile workforce. Nationally, the emergence of the rich peasants has generated acute tensions, which almost threaten to overwhelm the alliance of different classes represented by the Congress since the 1920s. Historically, the peasantry constituted the backbone of the Congress. But with its appetite for social and economic power stimulated by the affluence which it has already experienced, the newly enriched peasantry imposes upon the polity demands which are exceedingly difficult to fulfil. Indeed, there is some evidence to suggest that since the late 1960s, particularly in the states of north India, this class has deserted the ranks of the Congress to seek in fragmented political formations the satisfaction of its demand for a larger share of the gross national product. This development has conferred a great measure of instability upon the polity and renders the task of effective governance an exceedingly difficult one.[10]

To emphasise the social and economic challenges posed to the polity by the rich peasants is to refer to the obvious. Indeed, there exists a substantial corpus of literature in the social sciences which focuses upon the consequences flowing from this development, for instance, on the sharpening of localised social conflicts and the rise of new political formations which profess to speak for the newly enriched rural interest. However, if the enlarged appetite for social power of the rich peasantry was the only demand faced by the polity, then the problem would have been one of manageable proportions. It is equally important to remember, that a very substantial industrial sector has come into existence in India since 1947, a section of which is controlled by the State and a section by private enterprise. As in the case of the newly enriched peasantry, the industrial classes, too, have become more demanding in what they expect of the economy by way of consumption. Taken altogether, these developments have been responsible for the generation of a sizeable middle class, just as they have also been responsible for the generation of a substantial working class. Furthermore, the middle and the working classes have acquired social aspirations which are exceedingly difficult to satisfy within the framework of the multi-class political alliance that has characterised the electoral strategy of the Congress since the 1950s. To put it briefly, the different classes which had extended support to the Congress since 1920, and which continued to do so till the 1960s, have now fragmented into antagonistic social groups whose aspirations are difficult, if not impossible, to satisfy within the framework of a single political formation.

The groundswell upon which we have focused is sensitively reflected in the turbulence and fragility of contemporary Indian politics. The seminal development here is the break-up of the alliance between different classes represented by the Congress, since the late 1960s, because of the economic growth achieved in the first twenty years after 1947. The Congress now maintains its position in the political realm largely as a result of electoral alliances with a wide constellation of marginal classes and ethnic groups in Indian society. This is a phenomenon which is very well recognised by political activists as well as by social scientists. What is less well recognised is the fragility which the aggregation of electoral majorities by such a strategy imposes on the political system as a whole. The problem is further complicated by the fact that no alternative political organisation is visible, which has the capacity, or the vision, to cement a working relationship between those different classes and communities which underscored the functioning of the Indian National Congress, whether as the expression of organised nationalism before 1947, or as a party of social and economic reconstruction after 1947.

We have referred in the foregoing to some of the social tensions which characterise political society in India contemporaneously. We have referred also to the challenges posed by the emergence of these tensions in our polity. However, this is not to suggest that the problems facing India are so overwhelming, in their magnitude and in their quality, that they are beyond resolution. A society which has endured for three millennia must surely contain within itself the creative potential to face such challenges successfully. Moreover, it is important to stress that the challenges which India faces today, are a result of the successes, and not the failures, of the initiatives taken in the 1950s. If this is recognised, then we should be able to approach these challenges with a true assessment of India's capacities. Social scientists and political activists should be able to locate those areas upon which creative effort should be focused. If this is done, then the vision of a modern industrial community, capable of stimulating the moral as well as the material creativity of its members, may well be realised in the decades which lie ahead.

NOTES

1. R.S. Sharma, *Material Culture and Social Formations in Ancient India* (Delhi, 1983), Chapters V and VI. Also see Irfan Habib, "The Peasant in Indian History", *Social Scientist*, No. 118, March 1983.
2. See J.E. Carpenter, *Themes in Mediaeval India* , (Oxford, 1981), Chapter VII. Also see R.C. Zaohner, *Hinduism* (London, 1962), Chapter VI.
3. This is the principal argument of some authoritative scholars on the subject. See, in particular, M. Mujeeb, *The Indian Muslims* (London, 1965); Aziz Ahmed, *Studies in Islamic Culture in the Indian Environment* (Oxford, 1964) and A.K. Majumdar, *Bhakti Renaissance* (Bombay, 1965).
4. See, for instance, the views of one of the most influential nationalist thinkers of the 19th century, M.G. Ranade, as expressed in his essay "Indian Political Economy" in M.G. Ranade, *Essays on India Economics* (Madras, 1906), pp. 1-42.
5. I have spelt out this argument at some length in my essay "Nationalism and Social Change" in *Essays in the Social History of Modern India* (Oxford, 1983), pp. 1-30.
6. The classical work on secularism in India is D.E. Smith, *India as a Secular State* (Princeton, 1963). Also see R. Iyer, *Moral and Political Thought of Mahatma Gandhi*, (Oxford, 1973) and my essay entitled "The Varieties of Secular Experience" reproduced in the book cited in note 5 above.
7. See Bipan Chandra, "Jawaharlal Nehru and the Capitalist Class" in *Economic and Political Weekly*, Vol. X, No. 33-35, August 1975. Also see R. Kothari's "The Congress System in India" and G. Krishna's "One Party Dominance—Development and Trends" in *Party System and Election Studies*, CSDS.
8. A.H. Hanson, *The Process of Planning* (Oxford, 1966), Chapter XIII.
9. F.R. Frankel, *India's Political Economy 1947-1977* (Oxford, 1978), Chapters III and IV.
10. P.R. Brass, "The Congress, the Lok Dal and the Middle Peasant Castes: An Analysis of the 1977 and 1980 Parliamentary Elections in U.P." in *The Pacific Affairs*, Vol. V, No. 1, Spring 1981, pp. 5-41.

8

Jawaharlal Nehru, the Indian National Congress and the Anti-Fascist Struggle (1939-1945)*

As the three leaders of the great coalition against Nazi Germany, Attlee, Stalin and Truman, assembled at Potsdam in the summer of 1945, to determine the fate of an utterly devastated and war-ravaged Europe, the struggle for national liberation in India moved dramatically towards its climax. Yet even in the midst of their life and death struggle for the liberation of India from British imperialism, the leaders of this liberation movement, prominent among them Jawaharlal Nehru, maintained a keen interest in the course of world politics, partly out of humanitarian concern, but partly also out of the conviction that developments in Europe and elsewhere could not but affect the course of Indian politics. Indeed, when the Potsdam Conference ended in a declaration setting out, among other things, the fate of Germany in the post-War era, Jawaharlal Nehru was quick to react to the decisions of the three leaders who headed the anti-Hitler coalition. Voicing his satisfaction at the destruction of Nazism and of the regime of terror which it had established over European civilisation, Nehru observed: "German militarism had to be destroyed and the possibility of future aggression prevented."[1] Yet as a leader of a nation which was still subject to one of the three powers which had brought Nazi Germany to its knees, Jawaharlal Nehru was acutely conscious of the fact that the colonial and semi-colonial societies of Asia and Africa exercised, at that juncture, very little influence on the course of world events. The successful culmination of the liberation movements of Asia and Africa, Jawaharlal Nehru

*I am much beholden to my colleague, Miss Deepa Bhatnagar, for her assistance in locating materials for this essay.

believed, would decisively alter the balance of power in the international community; and among other liberated nations, India, with her vast resources in men and materials, and her tremendous industrial potential, would surely raise her voice in support of sanity and equity in the world order. "At the present moment the Big Three are deciding these vital issues," Jawaharlal Nehru stated, ". . . India has (not) been consulted . . . . Though India's voice may be powerless today, it will not be so in the future. I hope whatever influence India comes to possess will be used to evolve more stable conditions of world peace and freedom."[2]

Jawaharlal Nehru's reaction to the Potsdam Declaration rested upon a profound development in world history linked, on the one hand, to the changing interface between the imperialist powers of western Europe, and on the other, to a nationalist resurgence in the colonial societies of Asia and Africa. Since the dawn of the 20th century, nationalist movements of great significance had convulsed Asian and African societies, stimulating the moral and material creativity of their members, and encouraging them to throw off the overarching dominance of the West. Within India, Jawaharlal Nehru was one among hundreds upon thousands of young men who were drawn into the nationalist upsurge in the years after World War I. He brought to bear upon his participation in the liberation movement a number of questions about the objectives as well as the future of this movement. Was the liberation struggle a purely political phenomenon? Or was it equally a social and economic phenomenon? What was the relationship between nationalist politics within India, and the international politics that determined relations between the capitalist societies of the West and the colonial societies of Asia and Africa?

The answers to the questions posed by Jawaharlal Nehru were provided by the ideology of socialism which had become a significant factor in world politics, subsequent to the Bolshevik Revolution of 1917. The national movement in India, so Jawaharlal Nehru discerned, was an integral constituent of the global struggle of oppressed classes for liberation from exploitation and bondage. Within India, this global struggle drew upon the organised strength of the popular masses—in particular, the peasantry and the industrial working class—who were exploited and denied the fruits of their labour by the landed as well as the industrial magnates. Outside India, this global struggle was reflected in the conflict between the capitalist societies of the West and the colonial societies of Asia and Africa. Socialist Russia, with its novel system of producing wealth and of distributing it between different classes, was fully involved in the struggle between the exploiters and the exploited of the world. Increasingly, the liberal polities of the West, whose survival as capitalist societies was inextricably linked to the exploitation of their colonies, were turning to brutal forms of repression to retain their hold over the subject peoples whose wealth they appropriated for consumption. Increasingly, also, within the colonial societies, movements of national liberation, which were simultaneously movements seeking to end the oppression of the poor by the rich, were gathering strength through the organisation of the popular masses and their transformation from the objects into the subjects of history. By the 1930s, for instance, within India a liberation movement of great strength, resting upon the support of the intelligentsia and the toiling classes, and led by outstanding figures like Mahatma Gandhi and Jawaharlal Nehru, had struck deep roots in the soil. Jawaharlal Nehru, much more than his mentor, Mahatma Gandhi, realised that the success of their struggle was closely linked to the fate of democratic and progressive movements elsewhere in the world. Hence the close interest with which he followed events in Europe; and even more so, in the Soviet Union, which during the decades under consideration was engaged in a programme of reconstruction along socialist lines.

I

From the vantage point which he occupied as a leader of the liberation movement in India, Jawaharlal Nehru viewed with increasing concern the growth of fascism in Italy and Japan and the rise of Nazism in Germany. His commitment to the principles of socialism, as the most desirable means of reorganising human society upon a rational and equitable basis, conferred upon him a sensitive appreciation of fascism and Nazism as a social phenomena. Moreover, this perception was heightened—in a manner denied to socialists in Europe—by Jawaharlal Nehru's existential experience of British imperialism in India. Like all socialists, Jawaharlal Nehru believed that fascism and Nazism, with their frightful repudiation of everything that was creative even in bourgeois societies, came into existence "when a capitalist state was threatened during an economic crisis by socialist revolution".[3] However, so he also believed, over and above economic causation lay specific political factors; for instance, the fatal weakness of the Italian Risorgimento, which paved the way for the rise of Mussolini and his fascist gangs; or the gulf between social democracy and communism in Germany in the 1930s, which (in combination with other factors) enabled Hitler and his hoodlums to control state power, and establish a regime of unparalleled barbarity in the very heart of European civilisation.

As the citizen of a colonial society, however, Jawaharlal Nehru was able to discern a relationship between authoritarianism within and imperialism outside Europe which did not communicate itself readily to European socialists. This stemmed from his experience of the *Pax Britannica* in India. For whatever be the character of the British polity in its metropolitan base, the face which Britain presented to India was extremely unlovely. Indeed, the British Government in India, notwithstanding the facade of representative assemblies (elected by the vote of the exploiting classes within India) and the promises of constitutional autonomy in the future, became increasingly brutal in its suppression of the popular desire for political freedom and social equity. The horrifying incident at Jallianwala Bagh in 1919, when the British army fired upon a peaceful assembly of citizens, killing 1000 of them, was merely one among a number of episodes, which reflected the true face of the *Pax Britannica* in India. Indeed, Jawaharlal Nehru frankly looked upon the British Government in India as a fascist regime; in justification of which he could point to the manner in which organisations reflecting the popular will, like the Indian National Congress, had been repeatedly placed outside the pale of the law, and tens upon thousands of Indians denied their liberties as free citizens. He also believed that the fascist face of the British Government, as an instrument of imperial rule, could not be without repercussions on the character of the metropolitan polity. In the long run, liberalism at home and authoritarianism abroad was an untenable mix. This was also reflected in the extent to which conservative politicians, in particular, were willing to accommodate, through the policy of appeasement, the growing appetite of Nazi Germany and fascist Italy in the 1930s. For all these reasons, so Jawaharlal Nehru believed, fascism and imperialism (rather than the former alone) were the two principal evils of the time, which it was incumbent upon all progressive elements to fight with the resources at their disposal. As he put it: "The world is faced today with two obnoxious movements. They are Fascism and Nazism which are prevailing in Italy and Germany, and also in Japan. Fascism is a close relation of imperialism."[4] Or again: ". . . essentially imperialism and fascism are close of kin and one merges into the other. Sometime imperialism has two faces—a domestic one talking the language of democracy, and a colonial one merging into fascism."[5] Indeed, the two were extricably linked with each other; and what the nations of Europe were experiencing in the decades after World War I, the civilisations of Asia and Africa had suffered ever since their political autonomy had been destroyed by the aggressive expansion of European polities.

II

Jawaharlal Nehru's perception of the relationship between fascism and imperialism, on the one hand, and between national liberation movements and socialist movements, on the other, was sensitively reflected in the stance which he adopted in international politics on the eve of World War II. Indeed, ever since Nehru had attended, as a representative of the Indian National Congress, the Brussels Congress of the League Against Imperialism in 1927, he maintained contacts with some of the leaders of the socialist movement in the West, and through such contacts, he was able to extend the moral support of the Indian National Congress to those forces which stood for democracy and progress in Europe.

The crucial factor behind the growth of fascism in Europe, and increasing imperialist aggression in Asia and Africa, as perceived by Jawaharlal Nehru, was the vacillation—if not the actual connivance—of the Conservative statesmen who presided over the destiny of the British Empire. It was likely, for instance, that at any point in the early 1930s, Britain, if it so desired, could have checked German expansion by making it clear to Hitler that acts of adventurism on his part would be resisted by the British Government with all the resources it could command. But to take a clear stand against Hitler would mean supporting democracy in Europe, as well as in Asia and Africa. It would also mean making a choice between the Soviet Union and Nazi Germany. The conservative politicians who ruled over Britain were unwilling to make such a choice; because of their class position within the country; and also because of Britain's position within Europe as a whole. In the words of Jawaharlal Nehru:

> . . . If Britain had made it clear to Germany that in the event of violence being attempted, she would certainly resist it, Germany would have acted differently. It was within the British power to give this warning in the summer of 1938. Yet it was astounding to behold how safely the whole situation was planned out by Chamberlain's government The mission and the repeated surrenders to Hitler's demands are not merely accidental. They are the results of a calculated policy of surrender to fascist aggression.
>
> The fact is that England had to make a choice between Soviet Russia and Germany. If the British Government had genuinely desired an extension of democracy then Russia would not have appeared a greater danger than Germany. But the deliberate policy has been one of siding with fascism everywhere, either in Asia or in Africa.[6]

Not that the situation in Britain, or elsewhere in the capitalist world, was altogether without hope. Jawaharlal Nehru, for instance, was conscious of the tensions within the conservative leadership in Britain, which could bring about a dramatic change of policy towards the fascist powers.[7] Traditionally, so he argued, British foreign policy had been directed towards safeguarding the Empire and the routes which linked the metropolitan centre of the Empire to the far-flung colonies in Asia and Africa. But the emergence of the Soviet Union placed a new item on the agenda of British foreign policy objectives: the undermining, if not the total elimination, of the socialist threat to the regime of property in capitalist societies. The rise of fascism in Italy and Nazism in Germany posed a serious dilemma to British statesmen. At first blush, such a development could be regarded as a reinforcement of property and order in European civilisation. Hence the tacit support which Britain extended to fascism in Europe and Asia in the initial stages. But fascism was so pathological a variant of capitalism—its appetite for territory and markets so insatiable; and its political manifestation so nightmarish—that its leaders soon acquired the ambition of undermining Britain's position as a world power; establishing their hegemony over Europe; and looking for *lebensraum* in Europe, Asia and Africa. By the middle of the 1930s, therefore, the conservative leadership of Britain was split into two opposing factions. Those who put Empire before Europe, and wanted Hitler and Mussolini to be eliminated at all costs; and those who put Europe before Empire, and were reluctant to befriend the Soviet Union in order to control the growing appetite of the fascist powers. This is not to suggest that conservatives like Churchill, who were very hostile to Nazi Germany, and seriously concerned about the threat which Germany posed to the British Empire, looked upon the prospect of social revolution at home or abroad with indifference. Or that men like Chamberlain were reluctant to protect the Empire in their concern to stem the tide of social revolution. This is merely to highlight the differences within the conservative leadership in Britain as to the manner in which class and imperial interests could be protected; and the national power of Britain maintained at the level at which it stood in the closing decades of the 19th century, or the opening decades of the 20th century.

The social democrat in Jawaharlal Nehru, who saw fascism and imperialism as mirror images of each other, and who also looked upon the liberation of India as a process inextricably linked with the growth of socialism and democracy in the world, reacted to each instance of aggression by Mussolini, or the warlords of Japan, or Hitler, with feelings of horror and anger. On the other hand, because of their hostility to the Soviet Union, the leaders of Britain and France—at any rate the dominant establishment—virtually gave a blank cheque to the fascist powers in order to appease them and also to contain the Soviet Union.[8] At the very outset, Britain negotiated a Naval Pact with Germany in violation of the Versailles Treaty. France, threatened with isolation, rushed into the hands of Italy, and assured Mussolini of neutrality in the event of the invasion of Abyssinia by Italian armies. This arrangement was in turn reinforced through a secret deal between the French Foreign Minister, Pierre Laval, and the British Foreign Secretary, Sir Samuel Hoare; though public outcry at such an unscrupulous agreement forced Hoare to give way to Anthony Eden. Yet the exit of Hoare made no difference in British policy towards fascist aggression. A statement from Chamberlain spelling out Britain's indifference to Austria sealed the fate of this core region of the former Austro-Hungarian Empire, and led to the *Anschluss* of 1938.

Prior to 1939, the crucial battle between the democracies, on the one hand, and the fascist powers, on the other, was fought in Spain. Indeed, the Spanish Civil War was a dress rehearsal for World War II. The issues at stake were plain for everyone to see. Formally speaking, a legitimately elected republican government, with socialist elements as a part of the ruling coalition, was being threatened to death by a fascist clique within the country. Substantively, the fall of Republican Spain would bring about the encirclement of France, on the east and on the south, by hostile fascist formations. Yet even in the face of such grave danger, France and Britain refused to stir themselves, and take a firm stand *vis-à-vis* the fascist menace. Small wonder, then, that Hitler was encouraged to initiate yet another adventure in the Balkans. Small wonder, also, that notwithstanding their formal commitment to defend the territorial integrity of Czechoslovakia, Britain and France obliged the Czech leaders to concede to the Nazi demands at Munich, in the hope that they would thereby win for their countries durable peace.

Jawaharlal Nehru and other leaders of the liberation movement in India followed the fascist upsurge in Europe with growing concern. But events nearer home in Asia; for instance, the violation of territorial integrity of China by Japan; or the Palestine problem; evoked a deeper response from the leaders or the people of India than happenings in distant Europe. Indeed, even Jawaharlal Nehru, who was so deeply influenced by the culture of the West, spoke of China and her agony with a depth of feeling that was not discernible in his utterances about Europe:

> India's sympathy goes out for China for a variety of reasons [Jawaharlal Nehru stated]. Like China India is aspiring and fighting for national freedom. The forces of freedom in both countries extend to each other the hand of sympathy and support. They must band together against the urge of imperialism for exploitation and conquest. They must secure to prevent the use under imperial control of their nationals and soldiers in each other's territory. They must mutually defend themselves by refusing economic relations with the imperialist invader. They must prepare themselves for the day when they can strike a simultaneous blow at all imperialism. . . . The ancient friendship of the two peoples of China and India must now be reinforced by the new *camaraderie* of the two freedom loving nations.[9]

The importance which the leaders of the Congress attached to what can only be described as a common front against imperialism is admirably reflected in the support which they held out to their neighbour in the north. Jawaharlal Nehru pointed out how "thousands of demonstrations" were held in condemnation of the invasion of China; and "out of her poverty we extended our helping hand to them in the shape of food and medical missions".[10] The medical mission to which he referred consisted of a contingent of doctors which was sent to China. This mission attached itself to the Eighth Route Army commanded by Zhu De (Chu Teh) then engaged in hostilities with the Japanese army. The services rendered by the medical mission were acknowledged by Mao Zedong (Mao Tse-tung) in a letter to Jawaharlal Nehru which voiced the hope that "the Indian people will continue to help and aid us. . . [to] drive out the Japanese imperialists".[11]

The stance adopted by Jawaharlal Nehru towards fascism, or its specific manifestations in Europe, Asia and Africa, stemmed from his socialist vision and his cosmopolitan outlook. Yet it would be pertinent to ask: what was the position of prominent men within the Congress, as well as its rank and file, towards fascism in Europe and elsewhere? How did the leaders and the followers of the liberation movement, as a whole, view international politics?

Perhaps no simple answer can be given to these questions. Yet certain trends within the Congress are clearly discernible. At the very outset, it is important to remember that the towering figure of Mahatma Gandhi completely dominated nationalist politics in the subcontinent in the period under review. Gandhi looked upon fascism as the embodiment of evil. Yet he was also opposed to violence on moral grounds. As a result of this, Gandhi's opposition to fascism did not necessarily lead him to support war against fascism. Moreover, the Mahatma lacked the sensitive grasp of world politics which characterised the stances of Jawaharlal Nehru. Close to Gandhi within the Indian National Congress stood a group of conservative leaders, like Sardar Patel, or Rajendra Prasad, or C. Rajagopalachari, who shared the Mahatma's views on questions relating to war and peace. Also close to Gandhi, though the Mahatma did not fully share his vision, stood Jawaharlal Nehru and a small group of socialists who were unreservedly hostile to fascism. Yet the leaders of the Congress—even those who were committed to a socialist worldview—were not as sensitive to international as they were to national issues. Indeed, their primary impulse was to attack British imperialism at the first available opportunity, because British imperialism was the proximate enemy. All told, therefore, the leaders and the cadres of the Congress were opposed to fascism whether it reared its head. Yet they believed that since India, too, was an enslaved society at that juncture, their immediate responsibility was to liberate India, and then and then only join an anti-Hitler crusade.

III

As the Polish crisis came to a head in the autumn of 1939, the leaders of the Indian National Congress were obliged to take a concrete stand on the great issues of war and peace which confronted humanity with urgency hitherto unknown to history. On the initiative of leaders like Jawaharlal Nehru, the Congress had already framed its attitude to events in Europe and elsewhere. A resolution adopted at the Tripuri session of the Congress, held in May 1939, roundly condemned the policies leading to the Munich Pact and the recognition of rebel Spain. These policies were described as a "deliberate betrayal of democracy". In distancing itself from the British Government, or its liberal allies, the Congress voiced its opposition to "fascism and imperialism alike", and its determination to formulate its own policy as "an independent nation truly keeping aloof from both imperialism and fascism, and pursuing her path of freedom."[12] The Congress, at this juncture, was not an organisation solely interested in populist agitations. It had also established a firm grip upon the formal institutions of political power. Under the Constitution of 1935, the British Government had conferred a substantial measure of autonomy on the provinces of British India. In the provincial elections held under this constitution in 1937, the Congress had captured power in eight out of the eleven provinces where electoral contests took place. Indeed, apart from significant sections of Muslim India, all classes and communities had extended support in the 1937 elections to the Congress as the authentic voice of resurgent India and the spokesmen of her nationalist aspirations.

The outbreak of hostilites in September 1939 between Britain and France, on the one hand, and Nazi Germany, on the other, found the leadership of the Congress fully prepared to play their role in the anti-fascist struggle, *provided* the British Government formally acknowledged the people's desire for freedom. The Congress leaders reiterated their hostility to fascism immediately after the outbreak of war. They also took note of the proclamation of the Governments of Britain and France that they were fighting for "freedom and democracy and to put an end to aggression". Yet such a pronouncement was no substitute for firm action. The Congress leaders believed that India's entry into war could only be decided by the people; and they would reject the exploitation of India's resources for imperialist ends. Most important of all, the war put before the British Government an opportunity to secure the cooperation of the Indian people in the anti-Hitler struggle, provided it took expeditious steps to assure them of their freedom:

> If the war is to defend the status quo, imperialist possessions, colonies, vested interests and privileges, then India can have nothing to do with it [The Congress Working Committee stated in a resolution]. If, however, the issue is democracy and a world order based on democracy, then India is intensely interested in it. . . . But there is an inherent and ineradicable conflict between democracy for India or elsewhere and imperialism and fascism. If Great Britain fights for the maintenance and extension of democracy, then she must necessarily end imperialism in her own possessions, [and] establish full democracy in India. . . . A free democratic India will gladly associate herself with other free nations for mutual defence against aggression and for economic co-operation. She will work for the establishment of a real world order based on freedom and democracy, utilising the world's knowledge and resources for the progress and advancement of humanity. . . .
>
> The Working Committee [of the Congress] therefore invite the British Government to declare in unequivocal terms what their war aims are in regard to democracy and imperialism and the new order that is envisaged, in particular, how these aims are going to apply to India and to be given effect to in the present. . . . The real test of any declaration is its application in the present, for it is the present that will govern action to-day and give shape to the future.[13]

The British Government did not mince words in reacting to the challenge posed by the nationalist leaders of India. The Viceroy, Lord Linlithgow, reiterated the assurances first held out in 1917, namely, that the objective of British rule in India was "the progressive realisation of responsible government in British India as an integral part of the Empire".[14] A further concession was offered to nationalist sentiment insofar as Linlithgow also suggested that, after the cessation of hostilities, the British Government would consult various political interests in the country (including the princely rulers) to decide whether it was necessary to modify the Constitution of 1935.

The Viceroy's statement amounted to a virtual rejection of the legitimacy of the Congress and the nationalist aspirations which it represented. Jawaharlal Nehru, therefore, was quick to respond to such a statement. Dismissing the assurances held out by Lord Linlithgow as assurances fished out of the "dust-bin" of history, he described the viceregal statement as "a complete repudiation of all that India stands for nationally and internationally."[15] Nor was the Congress tardy in repositing to the Viceroy's move. The Congress Working Committee met at Wardha, in October 1939, to consider steps appropriate to the stance of the British Government. The leaders of the Congress felt that they could not embark upon any serious step, like a countrywide agitation, without adequate preparation. But as a preliminary step, they directed the Congress ministries in the provinces, where the Congress had secured a majority in the elections of 1937, to resign from office.[16] The resignation of the Congress ministries was meant to be a tentative step towards a renewed confrontation between nationalist forces in India, on the one hand, and the British Government, on the other. Yet a social democrat like Jawaharlal Nehru knew that whatever happened in India was not unrelated to developments elsewhere. In a confidential memorandum on Congress policy, Jawaharlal Nehru speculated about the likely course of events and about the desirable course of action for Indian nationalists in the years which lay ahead.[17] He felt that any hasty action would, in the circumstances, be wholly counterproductive. Nor could those engaged in the task of liberating India from the shackles of imperialism take any step that would, even inadvertently, assist fascism and Nazism. Perhaps a policy of watching out on events; and of taking timely and appropriate steps when necessary was what was really needed. Certainly, so Jawaharlal Nehru argued, those engaged in liberating India should apply pressure on the British Government in order to force it to reveal its war aims and its future plans for the Empire. From the nationalist standpoint, an undertaking to the effect that the future of India would be decided by a constituent assembly, resting upon adult franchise, and immediate steps that would assure the people of India of British intentions, would be the ideal state of affairs. However, whether the British Government would embark upon such policies was an entirely different matter. Indeed, with Winston Churchill, the most diehard of imperialists, assuming the office of the Prime Minister in May 1940, there was little likelihood of any liberal gesture towards India. In a speech made on this occasion, Churchill spelt out British war aims in phrases which admitted of little ambiguity:

> You ask what is our aim? I can answer in one word: It is victory, victory at all costs, victory in spite of all the terror, victory, however long and hard the road may be; for without victory there is no survival. Let that be realised: no survival for the British Empire, no survival for all that the British Empire has stood for; no survival for the urge and impulse of the ages, that mankind would move forward towards its goal.[18]

After such a statement, it was clear that whatever a British victory might mean for the Nazi dominated nations of Europe, so far as the people of India were concerned, they had little chance of regaining their freedom as long as Churchill was at the helm of affairs.

It remained for the Viceroy, Lord Linlithgow, to relate the overall objectives voiced by Churchill to the specificities of the Indian situation. Two developments, one within the country, and the other in Europe, prepared the background for such a consummation. In March 1940, the Muslim League, a party which claimed to speak for the Muslim community in India, resolved that the Muslims of the subcontinent would refuse to accept any constitutional arrangements which did not bestow on them an "autonomous and sovereign" status.[19] Shortly afterwards, in June 1940, France collapsed dramatically before an onslaught of Hitler's panzer divisions. Jawaharlal Nehru and the Congress leaders viewed with horror the growing strength of fascism; and the hegemony which Hitler had acquired over Europe after the fall of France. These developments obliged the leaders of the Congress to soften their position *vis-à-vis* the British Government in India. In expressing their shock over the tragic fate which had overtaken

France, they declared that if a provisional national government was installed in New Delhi, truly representative of the people, then the Congress would throw its full weight behind the defence of India.[20]

Yet even so conciliatory a stance merely earned for the Congress a rebuff from the Viceroy. In his statement of August 1940, Linlithgow told the Congress that, so far as drawing the people into the governance of India was concerned, he had been authorised to nominate representative Indians to the Executive Council; and also to constitute a War Advisory Council which would, among others, draw upon the Princely Rulers.[21] However, on the larger question of handing over power to popular representatives after the termination of hostilities, the British Government (in an obvious reference to the resolution adopted by the Muslim League in March 1940) would not yield control over India "to any system of government whose authority is directly denied by large and powerful elements in India's national life."[22] Jawaharlal decreed the Viceroy's statement to be a parting of ways.[23] Shortly afterwards, the Congress adopted a resolution advocating civil disobedience, though in view of the war situation, the resolution proposed individual rather than mass action on the part of satyagrahis.[24]

IV

The Congress decision to initiate civil disobedience (through individual rather than mass action) in August 1940 landed tens upon thousands of nationalists, both well-known and obscure, in British prisons. Among the prisoners was Jawaharlal Nehru, who had to spend the period between October 1940 and December 1941 as a guest of His Britannic Majesty! In the meanwhile, events moved towards a climax in the existing as well as in the newly opened war-fronts. Perhaps the most momentous of these was the invasion of the Soviet Union by Nazi Germany on 22 June 1941. Jawaharlal Nehru read the news of the invasion in Gorakhpur prison, where he had been incarcerated since October 1940, and wrote prophetically in his diary: "So Germany and Russia are at war!. . . . Somehow I expected war between these two sometime or other—but much later. . . . What will happen, it is rash to guess—Probably early German victories, even big victories—But this seems to sound the death-knell of the Nazi regime sometime or other."[25] No less significant was the entry of Japan into the war on 7 December 1941, through an attack on the U.S. Fleet stationed at Pearl Harbour. Thereafter, one country after another in Southeast Asia region fell into the hands of the Japanese in rapid succession. With the capture of Burma in March 1942, the triumphant Japanese stood at the very doorsteps of British India. Never had the British Empire stood in such dire peril as it stood in the spring of 1942. In its anxiety to persuade its Indian subjects to participate in the defence of India against Japan, the British Government released those Congress leaders who had been arrested earlier, in connection with individual civil disobedience.

The released Congress leaders assembled at Bardoli, on 14 December 1941, to take stock of the war situation. Apart from the proximity of India to the theatres of war in Southeast Asia, the central concern of the Indian leaders, at this juncture, was the course of events in the Soviet Union and in China. The Nazi armies stood at the gate of Moscow; and Japan had acquired control over vast territories in northern and central China. Jawaharlal Nehru and the Congress leaders looked on the Soviet Union as a repository of "human and social values" which were essential for the "progress of humanity". Similarly, China had displayed "unparalleled heroism" in fighting Japanese aggression. As the authentic spokesmen of the people of India, therefore, the leaders of the Congress extended their moral support to Soviets, and to the people of China, in the struggle they were waging against fascism. As a subject nation, India could do little more till such time as she was free of the British yoke.[26]

The lengthening shadow of war in Asia soon imparted a new urgency to the political situation in the subcontinent. The Japanese army, which had established superiority over the British army, moved towards South Asia with great speed, and with the fall of Burma in the spring of 1942, stood poised for a fresh venture upon the frontiers of India. At this crucial moment, there was every reason for the British Government to seek accommodation with the leaders of India, so that in the event of a Japanese invasion, both the people of India and their leaders would extend full support to the war effort. Within the coalition government the Labour leaders, particularly Clement Attlee and Stafford Cripps, put pressure on Churchill to resolve the constitutional problem in

India. Churchill faced similar pressure from Roosevelt, and China, too, supported to the full the Indian desire for freedom.

The task of negotiating a settlement with the political leaders of India fell upon Sir Stafford Cripps, who was believed to be sympathetic to the cause of Indian freedom. Yet the Cripps Mission was more of a propaganda gesture by the Churchill government—directed towards the United States and towards left-wing opinion within the Labour Party—than a genuine attempt to resolve the Indian problem.[27] The terms which Cripps carried with him appeared, at first blush, to be generous. But they contained the seeds of the balkanisation of the subcontinent, upon which issue Gandhi, Nehru and other leaders were determined to compromise not at all. Small wonder, then, that from the very outset Gandhi opposed the Cripps proposals, and he was able to persuade other Congress leaders, too, to reject them as proposals subversive of the unity of India for which the Congress had struggled for decades.[28]

The failure of the Cripps Mission gave relief to the conservative and imperialist groups within the British Government. But its effect upon nationalist circles in India was disastrous. Cripps' proposals and the flurry of political activity which they provoked conveyed the impression that Cripps was in a position to break through the constitutional impasse and pave the way for popular rule in India. But when the Cripps' mission ended in a deadlock, the Congress rank and file, and the people of India as a whole, were sorely disappointed and turned to their leaders with the expectation that they would initiate a movement which would deal a deathblow to British rule over India.

Gandhi, Nehru and other prominent leaders of the Congress fully lived up to popular expectations. In the second week of August 1942, the All India Congress Committee adopted a resolution calling upon the British to quit India and to leave its governance to the people and their representatives.[29] For a socialist like Nehru, to initiate a struggle against the British Government in August 1942, at a time when the Soviet Union was sorely threatened by the Nazi armies and Britain was part of the anti-Fascist alliance, was no easy matter. The debate within the Congress circles, more particularly between leaders like Nehru and those who were less concerned with international trends, is vividly reflected in the repeated redrafting of the "Quit India" resolution by the All India Congress Committee before its final adoption. Yet anger of the Indian people; and the deviousness (or worse) with which the Churchill Government handled the situation; called for an unambiguous expression of the popular will, so that an independent rather than an enslaved India could take its rightful place with other democratic countries in the global struggle against fascism.

The British Government, on its part, was fully prepared for a new round of agitation by the Congress after the failure of the Cripps Mission. In order to thwart any such movement, the leaders of the Congress were arrested as soon as the "Quit India" resolution was adopted. What took the British Government completely by surprise, however, was the scale and intensity of the popular response to the Congress call for decisive action. In the absence of the senior Congress leaders, who had been whisked away to Ahmednagar Fort prison, the urban and the rural classes of India, particularly in the west, the north and the north-east, rose in a mighty wave of protest against the British administration. Indeed, for the space of a month or more, organised government ceased to exist in many parts of India. In some rural districts—for instance, Satara or Midnapore—parallel governments were constituted, which performed most of the functions of a regular administration. At a moment when a Japanese invasion was imminent, nearly 90 per cent of the armies stationed on the Assam-Burma border of India were re-deployed in the interior regions to quell the popular uprisings. Tactically speaking, the Uprising of 1942 was defeated through the exercise of brute power. But the widespread support which it generated made it clear that henceforth British control over India would rest upon naked military power rather than upon the political collaboration of vested interests within Indian society.

Between the summer of 1942 and the Potsdam Conference of July 1945, the peace of the graveyard prevailed over the subcontinent of India. With the leaders of the liberation movement in prison, and the popular movement against the British Government suppressed through armies which had ostensibly been assembled to fight the Japanese, there was, for the time being, no effective platform of resistance to alien rule in the subcontinent. In the year following the Uprising of 1942, India made a horrendous contribution to the anti-fascist struggle in the shape of a man-made famine in which millions perished for lack of sustenance. Even the prospect of starvation on such a massive scale did not provoke any resistance, if only for the reason that British repression had stilled the voices of protest, temporarily although not permanently, in India.

When Jawaharlal Nehru and other leaders of the liberation movement in India were released from prison in June 1945, after an incarceration which lasted three years, the world situation had changed almost beyond recognition. The anti-Hitler alliance had brought Nazi Germany to its knees; and Japan, too, faced defeat in the proximate future. Yet in voicing his reaction to the Potsdam Declaration, Jawaharlal Nehru was giving expression to sentiments which were of a piece with the views which he had already expressed on international politics, and on the anti-fascist struggle, in the years prior to 1942. Even before India had acquired full control over her destiny, Jawaharlal Nehru had identified a foreign policy for his country, and for the Third World as a whole, which was to provide the basis for the non-aligned movement in the 1950s. This policy drew upon the historical experience of the erstwhile colonial societies of Asia, Africa and Latin America, and it rested upon a few seminal principles; that the former colonies of the world had good reason to come together in their continuing struggle against imperialism; that the growth of socialism was a highly desirable consummation for the Third World; that peace was the prerequisite for social development in the world; and finally, that with the advent of the nuclear age, war meant the annihilation of mankind, and it was, therefore, incumbent upon peoples everywhere to strive for peace. Perhaps these principles, which under-pin the non-aligned movement, are as valid today as they were valid when first enunciated by Jawaharlal Nehru in the late 1930s. They constitute the basis of a worldwide movement for peace and democracy, and hold out the prospect of moral creativity and material dignity to the citizens of both developing and developed societies.

NOTES

1. Interview by J. Nehru 4 August, 1945. *The Tribune* 6 August, 1945.
2. Ibid.
3. J. Nehru, *Glimpses of World History* (Bombay, 2nd ed., 1962), p. 945.

3. J. Nehru, *Glimpses of World History* (Bombay, 2nd ed., 1962), p. 945.
4. Speech by J. Nehru: *The Leader* 15 April 1934.
5. See J. Nehru, "Fascism & Empire" in *Eighteen Months in India* (Allahabad, 1938), pp. 122-6.
6. J. Nehru, "British Foreign Policy," in *National Herald*, 10 January 1939.
7. See J. Nehru's article entitled "England's Dilemma" in his *China, Japan and the War* (Allahabad, 1940), pp. 134-51.
8. Ibid.
9. J. Nehru's article entitled "Why India Supports China", in *Advance*, 21 August 1931.
10. J. Nehru, "India Looks at the World", in *The Unity of India* (London, 1941), pp. 335-42.
11. *Nehru Memorial Museum Archives* (hereinafter *NMM Archives*): Mao Tse-Tung to J. Nehru 24 May 1939, *Jawaharlal Nehru Papers* (hereinafter *JN Papers*), Vol. 45, p. 132. *JN Papers*, Vol. 14, p. 12 also contains a letter from Chu Teh to J. Nehru dated 26 November 1939 asking for further assistance.
12. *Indian National Congress, March 1939 to January 1940*: Being the Resolutions passed by the Congress, the All India Congress Committee and the Working Committee during the period between March 1939 to January 1940 (Allahabad, n.d.), p. 6.
13. Ibid. Resolution on the "War Crisis" adopted by the Congress Working Committee, 8-15 September 1939, pp. 37-43.
14. Editorial by J. Nehru entitled "The Answer", *National Herald*, 18 October 1939.
15. Ibid.
16. *Indian National Congress, March 1939 to January 1940* (See n. 12): Resolution of Congress Working Committee dated 22-23 October 1939, pp. 46-48.
17. *NMM Archives*: Confidential Note on Congress Policy by J. Nehru, 20 January 1940, JN Papers.
18. Speech by Winston Churchill, 13 May 1940 in House of Commons, *Winston S. Churchill: His Complete Speeches 1897-1963* ed. R.R. James, Vol. VI, 1935-42 (New York, 1974), p. 6220.
19. K.B. Sayeed, *Pakistan: The Formative Phase 1897-1948* (Oxford, 1968), pp. 106-18.
20. B. Prasad, *The Origins of Indian Foreign Policy* (Calcutta, 1962), pp. 177-9.
21. Speech by Lord Linlithgow, 8 August 1940: *Speeches and Statements by the Marquess of Linlithgow* (New Delhi, 1945), pp. 250-2. Also see J. Glendoven, *The Viceroy at Bay* (London, 1971), pp. 180-7.
22. Ibid.
23. See S. Gopal, *Jawaharlal Nehru—A Biography Volume One 1889-1947* (Oxford, 1976), p. 267.
24. *Indian National Congress, March 1940 to September 1946* (Allahabad, n.d.), Resolution of Congress Working Committee dated 18-23 August 1940, pp. 79-84.
25. See *Selected Works of Jawaharlal Nehru*, ed. S. Gopal (New Delhi), Vol. XI: Diary of J. Nehru dated 23 June 1941. p. 637.
26. *Indian National Congress, March 1940 to September 1946* (Allahabad, n.d.). Resolution of Congress Working Committee dated 23-30 December 1941, pp. 96-102.

27. N.S. Mansergh (ed.), *Constitutional Relations Between Britain and India—The Transfer of Power 1942-7* (Hereinafter cited as *Transfer of Power*) Vol. I; The Cripps Mission January-April 1942: L.S. Amery to Linlithgow 11 April 1942, pp. 756-8.
28. Ibid. Note by Stafford Cripps entitled "My Interview with Mahatma Gandhi" dated 27 March 1942.
29. *NMM Archives*. The "Quit India" resolution was the handiwork of Jawaharlal Nehru. He wrote a first draft on 5 August 1942. This was revised twice before a final version was passed at the Bombay meeting of the AICC on 8 August 1942, See *JN Papers*, Part II, File No. 31B.

9

The Historical Roots of Democracy in India

As we reflect upon the state of politics in the Third World during the closing decades of the 20th century, it is striking how few of the developing nations which were liberated from imperial bondage three or four decades ago have survived, in the late 1980s, as liberal polities. India stands as conspicuous example of a developing polity with a relatively stable democratic system. Indeed, both the institutions and the values of liberal democracy have shown considerable vitality and resilience in India; and many a prophet of doom, or worse, has been falsified by the manner in which the political elite has adroitly resolved problems of social integration and economic development at the same time as it has resolved problems of political succession and national survival. This is not to suggest that democratic institutions in India are wholly free of stresses; or that they do not face serious challenges; most important of all, the challenge of providing a life of dignity for tens upon millions of citizens. Yet despite such tensions, the range and vigour of political debate and the vitality of liberal institutions in India, over the past four decades, have attracted considerable comment from scholars and activists concerned with the dynamics of open societies.

It would be valid to suggest that most explanations of the strength of the democratic system in India dwell upon the post-1947 scene, and they attribute the resilience of democratic institutions in the country to the manner in which political elites and political parties have mediated between the formal institutions of politics, on the one hand, and a massive electorate, consisting of an amorphous constellation of social classes, religious communities and linguistic groups, on the other. While these explanations are by no means devoid of merit, they miss some essential characteristics of political society in India, since they do not look at the historical traditions which underpin contemporary politics. To gain a full appreciation of the vitality of democracy in India, and the manner in which the polity has fared in the decades since 1947, it is essential to examine both the traditions of "popular" participation in politics as well as the character of the struggle for freedom which emancipated the country from British rule in 1947. Only through such an exercise is it possible to gain insights into the strength of the values and institutions of liberal democracy within India.

I

The relationship of the pre-colonial State in India with the rural classes was radically different from the relationship of the State with comparable sections of society in the late medieval West. It is widely believed—although the subject is still a matter of scholarly debate—that feudalism of the variety which flourished in Europe did not find any place in the social organisation of medieval Indian society. Yet to deny the existence of feudalism is not to voice agreement with the marxist notion of a timeless Asiatic polity; or equally, with the notion of an unchanging traditional society, so dear to conservative social theorists. The distinguishing trait of the marxist as well as of the conservative delineation of the Indian polity lay in denying the fully articulated existence of private property; and in assuming the existence of perennial village communities, resting on a symbiotic relationship between petite landlords and substantial peasants, on the one hand, and artisans and craftsmen who fulfilled all the needs of the rural classes, other than agricultural needs, on the other. Both these assumptions are now known to be invalid. The institution of private property was firmly established in precolonial society. Moreover, the rural communities, whose existence is traceable to classical times, are also known to have gone through seminal changes in their technology of production; or in the principles on which they were organised socially; or in the spiritual values which provided them with an understanding of the profane and a vision of the sacred domain.

Perhaps it is much more valid to approach the State, in pre-colonial society, through the three levels at which classes and individuals were organised for political activity. In the first instance, it is necessary to dwell upon local society, made up, in its territorial embrace, of a cluster of villages centering upon a market town which could simultaneously serve as a political and administrative centre. These local units of society were presided over by a petty chief or a ruler, who was often tied through kin or clan solidarity to the dominant land-owning classes of the locality; and whose political authority was for that very reason reinforced by his primordial link with these classes. Below the landed classes, in the locality, lay a class of cultivators whose status approximated the status of tenants-at-will or share-croppers; while the nethermost layer of this miniature world was constituted of agricultural labourers or agrestic serfs. Intermeshed in the agrarian networks of local society were small communities of artisans and craftsmen, whose productive activity was shaped by the consumer needs of the rural classes; and who were entitled to a share of the gross agricultural produce, in kind or in cash (though more often the former), for the services they provided to their patrons. The internal structure of local society could vary substantially from one part of the subcontinent to another; depending upon the ecology of the region; or the stratified sediments of diverse social groups; or the nature of political authority at higher levels of the social order. Thus in the south, powerful corporations of merchants, artisans or landlords rendered the authority of the local ruler much more limited than was true in the north. However, despite such variations in texture and structure, the units of local society had considerable durability over time. They, therefore, provided the historical basis for the myth of a timeless and unchanging rural social order.

It would be appropriate, at this juncture, to dwell briefly upon the character of social participation in politics within the units of local society. All available evidence suggests that control over political power was exercised by the local ruler in close association with the petty landed classes to whom he was often tied through bonds of lineage or clan solidarity. Indeed, political power was distributed through local society in a manner which necessitated frequent consultation between the local ruler, also the lineage or clan head, and the landed elite of the locality, whenever any decision affecting the fortune of the community had to be taken. It would be no exaggeration to state that the subordinate rural classes, which actually carried the burden of cultivation, had little voice in the management of the polity and the economy of the local region; though the same was not true of the mercantile and artisan communities. Indeed, the merchants, who controlled rural credit, over and above consumer goods, played a key role in the circulation of the agrarian surplus within the larger region, or the pan-Indian world, to which the locality was linked. Besides, the political power of the local ruler, or his kin and clan fellows, was also kept in check by the counterpoised moral authority of the religious intelligentsia distributed within the locality. The members of this intelligentsia mediated between the belief and practice of the locality and the diverse high cultures of the region; and in doing so, they appropriated to themselves power and status out of proportion to the gifts of land, or goods, which were showered upon them by the landed elite, in return for legitimising the dominant position of this elite in society.

As our perception of ideology, power and the political economy in pre-colonial society gains in subtlety and in detail, it is becoming clear that the local polities, described above, were societal units of considerable durability over time and space. However, their linkages, in the first instance, with regional polities; and in the next, with a pan-Indian polity, were tenuous in the extreme; and led to those repeated integrations and breakdowns of kingdoms and empires which have fed into the myth that, prior to the advent of Islam in the second millennium A.D., India had no political history worth speaking about. Between the regional and the pan-Indian polities, it was the former which had greater cohesion and durability. It is nevertheless important to remember, that the regional polities never displaced the power of the local rulers, who presided, howsoever uneasily, over those localities and landed elites which were the true underpinnings of the political order. More often than not, the regional polities drew these chiefs or rulers into a proto-bureaucracy. Such regional polities also extracted, either in the form of tribute, or in the form of a tax on agricultural produce, the resources which provided the material basis for the sustenance of the regional order. In turn, these polities were linked through a tenuous system of subordination to a pan-Indian polity, presided over by a *chakravartin* ruler, who symbolised in his person suzerainty over the subcontinent as a whole.

The picture which we have presented of the pre-colonial polity, and the three levels—local, regional, or pan-Indian—at which it articulated itself, is brief to the point of caricature. Yet it sketches out the basic structure of this polity with substantial accuracy. What is conspicuously absent in this delineation is the power and authority which crystallised in the Absolute State of the post-feudal European world. It is equally relevant to remember that the most cohesive and articulate unit within the pan-Indian polity—or the regional polities—remained the local domain of the chief or the petty ruler; who was, in turn, crucially dependent upon the goodwill of his kinsmen and clansmen, distributed in the territories of his "little kingdom" as a land-owning gentry, or a dominant peasantry. Such a political system was characterised, on the one hand, by a striking decentralisation of power and an equally striking tenuousness of linkage between different political levels; and on the other, by the powerful voice which the land-owning gentry, or the dominant peasantry, exercised in the management of local affairs. What pre-colonial society in India possessed, therefore, was a political system in which the powerful social classes situated within local society were substantially outside the control of any authority beyond the locality. Instead, such classes enjoyed rights and privileges which enabled them to contribute in some modest measure to decision-making within regional and pan-Indian polities. The location within society of such classes and the voice which they exercised in politics, as a free peasantry or a petite landed class, was so formidable that this phenomenon has persuaded some scholars to argue that the institutions of liberal democracy were known to India from classical times. Such a belief carries little conviction. Yet in the absence of a centralised polity, the dominant rural classes within the local units of Indian society were able to appropriate resources, and provide the background to political decisions, which resulted in a trajectory of social development substantially different from the development of western societies.

II

The colonial State which emerged from the ruins of the Mughal polity, in the 18th century, was far more cohesive and centralised than the State which it had displaced. Yet a colonial polity was hardly an institution designed to strengthen the basis of popular participation in politics. Indeed, when there gradually emerged a westernised intelligentsia within Indian society, which claimed to speak for the "Nation" as a whole, its claims were promptly rejected by an imperial power reluctant to accept the members of this intelligentsia as the true representatives of the people.

As the colonial polity ripened into maturity, a novel variety of politics was introduced in the subcontinent, wherein leaders drawn from different religions or social communities tried to establish a political linkage between their constituents at the same time as they tried to relate their life-styles and culture to the life-styles and culture of the popular classes. Prominent among these leaders were men drawn from three social classes which were largely the product of British social engineering: the landed gentry; or the professional classes; or the commercial and industrial communities; which classes, whatever be the over-all state of the economy, did reasonably well for themselves. Under the new dispensation, therefore, classes which owed their genesis to imperial rule came together in the politics of association to offer a challenge to British domination. These associations, initially local, then regional, and finally, in 1885, national in character, reflected a wholly new political development in India. Instead of the old politics, which articulated itself most succinctly of all within the locality, the new politics was capable of exercising itself over questions quite different from questions that concerned social units, like caste or *panchayat* (informal judicial) institutions, which had thrived earlier within the micro-polity. The earlier political solidarities relied substantially on primordial loyalties. By contrast, the new associations were pyramidical in structure; associational in relations; and they relied upon altogether different social loyalties and social constituencies.

The entry of the landed, the professional and the commercial classes into the politics of association, therefore, was a novel phenomenon within the Indian polity, since earlier political formations functioned in a different manner. It is, moreover, pertinent that though these classes partook of an outlook which was largely shaped by their specific social background; they also articulated a wider concern for other classes and communities which went into the making of the Indian Nation. Once again, it is not fortuitous that such classes devised theories of nationalism which stressed the need for popular participation in the liberation struggle against the British Government in India.

It is appropriate, at this juncture, to reflect briefly upon the vision which these newly organised classes held out to themselves and to their less privileged countrymen. They envisaged a full-scale industrial transformation of India, with the objective of raising the levels of material production as well as the levels of social consumption. Over and above this, they also envisaged the full participation, in the decision-making process, as well as in the formal and the informal institutions of governance, of individuals drawn from the classes below them in the scale of society. Throughout the 19th century, both the peasants and the pastoral communities, living on the fringes of agricultural society, had been restive of imperial control; and had erupted repeatedly into local uprisings which were suppressed by the British Raj with a great deal of ruthlessness. In a manner of speaking, this restiveness of the peasant, or the tribal, was the time honoured way of expressing his hostility to the colonial regime, which lacked the social sensitivity of the traditional ruling class, largely because of the absence of any social contact, or community of sentiment, between the British Government and the wider civic society. The challenge before the new political elites, who spearheaded the nationalist resurgence in India, lay in drawing such popular classes into the associational politics that had come into existence under the colonial dispensation. The elites were equally interested in persuading these classes to support the credentials of the Indian National Congress, which in the 19th century, was largely a party of the upper and middle classes.

The manner in which popular support was secured for an elite organisation is well-known to scholars of the liberation struggle in India. Within the domain of symbolic politics, Mahatma Gandhi embodied the aspirations no less than the fears of the peasants, perched at different levels of rural society, as they were drawn into a worldwide market economy under colonial aegis. The Mahatma shrewdly realised the depth of religious feeling in the country. He consequently devised an idiom of politics in which political liberation and spiritual realisation were indistinguishable and mutually reinforcing objectives; just as this idiom was also utilised for the purpose of attracting different social classes and religious communities to a common platform, in the hope that such an experience would draw the social constituents of a plural society into bonds of allegiance to the overarching authority of a Nation-State.

By the third decade of the 20th century, the epic figures of the freedom struggle in India, men like Mahatma Gandhi and Jawaharlal Nehru, had achieved remarkable success in creating a coalition of the elite and popular classes against British imperialism. Both the institutional structure and the ideological texture of the politics of nationalism, as it crystallised at this juncture, was very different from the institutions and values of politics in the pre-colonial State; more particularly, politics in the local units of society, that were dominated by chiefs or petty rulers, on the one hand, and the landed elite, which was tied to the latter through kin and clan solidarity, on the other. In the institutional domain, nationalist politics was above all underpinned by a pan-Indian organisation, namely, the Indian National Congress, which was a party and a movement at the same time. Three tiered structure of the Congress replicated the territorial division of British India into provinces, districts and sub-districts, although the principle of linguistic rationality encouraged the nationalist leaders to bifurcate some of the provinces of the empire into smaller units. Thus corresponding to the territorial units of British India, stood provincial or district or sub-district level units of the Congress, linked to the fabric of civic society, within their allotted spheres, through appropriate means. The smallest organisational unit of the Congress was the committee of a dozen or so primary members; located in a substantial village constituting the nodal point of a cluster of rural settlements; which village often enjoyed considerable historicity as the fly-wheel of the local polity. However, the real difference between nationalist politics of the 20th century and pre-colonial politics, lay in the absence of any firm linkage between the locality and the higher levels earlier, in contrast with the firm bonding between the local organisation, on the one hand, and the district, the provincial and the pan-Indian units of the national movement, in the period under consideration, on the other. For the first time in the history of the subcontinent, therefore, a new forum of pan-Indian politics was created which linked the locality to the subcontinental polity through firm ties of representation and association. Within the framework of the Congress, linkages were also established with various organised groups like the professional classes, or the industrial workers, or the peasantry, or the tribal communities. Nevertheless, elite and popular mobilisation was achieved principally through drawing locally dominant leaders into the Congress; and utilising their influence for the induction of different classes or communities, which fell within their spheres of influences, into the struggle for political liberation.

Although the political alliance which had been conjured into existence by the nationalist leadership was a most formidable coming together of the elite and popular classes, it would be appropriate to dwell briefly upon the distribution of power within this alliance. Any attempt to do so reveals some disquieting features about the liberation movement. It is possible to mobilise the poor and the deprived in a society in two alternative ways. In the first instance, they may be mobilised through peasant associations or trade unions, which reach out *directly* to such classes, and organise them into a potent force within the polity. Alternatively, it is possible to use the power and influence of dominant interests within the localities (or larger regions) to draw the "wretched of the earth" into a large scale political movement. By and large, the nationalist leadership of India used the latter rather than the former techniques for popular mobilisation in the cities and in the villages. Such a political strategy was underpinned by the use of religious symbols, which reached out with great facility to the dispossessed, because of the hold which popular religion exercised over them. The result of such mobilisation was the creation of a conservative political consciousness which, despite the radical political face it presented to British imperialism, was not geared to the task of dramatic social transformation within Indian society. Indeed, the conservative impulse behind popular mobilisation enabled the British to hand over power to a nationalist leadership which presided over a structure of politics not qualitatively different from the politics which had been conjured into existence under the colonial dispensation. Despite its populist strength, therefore, the liberation movement in India possessed an ideological character which was titled in favour of the politics of gradual reform rather than the politics of dramatic social transformation.

III

In dwelling upon the ideological character of the nationalist leaders who captured power after 1947, we have referred briefly to the representative institutions, resting upon a restricted franchise, which the British had created prior to independence. An understanding of these institutions and their franchise base is necessary not only because it provides clues to the vitality of democracy in India; but also because they exercised considerable influence upon the character of nationalist politics. To fully comprehend the institutions of politics which the British had created in India, before 1947, it is also necessary to highlight the pre-conceptions which influenced their creation. Because of the cultural diversity and also because of the unique political institutions which had shaped Indian society over the centuries, the British believed that the task of framing an appropriate constitution for India had to be taken up on a basis radically different from the framing of constitutions in western societies. The strength of caste, community and religious sentiment created within Indian society solidarities, as well as cleavages, to which there existed no parallel in the West. A political society made up of macro-constituencies of language and religion; at the same time as it was made up of innumerable micro-constituencies, resting upon caste and tribal sentiment; could not lend itself to the creation of representative institutions similar to those which were created by the liberal polities of Europe. Instead, such a society was ideally suited to a Whig conception of the political order, in which the basic building block of a polity was a "class", or a "community", or an "interest", rather than an atomised individual. From such a perception of the Indian polity, the social engineers of the British *imperium* created political constitutions which sought to balance one linguistic group with another; just as it also sought to counterpoise religious and caste communities, as well as social classes, with one another. From the very outset, therefore, the constitutions which the British granted to India drew upon different religious communities and social classes to confer upon them representation proportionate not to their demographic strength but to their social and economic power. To put it bluntly, in the various constitutions which the British devised from 1909 onwards, concessions to the rising nationalist classes were counterpoised by the representation accorded to religious communites; or to the landed classes; or to minority groups; or to loyalist professional and commercial elites. Such constitutions were devised to heighten the existing cleavages within Indian society and they inspired associational politics which reflected the structure of power in Indian society as perceived by the imperial rulers.

It is hardly necessary to observe that, in mobilising the popular classes for the cause of nationalism, the nationalist leadership could not be indifferent to the constituencies created by the British Government. Indeed, these leaders had to expend considerable energy in building for themselves support in the constituencies mapped out by British constitutions devised in the decades before 1947. As a result of this, the nationalist movement was partly shaped by the tactical requirements of the representative institutions created, before 1947, at the pan-Indian level; or within the provinces; or within the districts and the localities of British India. Perhaps a classic example of the manner in which the British Government created counterpoised constituencies within India was the composition of the Delegation to the Round Table Conference, convoked in the 1930s, to initiate a dialogue between the growing nationalist forces, on the one hand, and the imperial political establishment, on the other. If the British Government had been guided by liberal principles, then a major group from the Indian National Congress, plus small groups drawn from a few other political parties, would have constituted the valid structure of a pan-Indian representation. Instead, this representation was characterised by an array of "special interests", deeply committed to the *status quo,* which were pitted against the articulate spokesmen of nationalism. Small wonder, then, that it was impossible to initiate a constructive dialogue between the representatives of nationalism and the representatives of imperialism at the Conference.

When the political leaders of India found themselves in a position to write a new constitution after the country had attained independence, they tackled this task in full consciousness of the problems which they had faced prior to 1947. Indeed, the nationalist answer to the Whig sophistry of imperialism lay in the concept of a Constituent Assembly, based on adult franchise, which would be at liberty to draw a novel constitution for India. However, since politics is the art of the possible, these leaders actually utilised members of existing legislatures, elected on a limited franchise, to create a Constituent Assembly, which drafted the constitution of India along liberal principles, taking the "individual", rather than the "organised interest", as the basis of the polity. Also in pursuit of liberal principles, the franchise was for the first time extended from 10 per cent of the population, to all the adult citizens of the new nation. At the same time, territorial constituencies of roughly comparable demographic strength were mapped out. The only exception to the liberal principle lay in the constitutional protection extended to some deprived groups, which had suffered social and economic exploitation over a great span of time. Indeed, the constitution also went beyond liberal principles to adopt the radical notion of the State as the great instrument of social welfare. In no other constitution is the responsibility of the State to create a secular society; or to promote the material well-being of the citizen, along socialist lines; so explicitly stated as in the constitution for India framed in 1950.

Perhaps the most dramatic change introduced by the new constitution was the extension of voting rights to every adult citizen of the nation. What it meant, demographically speaking, was the creation of a voting community of a couple of hundred million, instead of the 20 or 30 million who had been enfranchised, under imperial aegis, by the fourth decade of the 20th century. With reference to the three tiered structure of the polity, which has been sketched out earlier, the introduction of adult franchise meant that not only were the landlords and dominant peasants, who had controlled power within local society over a considerable span of time, a potent presence in politics; but the ranks of rural society below the propertied classes; namely, the intermediate castes, or share-croppers and tenants-at-will; and the untouchable communities, or agricultural labourers and agrestic serfs; were now active voting members of the polity, and exercised a voice, not necessarily in proportion to their demographic strength, in the business of governance.

The new polity of hundreds upon millions of voters, which emerged through the constitution of 1950, presented a massive challenge to the political leadership of India. So far as political action was concerned, this massive community could be mobilised through a plurality of political idioms. At one level, the leaders of the Congress, which organisation became more and more of a party without ceasing to be a movement, voiced an idiom which expressed popular aspirations in terms of expanding horizons of social production and an equitable system of distribution, for ensuring the moral and the material well-being of the citizen. This idiom, which rested upon an unresolved tension between the liberal and the radical vision of the "good society", was articulated at various levels—the pan-Indian; or the regional; or the local—by those within the Congress, who sought to attract the popular vote. Yet another idiom that was no less popular was the saintly idiom, which had been utilised by Mahatma Gandhi during the decades of the struggle for freedom. The strength of this idiom lay in the configuration of a society wherein, historically speaking, political institutions above the local polity had been quite fragile. The absence of firm political institutions; and the weakness of the linkage between the local polity, on the one hand, and the regional and pan-Indian polities, on the other, had created a situation wherein individuals of outstanding moral authority, who stood outside the formal framework of political structures, could by their example initiate social action on a massive scale. For these reasons Mahatma Gandhi was the premier instance, in the 20th century, of the moral exemplar initiating heroic political action across the class and communitarian orders of society. The saintly idiom was available as a political resource even after 1947 in a society in which the crystallisation of institutions was still relatively modest in scale. For the first two decades after 1947, a fusion of the liberal/radical and saintly idioms created a powerful coalition which enabled Jawaharlal Nehru to steer the Indian electorate through three successive general elections, in the course of which the Congress Party emerged as a dominant force.

Although the linkage between national and local politics within India had been considerably strengthened during the decades of the freedom struggle, or as a result of the social and economic changes engineered by the colonial regime, the gulf between the two still remains the crucial gulf within the polity. It has been suggested earlier, that one of the achievements of the nationalist leadership, during the decades of the anti-imperialist struggle, had been in forging relatively close ties between local society, on the one hand, and regional and national societies, on the other; just as it has also been suggested that an equally significant achievement of the freedom struggle lay in the creation of bonds of unity between the upper and middle classes, and the popular classes, made up of peasants and artisans and the industrial working classes. Despite the emergence of such bonds, idioms of politics which were effective at the local level remained distinct from political idioms which were effective at the national level. To put it more specifically, the idiom of local politics reflected the dominant strength of the propertied interest, at the same time as it reflected the primordial values of caste and community, which shaped the subjective no less than the objective worldview of all the social classes within the locality. The entire political debate within the country was, therefore, conducted at different levels and through the instrumentality of unresolved tensions between the idiom of liberal and radical politics, on the one hand, and the idiom of saintly politics and primordial values, on the other. Precisely because of such an amalgam of politics, it is possible to look upon the hierarchical orders of society, from the base to the apex, in terms of the aggregation of localities, anchored in primordial values, into a national polity, at the same time as it is possible to view Indian society, from the apex downward, as a massive liberal democracy, held together through a transformational humanism, which seek to confer the benefits of industrialisation and a modern scientific culture upon its citizens.

No account of the vitality of democratic values and institutions within India, four decades after 1947, would be complete without reference to the sweeping changes within the economy, and the effect of these changes upon the political fabric of the sub-continent. In the very first decade after independence, two major experiments in social transformation were initiated on a scale comparable to experimentation within the Soviet Union, in the 1930s; and within the Republic of China, in the 1950s. The objective of all this was to create a modern industrial economy within the country, at the same time as a transformation in social relations and in the technologies of production was engineered within the villages. So far as the vision of industrialisation was concerned, a massive programme was set afoot, which allocated to the State the responsibility of generating the productivity of basic items like steel or power, at the same time as private enterprise was called upon to stimulate the generation of consumer goods. Simultaneously, also, the great concentrations of landed wealth within regions and localities were broken up; and rights of property transferred into the hands of occupancy tenants and related social classes within localities. The political power of the Congress, in the first two decades after 1947, lay in an alliance between the industrial, the professional and the commercial communities, on the one hand, and the newly enfranchised dominant peasants of localities, whose influence also reached out to share-croppers, tenants-at-will, as well as agricultural labourers and agrestic serfs, on the other.

After an interval of two decades, however, the economic changes brought about through industrialisation and agrarian reform created a greatly transformed political scene in India. At one level, the efforts at industrialisation succeeded in generating a national grid of economic activity, public or privately owned, which rested upon the skills of a powerful class of entrepreneurs, managers and engineers, and last but not least, an industrial working class. At a different level, within the local societies which were the operative units of agrarian production, the dominant rural classes were able to seize the opportunities for growth created since the 1950s, but more specifically, as a result of the intensive agricultural development strategy adopted in the 1960s, to emerge as a powerful force in the consumer as well as the vote market; and the back-bone of the economic miracle which has transformed India from a deficit to a surplus agrarian economy. Through processes which are only partially understood by scholars or activists, the new dominant rural classes, whose productivity had expanded substantially in the period under consideration, appear to have moved out of the Congress voting system, into supporting regionally oriented or relatively narrow political formations. As a result of this transformation in electoral politics within India, the Congress had to work out a different system for conjuring into existence victory at the polls. The framework for a new majority was laid by Indira Gandhi, during the elections of 1971, when under the populist slogan of "*Gharibi Hatao*" (Banish Poverty), she successfully created a majority for her party, through an aggregation of the upper caste rural vote with the vote of under-privileged communities like *Harijans* and minorities like the Muslims. It would be no exaggeration to state that successive electoral majorities, since this election, have been created around such a calculus of electoral politics which provides substantial working majorities to the Congress at the same time as it confers upon the political scene a fragility flowing from the conflicting social and economic aspirations of the different constituents which go into the making of the new alliance. Of course, the general elections of 1977 and 1984 were exceptions to this rule, for reasons which it is not possible to spell out in a brief essay.

What of the future? Any attempt at crystal gazing for a polity of the scale and complexity of the Indian polity is an exercise fraught with the gravest danger. Yet the skill of the political leadership in generating economic growth and social change, at the same time as it has successfully created electoral majorities out of shifting political alliances, speaks well of the future of democratic institutions and liberal values within India. The politics conjured out of the raw stuff of existential reality, or flawed human materials, is necessarily a politics that does not gladden the heart of those who seek perfection. Yet despite their shortcomings, the values and institutions of liberal democracy have provided a measure of political stability to the subcontinent in a context characterised by a re-ordering of social productivity as well as of the distribution of wealth between different classes. That such a transformation of an agricultural into an industrial society is compatible with the values and institutions of liberal democracy is surely a profound lesson for other societies in the Third World, since the moral and material supremacy of the open society is a value which holds together men not only within nations but also within the world community.

10

The Place of Oral Sources in Historical Research

The discipline of history has, over the past two decades, undergone a very substantial expansion of its intellectual horizons. Two trends lie behind such an expansion. In the first instance, historians, influenced in particularly by scholars of the Annales School, have reached out to new disciplines in the social sciences in a bid to enrich modes of exploration and areans of enquiry. Secondly, the sources which underpin historical research have also grown in quantity at the same time as they have grown in quality. In this connection, the use of "oral sources" as the basis of historical writing occupies a very prominent place; and I propose, in the course of this essay, to reflect upon oral sources and how they can be drawn with profit into scholarly research.

Any enquiry into the place of oral sources in the reconstruction of our past inevitably leads us to examine the nature of history and the principles which undergird historical narrative and analysis. The discipline of history, as scholars understand it today, concerns the totality of relationships between Man and Society in the past. Further, the interest of the scholar in his discipline is more than just an antiquarian curiosity in the past of human society. Behind this interest lies the assumption that the past and the present are linked to each other through mechanisms of cause and effect. To the extent the past is causally related to the present, to that extent the historian seeks to unravel it in order to understand the world around him; in order also, to shape the future of this world.

The discipline of history crystallised in its present form, about a century ago, in the universities of Europe. The scholar whose name is prominently associated with this intellectual development is Ranke. Although it would be incorrect to suggest that Ranke is the father of modern historiography, we can nevertheless credit him with discovering those methods and techniques which characterise history in its contemporary form as distinct from the historiography of the centuries preceding the 19th century.

Ranke's distinctive contribution to history lay in two seminal areas. In the first instance, Ranke familiarised scholars with the use of archival materials; of documentary sources generated by the political actors of the past, whether they be emperors or kings; or statesmen or warriors; or popes or prelates. The crucial innovation which Ranke introduced—and this could bear emphasis in a seminar devoted to an evaluation of oral sources in historical research—was rigorous reliance on the written materials created by the political actors of the past, to the exclusion of later accounts of events and happenings. Prior to Ranke, historians had indiscriminately utilised contemporary sources, as well as sources generated *after* the occurrence of an event, in reconstructing the past. Ranke rejected such a method as unscholarly and unscientific. He sought to reconstruct the past "as it actually was". He, therefore, believed that only written materials generated during the occurrence of an event could be utilised as the basis of scientific works of historiography.

I have suggested that Ranke sought to devise a scientific method for the reconstruction of the human past. I would further emphasise that the use of the term 'scientific' in this context is not fortuitous. Ranke believed that the method which he had devised would enable scholars to write history with the same precision and rigour with which natural scientists unravelled the laws that determined the structure and behaviour of nature and matter. Ranke was firmly committed to positivism; to the belief that through utilising archival records for reconstructing the past, he could create knowledge which was no less rigorous than the knowledge created by the natural scientists who were involved in the exploration of inanimate matter.

I

It should be clear from the above that the written records

generated by the actors of the past are the basic materials from which a historian reconstructs his narrative.

What, then, is the place of oral sources in the scheme of historical research?

To answer this question, a crucial question if the pursuit of oral history is to be a purposeful endeavour, we have to review very briefly the manner in which the scope and content of history have changed since the time of Ranke.

In this context I would like, in the first instance, to dwell briefly on the social milieu in which Ranke's concept of historiography crystallised. As is well-known to historians, the 19th century was the age of nationalism in Europe. It was an age in which two developments were very much in evidence: first, it witnessed the break-up of culturally and ethnically plural imperial systems into autonomous polities, organised into powerful Nation-States which established (or sought to establish) monopolistic control over the citizens residing within their territories; secondly, the 19th century also witnessed the integration of scattered communities, subscribing to a common culture, and possessing a common ethnic identity, into cohesive national politics. The former process is exemplified by the break-up of the Austro-Hungarian empire; while the latter is reflected in the emergence of the German Reich in the third quarter of the 19th century.

Ranke was over and above everything else a product of the age of nationalism in Europe. As a result of this, the historiography which he advocated focused sharply upon the State, and upon political or religious institutions closely interwoven in the fabric of the State, as the proper subjects of scholarly exploration. Further, Ranke's historiography rested on the assumption that the men who mattered in society—the actual wielders of power—were a fortunate few, perched at the very apex of the polity, whose records, as preserved in the archival repositories of Europe, could reveal to the assiduous scholar the subtleties of the historical process. The historiography conceived by Ranke, therefore, was unabashedly elitist in its assumptions about the locus of power in society. Ranke's historiography, appropriately for an age which witnessed the emergence of powerful Nation-States in Europe, was also directed towards the State, as the one institution in society which lay at the very core of social reality.

In sketching out the historical assumptions of Ranke so tersely I may have presented a caricature of his views. Yet this brief survey will convey some idea of how history was conceived by scholars a century ago.

Since Ranke's days, a number of transformations have taken place in our understanding of history, as well as of source materials which can be utilised for research. The changes which have taken place in our understanding of the discipline touch two areas of history. In the first instance, few would, today, subscribe to the elitist view that only the political actors perched on the apex of society determine the historical process. There is a consensus in the scholarly community, contemporaneously, that to understand the past, we have to focus as much on the individuals in the median and lower reaches of society, as we have to focus on those who occupy its apex. To take a concrete example, to understand the Mughal polity under Akbar, we need to dwell just as much on the peasant-proprietor in a remote village; or an artisan in an obscure manufactory; as we need to dwell upon the scintillating figures which adorned the imperial court at Fatehpur Sikri.

Such an all-embracing conception of the historical process—the belief that history is concerned with the totality of relationships between man and society in the past—has obliged the scholar to cast his net much wider, than was done by Ranke and his contemporaries, in his quest for source materials. Needless to say, the historian who seeks to illumine the moral and material world of the lowly peasant, or the humble artisan, in the past, is confronted with novel technical problems. Such obscure men, are unlikely to leave for posterity the written records which princes and prelates and other outstanding men of the past bequeath to the scholar. To reconstruct history from below, as we call it, the historian is obliged to take recourse to ingenious methods; to legitimise new source materials as the basis of his research. Not infrequently, ordinary men and women in centuries past were illiterate. To the extent this is true, it would be impossible for historians, if they were to take Ranke's prescription literally, to write about such faces in the crowd.

However, the oral testimony of the past, the evidence of the spoken word as transmitted to us, comes to the rescue of the historian, who seeks to reconstruct the life, not only of rulers and statesmen, but also of common men and women, who toiled and struggled in centuries past. So far as the historians of Europe are concerned, they possess in the church an institution which has preserved a record of the life of ordinary people. In certain instances, as in the account of heresy cases in ecclesiastical courts, the church provides the scholar with a vivid oral account of what common men and women in the past felt, saw, dreamt, and feared. Perhaps the classical work of Ladurie, entitled *Montallon,* is one illustration of the manner in which the documentation created by the medieval church has enabled European historians to reconstruct "history from below" with an authenticity which borders on the incredible.

II

My observations regarding the growing scope of history, since the times of Ranke, make it obvious that oral source materials are coming to play an increasingly important role in the reconstruction of the past. This inference enables me to dwell briefly upon the valuable materials which have been created at the Nehru Memorial Museum and Library recording the activities of individuals who have contributed to the political, social and economic development of modern India. This project does not by any means exhaust the range of oral sources that can be generated to assist the historian in the reconstruction of the past. However, the materials to which I have referred comprise one corpus of oral sources that can enrich the historiography of modern India; and, therefore, deserve to be drawn increasingly into historical research.

The oral sources under consideration here can broadly be defined as autobiographical material. For reasons which need not delay us here, we do not have in India an articulate tradition of autobiographical writing. A majority of the prominent individuals who participated in social activity have, therefore, not left any written record of their experiences, or their contribution, to public life. The work in oral history being conducted at the Nehru Museum seeks to create through extended interviews, documentation which is almost a substitute for autobiographical literature. As such, this programme is generating a corpus of source materials which can greatly enrich a scholarly understanding of our recent past.* I shall speak very briefly, at this juncture, of the manner in which we generate our oral sources; and also draw upon some of the "oral autobiographies" in our archives to illustrate the nature and quality of this material. In any such endeavour, the most crucial decision is whom to interview. We are guided in this regard by the importance of an individual's contributions to public life; as well as by the extent of literature available about him. Having taken this decision, our next task is to establish contact with the person to be interviewed, and to carry out an exhaustive survey of the written materials, direct and indirect, which illumine his public career and private life. From such materials we prepare a questionnaire which is then communicated to him after securing his assent for an interview. This questionnaire is suggestive rather than exhaustive; and it gives the person to be interviewed an idea of the issues to which his reactions could enrich the historical record.

The most delicate stage of the exercise is the conduct of an extended dialogue with the subject on the basis of the questionnaire presented to him. The handling of this dialogue is as much of a science as it is an art. On the one hand, the interviewer has to equip himself with all available knowledge about his subject, as well as about the social and political milieu of his times. On the other hand, the interviewer has to be as unobstrusive as possible in securing from his subject a steady flow of valuable information. My colleague, Dr. Sharma, whose experience of a decade and more in this domain is unrivalled, believes that the interviewer "plays the role of a needle in a gramophone". What Dr. Sharma implies is that the interviewer has to wear a very low profile, yet gently lead his subject to reveal information about his past which is of historical interest.

The quality of the oral source materials being created at our organisation can best be appreciated by reviewing the "oral" autobiographies of two prominent individuals whom we have interviewed in the recent past. I would, first of all, like to look at the records in our oral history archives of the distinguished socialist and social worker, Smt. Kamaladevi Chattopadhyaya. Smt. Chattopadhyaya is in some ways an individual whose career is not altogether unknown to us. Born in a brahman family in Manga-

*The rest of this section leans very heavily upon the rich scholarly experience of my colleague, Dr. Hari Dev Sharma. I am much beholden to him for the unselfish manner in which he has shared this fund of experience with me

lore, the young Kamaladevi grew up in a very liberal domestic milieu where she was encouraged to think of a creative and purposeful career for herself. After her preliminary education in India, she proceeded to London to conduct higher studies in the social sciences. On her return to India in the late 1920s, Kamaladevi plunged into public life, devoting as much to the welfare of women as she devoted to nationalist politics, particularly of a socialist hue. Her contribution to the freedom struggle is as much a matter of public record as the pioneering role which she played in the organisation of the All India Women's Conference. But over and above these involvements was Kamaladevi's pressing concern for the "wretched of the earth," particularly those drawn from the weaker sex. Equally pressing was her concern for the revival of those traditional crafts of India, which could sustain tens upon thousands of impoverished artisans, at the same time as they contributed to a material and cultural renaissance in our country.

The autobiographical account of Kamaladevi Chattopadhyaya in our archives throws a flood of illuminating light upon the career and achievements of one of the most creative individuals in India. At the very outset, Kamaladevi speaks of the profound influence which her mother, surely a remarkable woman, exercised on her:

> Somehow the whole idea that women should be dependent on men was abhorrent to her (my mother). She felt that I should carve out a different pattern of life for myself. Now I began to earnestly engage myself in my studies. I went to a Roman Catholic convent school. The convent made a great impact on me. Perhaps, in a way, this background did prepare me for the kind of life I was to take on later—the great stress on austerity, simplicity of life—denying oneself unnecessary luxuries. Somehow, all this began to appeal to me more and more. At the same time, I also began to wonder why there were such big differences in the economic levels as also in social levels and there again was growing within me a resentment, a kind of revolt, and a desire that these things should be changed, that this was not right."

In view of the formative influences which moulded Kamaladevi's attitude to the role of women in society and to social exploitation and poverty, it is the reverse of surprising that she played so active a part in public affairs.Central to Kamaladevi's vision was the notion of a liberated woman, fully equipped to play a creative role, who would constitute the basis of a resurgent India. Since she was devoted to such an ideal, it is hardly surprising that she found herself associated with the All India Women's Conference since its very inception. Speaking of this association she observes in her oral testimony:

> Towards the end of the conference [the first AIWC] Mrs. Cousin told me that I was being requested to take up the General Secretaryship of this conference. The designation would be the Organising Secretary because this new body to be set up had to be organised actually from scratch; there was just not any foundation on which to build. Naturally I was very much frightened at the thought because I had never done any secretarial work before. And though I had some familiarity with the functioning of a women's body because of my association with the "Mahila Sabha" in Mangalore, I was never really actively connected with it. I was much too young at that time. But she did not brook much discussion on this issue and assured me of every help."

Kamaladevi Chattopadhyaya's involvement in the welfare of women by no means exhausted the rich diversity of her public life. Along with a gallant band of co-workers, she was active in the agitation which Mahatma Gandhi launched against the British Government in 1930. That this agitation rested, for the first time in nationalist politics, on substantial participation by women is a matter of historical record. However, Kamaladevi's reminiscences of this period bring home with a poignant vividness the scale of participation by women in the salt satyagraha. Speaking of this epochal struggle in Bombay Kamaladevi states:

> The next thing we did was to make small packets of illegal salt and to sell them. For this purpose, I visited several places, various markets, stock-exchanges and finally one day, I went to the High Court and tried to sell salt there. Everywhere we saw very great response. Where these salt packets were auctioned, we were able to raise large amounts of money especially in the stock-exchange where fabulous sums were raised. People were moved by great sentiment and fervour. It was a symbol of revolt of the people and the expression of their desire for freedom. The highest price that I could get for a packet of salt was 30,000 rupees, or might have been more.

Equally illuminating is her view of how a socialist could discern in

Gandhi a possible clue to the salvation of India's impoverished millions:

> Well, I had been reading Marxist literature; and as I said, from my early age, I had this disturbing feeling about the social differences, economic exploitation and there seemed no answer for it. So, I think, I became very much interested in Marxian literature, Marxian theory and began to study it. Then, when Gandhiji's leadership, emerged, I was largely attracted because he was the first and the only leader of that period who seemed to identify himself with the people, who seemed to define and interpret freedom in terms of the everyday life of the people which others had not done. With others, it had always been a question of political freedom in the sense of getting power from the British. So, to me this became more meaningful, here was somebody, who, in a more forceful and definite form was giving shape to what I had been vaguely feeling. So, that was the main sentiment or passion that drew me to Gandhiji.

No less significant than the testimony of Kamaladevi Chattopadhyaya is the recorded dialogue with the distinguished Marxist leader, S.V. Ghate, in our archives. Ghate is well known to scholars as one of the founding fathers of the communist movement in India. He was also very active in the trade union movement in Bombay during the 1920s and 1930s; and one of the revolutionaries involved in the Meerut Conspiracy Case. An organiser of great distinction rather than a theorist, Ghate dedicated his life to the Communist Party of India as a member of its Central Committee (1943-50) and as its Treasurer in 1953. The record which he has left behind with us speaks eloquently of the selfless service which he extended to the cause of socialism in India; and the manner in which marxists of his generation were as much concerned with the anti-imperialist struggle as they were concerned with the liberation of the working classes in urban and in rural society.

Ghate's account provides us with valuable insights into the climate in which the pioneering generation of marxists in India were attracted to political life. Describing his apprenticeship, he states:

> I finished my honours degree from St. Xavier's College [in Bombay]

> in 1923. By that time, of course, I had already come into the socialist fringe. In fact, my lodge [a sort of boarding-house] had become a sort of centre for discussions on socialism. I was in the lodge from 1921 to 1925, and it was there that I came into contact with Dange in 1922. I had a group of people. All of us used to discuss socialism, world events, etc. The lodge was going its own way and we were going our own. . . . So ultimately the lodge also went the way all other things under my "able" management did. It was 1925, the proprietor said: 'I will give it to somebody else to manage. You cannot manage. You have already gone into the communist movement'. I agreed that I could not manage it. So he said: 'All right. Let us give it to somebody to manage'. He became a *sanyasi* and I joined the communist movement.

The radical movement which Ghate and other young socialists of his circle fostered among the working classes of Bombay was momentous in its significance for nationalist politics in India. In 1928, barely a couple of years after they had initiated their activity, Ghate and the young marxists around him successfully organised a massive union among the textile workers of Bombay, which union led the workers in a heroic strike against the mill-owners. How the impoverished workers of Bombay were able to defy the combined strength of the capitalists, and the British Government, is vividly described by Ghate in his testimony. Speaking of the manner in which he and his associates reinforced the resolve of the workers not to surrender, Ghate states:

> We [the strike leaders and the workers] met regularly. One month, two months, three months, four months—nothing happened. The workers did not get any wages. We could not feed them every day by holding meetings. If you remember we had 800 meetings in the course of these six months and the people used to come and listen even if they did not have any rice-*kanji* in their houses. They used to come to the meetings, hear the speakers and go. Then later on when we collected funds, the Strike Committee decided that we should distribute food—two seers of rice, half a seer of *dal* and salt. This was all that was done and Rs. 20,000 to 30,000 worth of foodgrains were distributed during the later period—after, I think, four months or four and half months. The workers were actually starving. Their faces looked very grim.

That the textile strike of 1928 is virtually unknown today is eloquent comment on the manner in which some of the seminal episodes of the nationalist struggle in India have been relegated to the dustbin of history. Ghate's account is invaluable in rescuing this seminal constituent of our historical past from oblivion; just as it throws fascinating light on its sequel, namely, the Meerut Conspiracy Trials, through which the British Government tried to break up the infant Marxist movement in India. Ghate's account of the racy Trials, through which the British Government tried to break up the infant Marxist movement in India. Ghate's account of the Meerut Trial illumines the manner in which the radical leadership, isolated from its base in Meerut, was nevertheless able to offer determined resistance to the British Government. Even in the stifling climate of Meerut, the Marxist leaders were able to take an active interest in the momentous events of those times. On the eve of the Civil Disobedience movement, the Meerut under-trials, so Ghate observes, were visited by no less a person than the Mahatma himself, who sought to gain their support for the agitation which he was about to launch against the British Government:

> So on a particular date, time was fixed. He [Mahatma Gandhi] was to come there at 3 O'clock. The Superintendent told us to be ready to receive Gandhiji at 3 O'clock, and he would bring him to us. And things happened, we were told later, exactly the opposite of what the Superintendent wanted to happen. When Gandhi came—he had his watch tucked on his *pancha*—he came there with a host of people. . . . Then we sat round him. We gave coffee or tea to those who came with him. For him we had brought dry fruit which he kept on munching. Then we talked to him about the Chauri Chaura incident and his withdrawal of the movement as a result of that. Then he said: 'Look here, I am going to start a movement now. I want the assistance of all people. I do not want any obstruction. What is your attitude?' Dange said that we would have no objection to support the movement if he did not withdraw at the nick of the time because somebody had been murdered or some violence had taken place. To this Gandhiji said—the only main point that comes to my mind is—that he could assure us that he would not withdraw the movement, even if there was a slight violence here or there. We said that we would have no objection to support the movement if it was so. But all sorts of questions were asked by our people.

III

I do not propose to spend any more time on the oral history

documentation which we have created at the Nehru Museum through interviews with prominent participants in our public life. Suffice it to mention that these materials constitute a valuable data base for scholars who are seeking to reconstruct our recent past. It need hardly be emphasised here that oral sources should be utilised by the scholar in conjunction with other sources rather than as a solitary basis of historical reconstruction. I am striking a note of caution at this juncture because the scholar who seeks to write rigorous history must draw upon a variety of sources, all of which sources he ultimately transcends in his work. Oral sources, when viewed in such a perspective, are no more or no less valuable than other sources, and it is only by taking oral evidence in conjunction with other forms of evidence that the scholar can hope to discern the truth about the past.

I would, in conclusion, like to touch briefly upon other varieties of oral sources which can profitably be utilised by the historian in his researches. It is well known that till very recently, the level of formal literacy in India was low, with the result that the oral transmission of ideas and traditions occupied an important place in our culture. The historian who seeks to portray the past in the round—who is as much concerned with elite history as he is concerned with the moral and material culture of the lowly classes—must draw upon a wide range of oral sources if he is to be true to his task. We are very rich in our oral culture and it is incumbent upon scholars to record this culture at a juncture when changing mores of cultural transmission have not totally destroyed it. This task of recording and preserving the oral culture of our society is all the more important in an era in which social theory, particularly in the realm of linguistics, has placed in our hands powerful tools for reconstructing reality and remoulding it nearer to the heart's desire.